Nathalie Dupree's
COMFORTABLE
Entertaining

AT HOME WITH EASE & GRACE

THE UNIVERSITY OF GEORGIA PRESS

Athens

Published in 2013 by the University of Georgia Press
Athens, Georgia 30602
www.ugapress.org
© 1998 by Nathalie Dupree
Photographs © 1998 by Tom Eckerle
All rights reserved
Designed by Jaye Zimet
Set in Bembo
Printed and bound by Imago

The paper in this book meets the guidelines for permanence
and durability of the Committee on Production Guidelines for
Book Longevity of the Council on Library Resources.

Printed in China

13 14 15 16 17 P 5 4 3 2 1

Library of Congress Cataloging-in-Publication Data
Dupree, Nathalie.
[Comfortable entertaining]
Nathalie Dupree's comfortable entertaining : at home with ease and grace.
pages cm
Originally published: New York : Viking, 1998.
Includes index.
ISBN 978-0-8203-4513-0 (pbk. : alk. paper)
1. Entertaining. 2. Cooking. I. Title. II. Title: Comfortable entertaining.
TX731.D824 2013
642'.2—dc23
2012034506

Nathalie Dupree's Comfortable Entertaining: At Home with Ease and Grace was originally
published in 1998 by Viking Penguin, a member of Penguin Putnam Inc.

This book is for all those who want to issue hospitality with ease and grace—especially the young women my friends and I wish we could have taught more—Audrey, LuLen, Gail, little Marion Sullivan, Mary Rawson, and Margaret Foreman.

ACKNOWLEDGMENTS

Once again I am indebted to many people—my husband Jack, who found my agent, Angela Miller, for me, and supported me every step of the way, and my good friends and helpers, Kay Calvert and Richard Lands, without whom the manuscript would not have been possible. Kay has loyally worked for me for over twenty years, and Ric has helped me since the taping of *New Southern Cooking*'s second series, over ten years ago. They are an invaluable part of my team.

Recipes and tips were also generously provided by Marion Sullivan, Peggy Foreman, and Carole Landon. All the testers were priceless, as were the friends who read the manuscript and made comments, who gave recipes, who lent their houses for the photo shoot, and those who volunteered to help. These include Spring Asher, the Australian Meat and Live-Stock Corporation of New York, Traci Badenhausen, Victoria Cohen, Merrill Davis, Penny Goldwasser, Elise Griffin, Bud Koram, Elizabeth Land, Sara Levy, M. Cory Lewis, Sandy Linver, Elliott Mackle, Barbara Morgan, Karen Oakley, Drexel Pringle, Lydia Rajczak, Anne Rand, Pat Royalty, Patricia Scott, Todd Weinstein, Virginia Willis, and Wendy Wolfenberger. Reading *China and More* provided valuable assistance with propping.

Amy Mintzer gave incredible editorial support, as did my editor, Carole DeSanti. Her assistant, Alexandra Babanskyj, is ever helpful and cheerful, thank goodness. Tom Eckerle, the photographer, is enormously pleasant and easy to work with. The beauty of this book is due to Jaye Zimet, design director. I am truly grateful for her skill and grasp of my message. She translated my vision into photos as beautifully as I could have hoped for. Two other people aided immeasurably with the photographs: Penny Goldwasser, my interior designer, who is my mentor in the visual and arranged to use homes of other clients for the photography, and Virginia Willis, who has gone from being my apprentice years ago to a top food stylist for print as well as television. My producer Teresa Statz is a great aide in translating print into motion. Thanks to the loyal GPTV crew as well. Special thanks to Howell Raines for the use of his home for the cover.

CONTENTS

CONTENTS

Nathalie Dupree's COMFORTABLE *Entertaining*

INTRODUCTION

Comfortable Entertaining: What It Means

I hosted my first formal party at the age of ten. My eleven-year-old sister and I married off our four-year-old brother to a little girl in the neighborhood. We planned the entire wedding—from finding the bridal gown and the groom's suit to rounding up cookies, which we baked, and cheese straws, which a neighbor graciously donated. From that day on, I knew I loved giving parties.

By the time I was in my teens, my parents were divorced, my mother was working as a low-paid government clerk, and funds for entertaining were nonexistent. I did it anyway. I served iced tea or Cokes with chips and onion dip, and we had a great time. Those parties at Mother's included so many teens crammed into our small apartment that she hardly could move. (Her philosophic response: "At least I know where you are.")

Entertaining is a mindset, an attitude as well as a practice—not quite an art form but more than a craft. Like most artistic endeavors, it is a marriage of personal expression and technique learned through observation and experience. An excellent host may well be self-taught, with the desire to entertain in a way that is graceful and comfortable. A good guide can help you avoid catastrophes—or at the very minimum, put them into perspective. This book talks about my mistakes as well as my successes, what I have learned not to do as well as what I hope you will learn to do.

What do I mean by comfortable entertaining? The *Oxford English Dictionary* defines comfortable as "affording mental or spiritual delight or enjoyment." (Also "free from pain and trouble"—let's keep that in mind as well.) To entertain, it says, is not only "to provide sustenance for a person," but also "to take upon oneself an obligation." The key ingredient in entertaining is the desire to be hospitable.

During my freshman year in college, I lived with my father and stepmother. It was a dramatic change. As ranking colonel on an army post, my father lived in what seemed to me an enormous house. There were protocols for every aspect of daily life, especially entertaining, which was itself inextricably linked to the obligations and rituals of military life. The lessons I learned during those years also contributed to my knowledge—positive lessons about how to give structure and organization to a gathering as well as negative lessons in what to avoid. The food was much better than the sodas and chips I provided at my mother's, and the napkins were folded absolutely correctly, but the rigid ambience didn't foster lighthearted fun.

Good and bad, much of what I know about the heart of entertaining I learned from my parents. Make your guests comfortable in your home. Welcome them, truly welcome them: Being delighted they are there is the spirit of entertaining. Being well enough prepared so that you can enjoy yourself with them is the practical key. Everything else—menus, decorations, table settings—comes after. Comfortable entertaining embraces the key ingredients: the host and the guest.

Practice What I Preach

You can only learn to host successfully by doing it.

Although practice doesn't lead necessarily to perfection, it *is* the key to better entertaining. In fact, perfection isn't the goal, and neither is professional-level catering or competition with a top restaurant. The goal is your comfort and the comfort of your guests, and nothing will be comfortable to you if it isn't familiar.

So how to begin? Not with a black-tie, sit-down dinner for twenty. Start small with what you know. Little by little, add to that experience, and soon you'll be as much of a pro as you need to be. Only through entertaining will you find your own style of entertaining. Through cooking for friends you will develop a core of recipes that you're comfortable making and serving, that you can embellish or simplify as the occasion demands. As with other meaningful endeavors, your entertaining style likely will reflect your personality.

If you're most comfortable in a casual, laid-back atmosphere, when you think of entertaining you may be inclined to buy some paper plates and napkins, throw burgers on the grill, and let everyone serve themselves. This is not to suggest there won't be times when even you will want to set the table with cloth napkins and good candlesticks and offer more exotic fare. But if burgers are your style, go for it! Casual reflects you and therefore best serves your guests.

On the other hand, perhaps your pride and joy is your exquisitely decorated home with your porcelain collection prominently displayed. Maybe you dream of setting the dining table for twelve with your finest linen and crystal (even if it's been gathering dust since your wedding). An invitation for burgers on the grill? Probably not. If your style is formal, you will be more comfortable amid the formal trappings. And your guests will recognize these gestures as signs of welcome.

As you entertain, you will probably find that your own comfort level—your individual style—lies somewhere in between.

My favorite former husband was imaginative and especially clever when it came to changing the look of a room. (We once wallpapered the sleeping part of our tiny New York L-shaped efficiency apartment with wrapping paper from Bloomingdale's.) For a party, he would drape our beat-up tables with shawls or quilts and add candles and flowers. Our guests would arrive to an elegant, "new" apartment with an exotic atmosphere.

The important thing is to let it develop. A presentation that is false for you will feel contrived, which may result in both you and your guests being uncomfortable. That's not to say you shouldn't decorate or move furniture for a party, or adapt your style to the occasion. After all, high school gyms and church basements can be transformed into discos and romantic islands.

To paraphrase the ancient Chinese wisdom, a dinner party of a thousand courses begins with a single step. So let's begin.

For first-timers, invite one friend for a meal. Prepare one little thing you have cooked before, or even purchase "carry-out." Pick up around the house. Set a nice table. Be ready at the time you've established. Welcome your guest. *Et voilà!* Bask in the glory of your ability to entertain.

Or plan a picnic. Make some lovely sandwiches and buy a couple of brownies from your favorite bakery. Select your favorite spot in your favorite park and venture forth with basket and cooler in hand. Spread out a blanket. You're a host.

You're Not Quite Finished Yet

*N*ow that you have offered your hospitality, do you feel the warmth and welcome you have created, both for yourself and your guest? Good!

Now ask yourself what you would have done differently. Did you leave yourself enough time for a shower before dinner? Would it have been nice to have had something for you and your friend to munch on while the dinner heated? Could you have saved yourself some stress by buying the brownies the day before instead of en route to the park? Make notes. Try again. Invite your friend back. Ask another. Practice.

Of course, you're not just practicing. You're entertaining.

Nathalie's Golden Rules
for Comfortable Entertaining

Entertaining is a grandiose word for showing hospitality to people whom you want—or need—to have in your home. In reality, most occasions include some mix of want and need, desire and obligation. You want to make dinner for dear friends who are visiting from out of town, but because of their schedule you need to do it on a night that's not really convenient for you. You want to throw a little party for a colleague who's been promoted, but you need to invite everyone in the department—more people than you've ever fed before. You are obligated to take your turn hosting a group's meeting at your home, but you want to do it as nicely as others have and without too much stress. Or you just want company—to spend some time with someone.

Sometimes we welcome friends and family into our home with joy and gladness; sometimes we just get cornered. But all those times can be made more pleasurable if you take to heart the principles of comfortable entertaining.

1. *Think about who's coming and why before you think about the menu.* If you give some thought to the purpose of the gathering, to the guests, to their needs and your own before you start picking recipes, you'll be off on the right foot.

2. *Serve what you know.* There are two reasons for this: First, true hospitality is not about impressing others but it is about expressing yourself, and you do that best with dishes that you are comfortable with, that you have cooked often and made your own. The second reason is practical: Attempt something unfamiliar and you might end up with a nervous breakdown and hungry guests.

3. *Be realistic.* Be generous with yourself when deciding how much you can handle. Stay within the comfort zone of your capabilities and you won't go wrong. A confident host is a gracious host. Really, there's little that's more unpleasant than a host who's been too ambitious: A host who's distraught or near nervous collapse from the failure or success of the flambéed pheasant or the origami napkins is not going to do a good job of making her guests welcome. (If the *pièce de résistance* is something you can create in advance, however, shoot for the moon, knowing that if it doesn't work, you will have time to do something else.)

4. *Plan ahead, start ahead, work ahead.* Get as much done as possible in advance. It is better to reheat than to be frantically preparing while your guests watch from the edge of their seats, or worse yet, sit in the dining room while you slave away in the kitchen. Planning enables you to space out your efforts. Do some planning, and don't procrastinate.

5. *Make yourself and your guests comfortable.* Different guests and events have different requirements, as do stages of life. Chances are an elderly guest won't be happy

to see hot and spicy food, and children will be upset by whole fish. Sitting on the floor may be ideal for your best friend and all wrong for your boss. When I was a student, I entertained differently from the way I did as a restaurateur. Know your guests and know yourself.

Why do I call these my Golden Rules? I believe that food is nourishment for the soul, as well as the body, and that spiritual sustenance is offered along with dinner when we entertain. The joys and pleasures you give your guests are those you would be grateful to receive.

Comfortable Entertaining: How It Works

Every occasion begins with a desire, an obligation, or a creative impulse in the mind of the host. If the next impulse is to write down the menu, fight it. That's way down the line (unless your creative impulse came from a culinary theme or event, such as a shrimp boil or a cookout, and even

---

This is a cautionary tale about Golden Rules #2 and #3.

I once lived in what was called the oldest house in Greenwich Village, a very tiny house on Bedford Street. My roommates and I regularly had "at-homes" on Wednesday nights, when we served wine and cheese and not much else, encouraging our guests to bring wine as well. At one of these at-homes we decided we would roast a suckling pig for Thanksgiving the following week. One of the regulars said he would bring the pig and we set about inviting others.

Thanksgiving morning came: no pig. We couldn't reach our pig-buying friend, so we rushed out and, somehow, found an 18-pound pig for sale Thanksgiving morning (the magic of New York). After we stuffed the pig with fruit, we skewered him with straightened-out coat hangers and put him over a small wood fire. (He barely fit in the fireplace.) The pig toppled into the flames a few times, and a very poor draw in the chimney soon had the house moderately smoky. Then my boss and his family showed up.

Cooking the pig over low heat was the best we could do, and the pig didn't get done until well after it was time for my boss to take his children home to bed.

Ultimately, the pig was succulent and meltingly delicious—for anyone who cared enough to stay. But oh, to have had a fall-back plan like a turkey or ham in the oven, and a sense of what to do when we found ourselves in trouble.

I used to think of this as a disaster story (and I'll always wonder if the episode moved me away from advertising as my career), but it was a thoroughly exciting Thanksgiving. And since I believe you can never be punished for gathering friends together, maybe if I'd been a better holiday planner/pig roaster, I wouldn't be writing cookbooks; I'd be in advertising, and nowhere near as happy.

then you should hold off on constructing the actual menu). Though many people who love to entertain also love to cook, there are many considerations that supersede gastronomy—venue, time, logistics, guests' food allergies, and budget among them. Whether you're starting with the realization that you have no choice but to make dinner for your in-laws on Saturday night or with the passionate desire to throw yourself an extravagant housewarming party, the process and the principles are the same: They are Planning, Preparation, Presentation, and Participation.

Nathalie's Party-Pitching Principles: The Four Ps

*P*LANNING As soon as that entertaining impulse strikes (and it can hit you anywhere, at any time), start planning. You'll need both a master plan, which defines and refines your vision for the gathering, and a tactical plan: what has to be done and when. An experienced host with a guest list of one may complete a master plan mentally in five minutes. A novice considering an event for forty may write it over several days. In either case, the components are the same.

Ask yourself the same questions a reporter does before writing a story: Who (is invited)? Why (am I giving this party)? When and Where (will it be)? What (will I serve)? And the two Hows: How (will I serve)? And How (am I going to accomplish this)? As you figure out the answers to who, why, when, where, what, and how you are going to serve, you are developing your master plan. The second how—how you accomplish it—is your strategic plan.

DEVELOPING THE MASTER PLAN
1. Start with the guest list.
2. Set the place and date and time.
3. Decide how much you can afford, in both time and money.
4. Decide what to serve.

The guest list

ᴥ Make a *first* draft of your guest list. You'll need to revisit it after you've worked your way through 2, 3, and 4 in the list above.

ᴥ It is important that each guest feel comfortable and enjoy the company of the group. Odd numbers should not be a problem, as long as a guest doesn't sit like a bump on a log with no one to talk to because the table arrangement gives him/her no companionship. (In fact, five is a wonderful number for a dinner party, maybe my favorite.)

ᴥ Remember that there are talkers and listeners. It helps to include a talker or two when you are entertaining more than six people. But a major talker can dominate a small group to the exclusion of others, which is undesirable.

ᴥ To determine how many is comfortable, particularly for large parties, remember the mingling theorem: the length of the party divided by the number of guests equals how much time you'll have to visit with each one. (A two-hour party is 120 minutes, so with sixty guests the host has 2 minutes per guest.)

Decide when. The date and time may be determined by the occasion—breakfast, brunch, lunch, after the game, tea, cocktails, before theater, dinner, dessert, midnight snack. The "when" may also be influenced by your budget or by the nature of the event. A last-minute supper is tonight; a wedding or bar mitzvah may be planned a year ahead. So . . .

Set a budget. For some reason, the only party givers who consistently set budgets are college students with $40 to spend on beer and pretzels and parents planning to spend a hefty chunk of their life's savings on a daughter's wedding. Your party is probably somewhere in between, but you, too, can benefit from a budget. The amount of money and time available will influence the number of guests, the type of gathering, and the menu.

For a casual dinner, you may not need to think twice about a budget. For a large party, if your response is either "It doesn't matter how much I spend" or "I want to spend as little as possible," you are probably headed for trouble. Be realistic.

Budget for:
ᴥ food
ᴥ beverages
ᴥ decorations, including candles and flowers
ᴥ additional plates, glasses and flatware, laundry expenses
ᴥ any serving and cleanup help (before or after)

If you foresee the guest list might create awkward situations, plan the menu and special touches as conversation ice breakers. I was asked to host a dinner party to introduce a recently appointed city officer to the leaders of various charity groups. After the invitations were issued, I realized there were many difficult elements among the guests—ex-spouses, ex-employees, competitors. I planned an eating-implement and finger-food party. (I also used a seating plan.) Asparagus tongs, lamb chop holders, marrow spoons, fish knives, and forks were among the tools I used to set the table. Everyone was intrigued. Partly because of the novelty of the flatware interspersed with the finger food, the conversation flowed easily, away from the personal, which is, after all, the purpose of a conversation piece.

Now budget for your time:

🌢 How *much* time do you have to give to this event, and what kind of time is it? If you are working full-time and have small children, your available preparation time may come in bits and pieces, an hour here, 15 minutes there, spaced out over weeks. Others may be able to dedicate a whole chunk of time—like an entire weekend—to prep, cook, and freeze.

🌢 Consider the *value* of your time to you, weighing preparation time against the cost of ingredients. A casserole can be cheap, but it might take the better part of three days to prepare. Salmon or tenderloin can be pricey but take less time and energy from market to table.

🌢 Consider your time *priorities*. Know what you realistically can and can't do. If you feel the house is more important than the menu, so be it. Purchase the best carry-out you can find or afford, put it in your own serving dishes, name it something special, and enjoy.

Decide where. Even if the party is going to be at home, there are still "wheres" to answer. You have more options than you may realize at first:

🌢 Assess locations for both space and equipment to help determine where you will entertain. Is your dining room too small to seat twelve? Could you set a small table by the fireplace for an intimate dinner for four?

🌢 Check tables and chairs, refrigerator/freezer space, grill, oven, stovetop, and the serving areas for food and beverages. This review will generate some questions about needed equipment. Will you need to rent or borrow additional tables or chairs? If you set up a bar in the hall, will it block the coat closet? Should you add a card table for coffee and tea? Where will the coats go?

When my husband-to-be, who at the time was not experienced in entertaining, and I were courting, he invited me to Oxford, Mississippi, to meet his friends. Jack planned a dinner featuring fried catfish for twenty at a restaurant with only four tables. The quaint Busy Bee Cafe was run by an elderly lady, Miss Isaiah, a legend in Oxford. Although the café was a far cry from a white-tablecloth restaurant, my beau set out flowers, place cards, and wine. His enthusiasm that evening produced an air of glamour felt by all. And I was impressed.

Decide how you will serve. Out of necessity this decision dovetails with the "where" and the "when," but it has the most effect on what you will serve, which comes next. Here are some of the usual choices:

🌢 Hors d'oeuvres can be set out or passed

🌢 You can serve from a buffet or at the table

🌢 With a buffet, your guests can sit down to eat or stand

Okay, *now* it's time to plan the menu.

SETTING THE MENU: *The Big Questions*

The menu should take into account all those decisions you've been making about who, where, and when. Here are the Big Questions:

❡ Consider your time: The menu determines what can be done ahead in terms of shopping, cooking, and even decorating.

❡ Consider where you are: Do you have the cooking and serving equipment to manage your menu choices? That is, if you're toting a picnic, the food needs to be portable.

❡ Consider how you're serving: If you are planning a stand-up party—however formal or casual—everything you serve must be edible with one hand alone, whether with finger or fork. If it's a sit-down dinner, you need to decide if you are plating the food before it is served, passing bowls family-style, or serving from behind the guest (like a butler). If you will be without help in the kitchen, don't attempt to individually "plate" more than one course, and then make it either the first or the last.

❡ Consider whom you've invited: For a smaller party, ask guests in advance if there are any foods they can't eat. Plan your menu accordingly, particularly in the case of genuine allergies or religious restrictions, but don't feel you have to accommodate every dieter's demands. Serve enough variety so that everyone will have something to eat, even if not a whole meal, without burdening yourself unduly.

Now select foods that fit within those parameters.
Balance is key to a comfortable, workable menu, not just the balance of foods but the balance of time. A large piece of meat will take a long—but unattended—time to cook, and therefore is the easiest thing to do as long as you have a block of time when you'll be home anyway. Smaller individual entrées, like scallops, take less cooking time but probably either are more expensive or require more of your attention and time to prepare.

You do want balance on a menu, as well. Consider the combinations of flavors and textures, and strive for an overall effect that will be delightful for your guests and manageable for you.

A cocktail party may seem like an easier alternative to a full-fledged dinner party, but it's probably the most expensive kind of party you can give in terms of both money and time. Bite-sized food is costly to purchase; if you make it yourself it is very time-consuming. (For tips on making it easier, see page 172.) You'll have a big liquor bill, since people drink more standing and munching and mingling than they do sitting (that's the point, after all). Per hour of consumption, drinks are more expensive than food. (I, personally, believe that alcohol should never—no exceptions—be served without food, including a substantial protein. I also realize this statement well may ignite The Great Debate. For the affirmative side, I only can cite "Nathalie Dupree's First Rule of Serving Alcohol.")

One of the least expensive ways to entertain nicely is a brunch. Brunch involves little or no alcohol and can use eggs, fruit, and bread as its core without compromising.

Avoid using the same prominent ingredient or cooking method in every course—the usual culprits are shellfish, cream, tomatoes, individual spices, and fried foods.

Use recipes you know, or ones you can experiment with ahead.

Now refine the guest list. In light of the budget, the location, the date, and the menu, are there problems with your original guest list? How many people can you invite? (In the past, I've frequently forgotten to count myself. Now I complicate the problem by tending to forget to count my husband, as well as myself. So I have to check to be sure I haven't overinvited. At one dinner party, husband Jack and I ended up perched on a windowsill in the corner of the dining room.) How many elderly and/or frail guests do you expect? Will you be able to accommodate their needs? Among your guests, is there someone you can count on to help, or will you be doing everything? And can you? Once you are satisfied with the list of guests, you can think about inviting them.

Invitations. In collecting information for your invitations, no matter what their form (printed, verbal, or electronic), it is important that your guests have everything they need to know: date and time, certainly, and possibly who will be there and why you are gathering, as well. Be explicit about what your guests can expect—light hors d'oeuvres, sit-down meal, buffet brunch; casual clothes, black tie, Sunday best. For some gatherings, I find it helpful (for guest and host!) to include a beginning and an ending time—for example, 7:30 until 9:30.

A NOTE ON RSVPs

I have found the longer the guest list, the less likelihood of an appropriate number of RSVPs. In today's busy world (or that, at any rate, is the excuse), people often don't respond even to a written invitation. This has become so consistently true that I usually don't even request an RSVP for larger parties. For events where the "head count" is critical, the host, unfortunately, must assume a proactive role in eliciting responses. A follow-up call is usually a good idea for any sit-down meal.

If you are going to request RSVPs, please consider: Who will accept them? Will your children write down the messages? Are you willing to let RSVPs fill up your business VoiceMail to the exclusion of a message from an important client? How do you plan to respond to the responses?

Be sure to keep a list of the replies. Don't trust your memory, especially for large gatherings.

Think about what you will do if a guest asks to bring others—adults and/or children. Know the answer before the question arises, and be prepared to respond diplomatically whatever your decision.

It has been my experience that "RSVP—Regrets Only" unfortunately doesn't motivate people to respond as they should.

Deliver (via mail, telephone, e-mail, or fax) the invitations and hope for RSVPs. Don't hold your breath.

THE STRATEGIC PLAN: *The Big "How"*

So how *are* you going to get everything done? You're going to need a strategic plan, a list of what needs to be done and when it's going to be done: It's that complex and that simple.

Whether your dinner party is tomorrow night, or the wedding is in six months, start a list and a timetable and add to it. Include the dates and times you intend to work on a specific task. (Remember to keep your list where you can find it—I keep mine on the refrigerator—and write individual items on your calendar. You'll be more inclined to treat it like a real commitment.) Strategic-plan highlights include cleaning, laundry, setup, shopping, decorating. Remember the food—preparing in advance, freezing, defrosting, reheating, beverage chilling. Be sure to cover the finishing and serving details.

Review your workplace. Check the freezer and refrigerator for space, as well as the oven and stovetop. Is there enough room for plated salads or desserts? Are there enough heating elements to prepare or reheat the dinner? This is the time to fine-tune the menu. Note on the timetable where everything is to be reheated or cooked—microwave, stovetop, oven—and where you will put the hot pans when they come out of the oven. Is there enough space?

Plan the shopping. Remember to make time for this! Your shopping list should include groceries, ice, beverages, coffee, and tea as well as candles, paper supplies, flowers, or other decorations. This is not as daunting as you might think. Divide the list into perishables and nonperishables, and purchase the nonperishables as far in advance as you can.

Organize extra hands. Write a list of duties for those assisting—children, spouse, friends, paid help—then make contingency plans. Unpaid help is not always reliable, and even paid help can let you down. Determine your "wants" as well as your "musts." Yes, bows tied to the chairs would be pretty, but the main course is crucial. Set priorities.

Plan your cooking time. Map out a plan for when you are going to do what. Remember what you noted about how much and what kind of time you have available. (See individual

One of my friends from grade school, Juliette Lam, is now a top corporate interior designer. Her husband's parents are Chinese restaurateurs who taught her a great deal. We all know how well she does Chinese cooking from scratch. But when she flies in from Kuwait or India and wants to have us in her stylish home the next day, she sometimes purchases the best local dim sum and serves it up beautifully on her antique Chinese plates with no apologies. Whether or not she cooks it herself is not crucial to her guests; it's the hospitality and charm that matter. And the evening is always memorable. Faced with similar time constraints, you might decide that you don't want to miss out on the cooking, choosing to hire someone to help with the silver instead.

One of the most outstanding memories of grace under fire is of my friend Danielle Depleuch. Once, in Paris, I invited her to join me for dinner at a three-star restaurant, since my traveling companion couldn't go out to eat. (In a three-star restaurant, they are not happy to see someone dining alone—they keep thinking about the person who could be sitting opposite you, spending more money and entertaining you.) We had a thoroughly memorable meal of incredible delicacies. Danielle turned right around and invited us to dinner the next night, one of the few times I have ever been invited to a French home for a meal. We accepted with alacrity, as Danielle was famous for the production of fine fois gras on her family estate. She was in Paris, however, on a shoestring budget. But, as she welcomed us into the tiny Parisian flat, a wonderful aroma greeted us and there was not even a hint of apology in her manner. The kitchen was large enough just for her. There was no dining room. But the bedroom was immaculate, an African-print throw on the bed, a lighted candle on a tiny bedside table. The four of us ate a marvelous meal of leg of lamb and flageolets (tiny beans) on the bed, perhaps one of the best meals I ever had, and a truly elegant presentation. It was no surprise Danielle became the personal chef to the premier of France.

chapters if you're preparing a menu from this book.) For a big party or a complicated menu or just to give yourself confidence on your very first forays, make a countdown plan for heating, finishing, and serving.

Plan relaxation time. Block out time for yourself to rest and get ready. Three or four days before a Really Big Party, take the evening off. Go to the movies, curl up with a book. For a small dinner party, give yourself at least an hour, preferably two, for putting your feet up.

Plan some contingency time. Build in a window for the unexpected—last-minute calls for directions that can tie you up for half an hour, a run to the store to replace the spilled sugar, even a call to pick up a stranded guest at the train station.

Set the drop-dead time. This is the most important! What is the very latest time you can change your plan and still feel calm and in control when your guests arrive? Whenever that is, usually P (party) minus about two hours, is your drop-dead time—budget for it. At drop-dead time, you stop fussing, make a decision, and stick to it. Now is when you decide once and for all whether you'll light the coals or grill indoors. Now is when you say "It's too late to iron the tablecloth, or make a second dip for the vegetables." What's not done by drop-dead time can't be and you must admit it. If you set your drop-dead time well in advance of the day and write it on your timetable, it will be pre-ordained and that much easier to stick to. You'll thank me.

$\mathcal{P}$REPARATION Congratulations! You're on to the second P.

How much to prepare. There is no easy answer to determining quantity. There are many variables—the time of day, the age and weight of the guests, the formality of the occasion, the manner in which the food is served—the list goes on and on. Generally, people rarely eat more than a half pound of food total at one sitting. (Sure, many restaurants sell a 12-ounce steak, but most diners take part of it home.) A pound of food prior to preparation "shrinks" to one-half to three-quarters of a pound when cooked, which should be ample for each person for dinner. Better the happy dilemma of leftovers than empty serving dishes and hungry guests.

Cleanup: In advance. Assuming your house is clean on the surface, tidying is more important than deep cleaning before a party. When scheduling time for cleaning before the party, only you know the answers to how much needs to be accomplished, but there are important basics. At the top of that list is the bathroom—the cat litter clean, the commode and sink sparkling, and plenty of toilet paper, tissues, soaps, and towels on hand. (I have found through unofficial surveys that guests will use anything except starched linen towels to dry their hands, so I no longer put them out. I have replaced them with terry-cloth fingertip towels, which are stacked in a pretty basket.)

Just before your guests are expected, check again to be sure that surfaces are clean, the bathroom appears immaculate, and the sink and the dishwasher are empty. Fair warning: Be prepared for the curious whose "need to know" may extend to the medicine cabinet, the shower, the linen closet, and who knows where else. (I normally schedule time for a nap before my company arrives and sometimes the bed doesn't get made. Whether the bed is made or not, I usually consider that room off-limits and close the door. I'm amazed when guests enter the upstairs bedroom anyway.) Don't start a load of dishes unless there is time to put them away before your guests arrive. In an emergency, put dirty dishes and/or last-minute cooking equipment out of sight in a spare cooler or dishpan. It's essential to have the sink and dishwasher empty to clear to during the meal.

During. Have a plan for clearing the table between courses and for removing used plates, glasses, and so on if it's a buffet. Try not to clutter kitchen counters with used plates and silver; you will probably need those surfaces later for putting down hot pans, carving, and serving. If I have a minute while I heat up a course, I might put dishes in the dishwasher. Remember that too much kitchen activity during the meal might well

You may face the option of choosing to hold your party in the Great Outdoors. If the temptations are obvious, so are the risks. Consider the weather. As a rule, I suggest avoiding large, unsheltered, outdoor events during the more unpredictable months. (See page 288 for tent information.) But even in June in Southern California, things can happen. If you plan to have a party of any size outdoors, remember that it is best to simultaneously plan the same party for indoors and set a drop-dead time for deciding which it will be. Then relax. Unexpected rain, heat, or cold can be the foundation for disaster or an excuse for happy spontaneity. And the weather is one thing you can't do anything about.

After you have learned, through practice and experience, the rules for menus, it is occasionally fun to really break them. One of my more memorable dinners was all asparagus. The "whys" were celebrating Spring (asparagus season) and a friend's terrific job change. I began with asparagus Chinese-style with soy and ginger; the second course was asparagus soup; then came asparagus and orange salad; the entrées included asparagus and shrimp in butter sauce and asparagus and chicken stir-fried. And finally, I served asparagus in an apricot sauce. The only thing I didn't do was dip the asparagus in chocolate. Maybe next time.

have guests jumping up with offers to help, which ruins the flow of conversation and of the evening.

After. Include this in your strategic plan to ensure that you have the time, the help, and the equipment that you need. Even if you prefer to do most of your cleaning the following day, do check surfaces that might be damaged by spills or leaks, remove all glasses, and wipe up. Beyond that, decide what will work for you. I find that I actually enjoy post-party cleanup time. Near the end of large gatherings, a friend will usually pitch in. Rinsing dishes and loading the dishwasher provide time for companionship—often it's the best time for a real talk.

$\mathcal{P}$RESENTATION You are the producer and the director for this presentation. It's opening night, and you are in charge. It is your cast, your script, your location.

Part of entertaining is showmanship. Take a simple meal, dim the lights, add candles, *et voilà!*—instant theater.

Your considerations are the same as any director's: a beautiful set, effective lighting, mood-enhancing music, and the fluid movement of the actors. The presentation of the food is another way to add to the mood. My cooking teacher always said that people eat with their eyes first.

Tables. Conversation naturally flows better—side to side, as well as across without shouting—at a round table that comfortably seats six or eight. With a little squeezing such a table can accommodate a few more. A round table is also ideal with an odd number of guests because it doesn't emphasize the paired and the nonpaired. Among people who entertain frequently, most prefer round tables.

Which is all well and good if you happen to own a round table. I don't.

My dining room table, which I inherited from my mother, is oval. The room is small and no round table of size would fit.

How long should the cocktail hour be? I'm rarely willing to put off dinner for more than forty-five minutes after the invited time. There does have to be some time for most people to relax and cluster a bit before they go in to the table and to allow for late arrivals, but people have a right to be served food within an hour of the time they arrive. A secondary reason is that much more than that between arrival time and serving time necessitates the host spending more party time in the kitchen—putting food in the oven, heating it up, or removing it from the refrigerator, when otherwise food can be slipped into the oven when the first guests arrive, or when a discreet timer goes off in half an hour. When you are writing your time chart, remember to work backward from when you want to serve.

There is no formal obligation to serve anything to eat before dinner, but I always keep a munchie on hand. Even nuts will do, or olives, but something is needed for munching. Nonalcoholic drinks must always be served alongside alcoholic. (Although this comes under the heading of know your guests, or know your crowd, but it's especially important when you don't know your guests.)

And besides, my life isn't perfect, so why should my dining table be? When the leaf is added, the table will seat ten semi-comfortably and twelve in a pinch. If the guest list reaches twelve and if the guest list and occasion accommodate it, I usually set two tables for six—one in the dining room and the other in the adjacent kitchen hall. Two rooms, two tables make it awkward for me to serve alone, so I enlist one person to help from the other table. Because space is at a premium,

After my second year in college, I was living in a loosely run boardinghouse for international students in Cambridge, Massachusetts. It was there I had my first encounter in cooking for more than a few people. The cook became ill, and I volunteered to fix the meals while she was out. (I was a bit behind in the rent and this was an easy way to make up the difference.)

The first evening I cooked tuna casserole. Since the recipe served four and there were eighteen in the house, I multiplied the ingredients by five, including the fat for cooking the onions. In the too-small pan, I couldn't stir it well enough for the sauce to thicken. My baked casserole ended up with four distinct layers—grease, milk, flour paste, and tuna, which had sunk to the bottom. I skimmed off the top layer of fat, stirred the remaining concoction, added some green peas, spooned the rather soupy mixture over toast, and dubbed it Tuna Fish à la King.

The next evening Uri, an Israeli student, helped me cook spaghetti and meatballs. Again I multiplied the quantities by five. Uri, however, was a literalist. The recipe read, "Form 20 meatballs," and that's exactly what he did—even though we had five times as much meat as the original recipe called for. Just before it was time to serve, I discovered Uri's twenty baseball-sized, barely cooked meatballs in the oven. I broke up the meat, sautéed it, and served spaghetti and meat sauce to rave reviews. The moral of the story: Be careful when you multiply . . . and don't announce what you're planning to serve until it's on the table.

I do not use armed chairs. In fact, I occasionally resort to card-table chairs to squeeze in more people.

With a very large table and fewer guests, maintain the cozy atmosphere by seating them together at one end, perhaps with a cluster of flowers at the other.

Lighting. Lighting is crucial, especially if guests will be sitting for a couple of hours looking at one another. It should be as soft and flattering as possible if your goal is muted, thoughtful repartee. If, however, your aim is a loud, jazzy party, turn up the lights and the music and conversation will become more boisterous.

Music. I love the idea of soft music floating through the rooms to greet my guests. I usually have it playing when guests arrive, providing a festive mood. But as the party progresses, conversation can be forced into competition with that same music. When the music takes on the distinct characteristics of another voice, I turn it off. Later, when the tone of the gathering becomes mellow, I introduce my favorite soft, flowing jazz.

A note to guests: Don't bring flowers that are not in vases. It is distressing for a host to have to leave the guests to find a vase, fill it, and find a place to put it! Flowers are best sent a day ahead so the host has time to position them. Wine can be welcome, but if it doesn't fit well with the meal, it can be reserved for a later time.

Flowers. Although I took classes at Constance Spry in London, arranging flowers is not my forte. Whether you're arranging or buying, table flowers should always be below the sight line of those seated.

Although I do love flowers, there are many other centerpiece and decorating possibilities. Free your imagination. A centerpiece is a focal point drawing attention to the dining room, buffet, beverage, or dessert table and the food. Look around your home. Do you have a collection of pottery, figurines,

One thing you can't control—and believe me, I've tried—is where your guests will cluster. No matter how you plot or plan to create space, people still herd. The doorway between my front hall and living room attracts guests as if it had garlands of mistletoe stuffed in the molding. The living room, a few feet away, can sit empty while twenty people crowd in that doorway. At first this bothered me, but I have learned to accept it. They have chosen the spot where they are the most comfortable. If my guests are comfortable, I guess I can be, too.

or wooden boxes? If they're attractive and won't get in the way, they might make a lovely centerpiece.

Whether you decided to use flowers or objects, decorations and centerpieces are among the best ways of displaying your personal style.

Special touches. Making each guest feel treasured and welcomed, can be particularly difficult if you are entertaining a large group. I have learned, although it's not been easy, to accept that I can't offer abundant servings of individual attention to a crowd. (Remember that mingling theorem.) This is where special touches come into play.

Truth be told, people don't always remember the menu, but they usually do remember the trappings—dining by candlelight on the terrace, lanterns lighting the driveway, the music selections, the unusual invitation, the clever place cards, a favor to take home.

But do remember: You will undo all your good intentions if you're cranky because you stayed up too late the night before wrapping favors or if you're frantically lettering elegant place cards instead of having cocktails with your guests. Remember your priorities.

$\mathscr{P}$ARTICIPATION Perhaps the most important P is participation. If you and your guests don't participate, what difference did all your efforts make?

As a host, you must be sure that you've accepted the decisions of the drop-dead time with good humor—and if the shrimp is bad or the rug unvacuumed you must shrug it off and laugh.

Your job is to make your guests feel safe, wanted, and joyous, to keep their time with you as pleasant as possible. That starts with making sure they are greeted, that they meet people interesting to them, that you feed them before they drink too much, that you keep things moving, whether it's conversation or dirty glasses, and that you see them safely on their way home, secure in the knowledge that you were delighted to have them there, because you wore a happy face the whole time they were with you.

Their job is to revel in all the doors you open for them and respect the closed doors of your life. They are supposed to be good sports, to refrain from criticism of your best efforts, and to take cues from you about what behavior is acceptable—whether joining in lively debate on sex, religion, and politics, or in basking in a bride-to-be's radiance. They, like you, should put on a happy face and be glad they are there.

Be there for your guests and be who you are. And enjoy yourself: It's your party too.

How to Use This Book

*A*head are twenty menus, beginning with a breakfast, then simple suppers easily planned and prepared by one person, and ending with full-fledged, all-out, no-holds-barred holiday meals. In between are more elaborate sit-down dinner parties, fork-only and finger-food-only buffets, both casual and elegant, and cocktail parties. The menus are organized according to how they are presented—Sit-Down Meals, Fork Meals, and Finger Meals. Of course, many "sit-down" meals can be served around the coffee table or on trays, and many of the "standing" menus would work just fine in the dining room. In some instances, I've suggested alternative ways of preparing and presenting the meal, but all the menus and recipes have been chosen for their flexibility and adaptability.

Each menu includes a brief introduction to give you an idea of why I like this menu and how you can use it, a cooking time line to help you with some of the logistical considerations, and then the recipes.

Cooking a goose or a duck for the first time can lead to a delicious meal or a calamity. It can be a bit tricky, and so it's a good idea either to cook ahead and reheat (which is usually better for duck, anyway, as it turns out), or invite very, very good friends. My first experience in cooking duck was in a rented apartment in Washington, D.C., that had a very small kitchen. I compiled a recipe that was a pastiche of recipes from small pamphlets written for liquor companies, heavy on the Grand Marnier (an orange liqueur) and light on good directions.

The only pan to be found was not a roasting pan but a cookie sheet with no sides. I stuffed the duckling, and forgetting entirely about my episode with the fatty pig some years before, I didn't take a thought for the fat of the duck. I placed it on the cookie sheet in the oven, served my guests a drink, and sat back to wait for it to be done. We were all a bit excited, as it was everyone's first home-cooked duck. After half an hour or so, we smelled smoke. The duck was making marvelous sizzling sounds from the oven, but smoke was oozing from the sides of the oven door. By the time we opened the door, the oven floor was in flames. All the duck fat had slid off the cookie sheet onto the bottom of the oven. Fortunately, we had a few clever people with us. As a fireman guest on my cooking show told me, the first thing to do when you have a kitchen fire is to cut off the source of the heat, in this case, the oven. The next thing is to smother the fire. Do this by sealing the oven doors, covering the cracks with heavy towels, or covering the flame itself with a towel heavy enough to smother it. Keep the fire contained. Do not run through the house with the offending blazing pan, as that may set the whole house on fire. Do not throw flour or baking soda or salt onto the fire unless you are a chemist and know what will explode. Use a fire extinguisher only as a last resort, preferably after you've called the fire department for advice. With luck, you may put out the fire simply by smothering it, then be able to open the oven door, clean up the mess, and do as I did, put the duck into a sided pan and continue cooking it. It makes for an hysterical story, and you and your friends will never forget it. But better they should remember how delicious it was!

Use the whole menu or selected parts of it and add your own favorite dishes. As you gain confidence, try doing the same menu in another way: Take a sit-down dinner on a picnic or use the recipes in new ways by trying the variations or serving small portions of a main course as an hors d'oeuvre.

Last, there is a chapter of additional core recipes, some of which are great in emergencies, others of which require more planning. What makes them core recipes is that regardless of changing circumstances, changing food fads and fashions, you can always rely on them.

Learn the elements and practice the entertaining basics, and you will gain the confidence to add the fanfare. Once you are comfortable with a few core meals and a few practical principles, you will be ready to welcome people into your home with ease and grace.

On the menus, recipes followed by asterisks can be store-bought.

Multiplying Recipes

Most recipes can be safely multiplied to feed more people.

&. *Never multiply a recipe by an uneven number. It's conventional wisdom among experienced cooks that it doesn't work, maybe because the math is too hard to keep up with.*

&. *It's safer to arrive at the right numbers by doubling a recipe (on paper) and then doubling it again than it is to try to multiply by four, especially if you're not mathematically inclined.*

&. *As with many things in life, you need to use your judgment and rely on your own taste. Not all ingredients need to conform to strict mathematical rules. For instance, the amount of fat needed for sautéing needn't be doubled even if you are doubling the recipe. You still only need to cover the bottom of the pan to sauté even twice as many onions.*

&. *Timing is trickier than quantities. When doubling a recipe, timing by the clock might not have to be multiplied by two—or it may take much longer, depending on the pan size. Watch for the indications mentioned in the recipe—bring to the boil, heat until soft, stir until brown—and ignore the number of minutes. The result is more critical than the amount of time it takes. Buy an instant-read thermometer, one of a cook's best friends.*

&. *Before you start preparing the recipe, write down the multiplied ingredients and the quantity. It is safer than trying to do it in your head. With a written record, if something does go wrong, you might be able to figure out and correct any mistakes due to faulty multiplication.*

&. *And remember, food multiplies. According to some mysterious spiritual law, a recipe for four multiplied by four usually will serve more than sixteen. Remember the parable of the loaves and fishes, or you might have an enormous amount of leftovers.*

SIT-DOWN MEALS

A simple sit-down meal is the most natural way to share our table with friends, since it's the way most of us eat most of the time. It's an easy way to begin if you are new to entertaining. Of course, the term "sit-down meal" (breakfast, lunch, or dinner) encompasses a very wide range of possibilities, from a weeknight supper of spaghetti and salad, served family-style, to a multi-course extravaganza complete with formal service, lots of forks, and your good silver. Though one extreme requires substantially more time and work than the other, your own comfort—and therefore that of your guests—can always be increased with a little planning and a little practice.

These menus will give you an idea of how to plan a meal—whether impromptu or long planned—for guests and of ways to organize your own favorite recipes.

Don't be afraid to be known for serving one of these menus, or any of the individual components, over and over. They are included here because they wear well with time and should become regulars in your repertoire. Once you've done several of these meals, you'll see new ways to mix and match the recipes for yourself, taking your favorites from each of the menus and putting them together in new ways.

Everyone should have a core of recipes that can be served simply and casually or dressed up for fancy times, that require a minimum of cooking equipment, and that use ingredients readily available from the local grocery store. When you find a recipe that works for you in this way, add it to my list of core recipes in the back of the book.

Breakfast for Six to Thirty
at 7:30 a.m.

Orange Juice

Orange and Banana Salad with Yogurt Dressing

Melon Cubes with Slivers of Prosciutto

Spinach and Mushroom Strata
(Overnight Casserole)

Bacon and Swiss Cheese Strata
(Overnight Casserole)

Brioche★

*F*or many of us, the morning is the best time for entertaining. We are the most alert, we can meet, love, laugh, and move on to the business of the day.

If you believe, as I do, that successful hosting—entertaining—is based in large part on the Golden Rule, then breakfast is a good time to begin, because starting friends and loved ones off right in the morning is a wonderful thing to do. Think about how you feel when things aren't right for you in the morning, and you'll want to do right by your guests, giving them what they want—actually, need—to eat and drink and feel comforted, soothed, then exhilarated at the prospect of the day ahead. It is an important time to put on a happy face for your guests, rather than greet them harassed, tired, or grumpy. You want it to appear that it was no problem. Keep it simple, and it won't be.

I can't emphasize enough how important it is to be ready well ahead of the time that you expect your guests to eat, especially when you are entertaining weekend guests. In that case, the self-service coffee area should be ready as early as 7:00 A.M. for those who like to begin their morning right away with coffee. A drop-dead time is *crucial* so you know when you are in trouble, in which case throw yourself on the mercy of the early birds who probably are the kind of people who love the early morning and have been wide awake for hours.

This menu is especially handy because almost all of the preparation can (and should) be done by the night before, allowing the host a degree of leisure in the morning. If you're serving in the late morning or early afternoon, put out a bowl of whole fruits and a few tasty snacks, and this brunch menu should prove hearty enough to carry everyone through to an early supper.

There's a final reason why a lovely breakfast is the perfect way to start entertaining: The person or persons who share your home are already available and willing to be practiced on!

If you are expecting a large number, adjust the menu and determine if you are going to have enough seats, serving dishes, china, flatware, linens, and containers for jam. Read through the introduction and the "Buffet for Twelve to Fifty in Four Hours" (page 172) to find tips for large-scale entertaining before you proceed. Either make one strata multiple times, preparing double batches as necessary, or make a variety. If you are serving thirty people at a sit-down occasion, you may find it easiest to cook the strata in the smaller-size baking dishes indicated, so you will be able to have several stratas for each table. The fruit salads should be multiplied up as well. If you are serving both salads they will serve twice as many as the number indicated on the recipe, as people will take less. As a guideline, for thirty people, make four times as much of each salad and five stratas. For six people, make one strata and one of each salad, planning to have leftovers for a gracious plenty, or make just the melon salad.

Brunch has usually been an easy meal for me, so I was startled at the difficulty in adjusting the same menu to 7:30 A.M., when I volunteered recently to host a breakfast meeting of my career women's group. There were several things I didn't count on. First, it was early summer and I thought surely I could use the deck! (The truth is, I'd recently had my living room redecorated and I wanted to show it off, uncluttered with tables, so I didn't want to put up inside tables if I could avoid it.) It's one thing to have an eye on the sky hours before a party is scheduled; it's quite another to face the "in or out" decision when you're barely awake and guests are arriving momentarily.

So I fiddled around when the weather looked ominous. I waited until 6 A.M. to set the tables out, and then vacillated. My dear husband was hauling tables for thirty in and out of the house at 7:15 when the first guests showed up early. (Another thing I hadn't considered: 15 minutes early at 7 A.M. feels a lot different from 15 minutes at 7 P.M.) They huddled in a corner, poor souls, out of the way of the moving tables, without coffee. I'd been so distracted I'd forgotten all about it. The meeting started late. Someone said, "Nathalie looks harassed." That pulled me up short. Even for thirty people, the menu could not have been easier, but I hadn't heeded my own advice about a drop-dead time. It didn't rain, after all.

Cooking Time Line

Remember, each day, check your preparations list for things like cleaning, shopping, setting the table, and drop-dead time. If you elect to use a store-bought item (or more than one), make sure it's on your shopping list (and obviously, then, you don't need to make it).

UP TO 3 MONTHS BEFORE

1. Make the brioche and freeze.

UP TO 2 DAYS BEFORE

1. Cut the melon cubes, oranges, and prosciutto. Refrigerate separately. Do not cut up the bananas ahead.
2. Prepare the yogurt sauce and strata(s) and leave in plastic bags.

UP TO 1 DAY BEFORE

1. Remove the brioche from the freezer and leave out to thaw.

The Day

UP TO 2 HOURS BEFORE

1. Preheat the oven. Put the strata(s) into baking dish; cover.
2. Set out the melons with the prosciutto, oranges, and bread.

UP TO 1 HOUR BEFORE

1. Put the strata(s) into the oven to cook.
2. Slice the bananas and toss with the oranges. Set out with the yogurt sauce.

SERVING COFFEE TO GROGGY MULTITUDES

Perhaps the most important tip of all about this menu is to be sure you have plenty of coffee. Considering the number of guests, and remembering that each will drink two or three cups, you may want to rent a fifty-cup coffeemaker in addition to whatever your regular pot makes. If so, you should be aware that it takes almost an hour to perk, and that it pulls a lot of electric current. Test it out beforehand to be sure that it doesn't flip a circuit breaker. A thirty-cup coffeemaker is a good investment. It takes about 30 minutes to perk, uses less power then the fifty-cup model, and is less likely to cause power trouble. Alternatively, use a large thermos to keep one pot of coffee hot while another is brewing. In either case, remember to plug in the coffeepot in time for the first guests to have a cup.

I suggest putting coffee, the makings for tea, and your juices out in a different place from where the food will go. That way, guests can help themselves without interfering with the food service. It's true that coffee is a big thing these days, somewhat comparable to wine with lunch or dinner, but don't get caught up in the mystique of the terribly expensive or flavored types. Just buy good coffee and your guests will be happy. Most people want their coffee to have caffeine in the morning. As there is an occasional decaf drinker, make a pot of this in a small coffeepot and label it decaf.

As for tea, pour boiling water in a hot beverage carafe and put it out with a selection of caffeinated, decaffeinated, and herbal tea bags. Don't use a carafe that has been previously used for coffee—your tea will have a coffee taste to it.

Do not stack the cups and saucers separately and expect your guests to match them. Each cup should be on its own saucer. A pile of small, pretty paper or cloth napkins would be nice. Use a "spooner" (an old-time spoon holder that looks like a wide-mouthed vase is a staple in the South), a beautiful glass, or a vase for the teaspoons, or put the spoons on the saucers.

Orange and Banana Salad with Yogurt Dressing

SERVES 4 TO 6

I so love the fresh taste of ambrosia that I combine bananas and oranges all year long. The yogurt dressing expands the whole salad, but the salad is very refreshing even without the dressing.

2 navel oranges
1 to 2 tablespoons
   chopped mint
3 bananas, sliced
   Yogurt Dressing
   (below)

Grate the peel from the oranges and reserve for the dressing. Then peel the oranges, removing all the white pith. Cut the oranges into ¼-inch slices to make wagon wheels, or section them, removing all membranes.

Combine the oranges and mint. Refrigerate, covered, a couple of hours or overnight. Add the bananas no more than 1 hour before serving.

Put the salad in a pretty glass serving bowl and serve with the yogurt dressing on the side.

YOGURT DRESSING

MAKES 1 CUP

Low in fat and tasty, it's welcome with any fruit. If you're using the dressing with oranges, remove the peel first, before juicing the oranges.

1 cup plain yogurt
1 teaspoon grated
   orange peel
2 tablespoons fresh
   orange juice
4 teaspoons honey

Combine the yogurt, peel, orange juice, and honey. Refrigerate, covered, until needed. Serve on the side with fruit or pound cake.

Melon Cubes with Slivers of Prosciutto

SERVES 4 TO 6

My husband and I regularly ripen store-bought melons at room temperature for several days, then cut them up and store them in plastic bags for our breakfast. (We learned this from the way they are sold pre-cut in grocery stores.) This recipe is the way we dress them up for weekend guests, brunches, or starters. Cantaloupe is preferred, but honeydew works in a pinch. The most important thing is the ripeness.

1 cantaloupe or honeydew melon
¼ pound very thinly sliced prosciutto

Peel the cantaloupe. Cut it in half and remove the seeds. Cut the melon in cubes or scoop out balls. Place in a plastic bag for up to 3 days. Cut the prosciutto slices into ¼-inch-thick strips and store, wrapped separately. Toss the prosciutto with the melon no sooner than 30 minutes before serving.

Pour into a pretty serving bowl or a melon basket (page 95).

VARIATIONS

Multiply by 6 to serve 30 people.

❧

Wrap the melon with prosciutto strips and secure with a toothpick. Serve as an appetizer or munchie.

SHOPPING TIP

Melons

When purchasing cantaloupes look for even "webbing." The greener the exterior, the less ripe it is. Melons continue to ripen when picked, if kept at room temperature. It is all right to use them when they have a few soft spots, although the soft spots may have to be removed.

Spinach and Mushroom Strata (Overnight Casserole)

SERVES 6 TO 8

While strata means "layers," and the dish used to be assembled in layers, here is a quicker, easier way to come up with an overnight casserole. I find it easier and safer to store the assembled casserole in double best-quality zippered plastic bags than to put the casserole in a dish, where it takes up too much room. In an emergency it may be assembled and baked right away—it won't puff as much but is perfectly fine. The casserole may also be baked ahead and reheated but will not be as light.

4 tablespoons (½ stick) butter
1½ to 2 pounds mushrooms, sliced
1 pound fresh spinach
10 slices bread
1½ cup (½ pound) finely chopped Brie or creamy goat cheese
9 large eggs, lightly beaten
1 teaspoon Dijon mustard
3 cups milk
½ to 1 tablespoon chopped fresh tarragon, or ½ teaspoon dried
Salt
Freshly ground black pepper

Preheat the oven to 350°F. Lightly grease a 13x9x2-inch baking dish or two shallow 1½-quart casseroles.

Melt the butter in a large skillet. Add the mushrooms and sauté until soft, about 5 minutes. Meanwhile, tear off the tough stems of the spinach. Wash thoroughly and add the still damp spinach to the mushrooms. Cover the pan and cook until the spinach is wilted, about 5 minutes. Strain and reserve any liquid. Set the mushrooms and spinach aside.

Meanwhile, remove the crusts from the bread and cut it into cubes. Mix the bread, cheese, spinach, and mushrooms. Pour into a zip-type plastic bag. Mix the eggs, mustard, and milk. Add the tarragon and season to taste with salt and pepper. Pour the egg mixture into the bag and seal, carefully squeezing out the excess air. For safety, slide this bag, zipper end first, into a second zip-type plastic bag and seal. If possible, refrigerate overnight.

An hour before serving, spread the mixture evenly in the baking dish or casseroles. Cover with a lid or foil and bake for 30 minutes. Uncover and bake another 30 minutes. May be refrigerated several days or frozen up to 3 months.

VARIATION

Asparagus, Brie, and Pear Strata

Substitute 3 pears sliced in wedges for the mushrooms and 1½ pounds blanched asparagus pieces for the spinach.

TIP

There is a strong variety of tarragon on the market, called Mexican tarragon, as opposed to French. I find it very harsh, so I'm careful not to overuse it.

Bacon and Swiss Cheese Strata (Overnight Casserole)

SERVES 6 TO 8

This is strata's answer to quiche. I frequently use it for Sunday-night supper along with sliced tomatoes or a simple salad, particularly when I have weekend houseguests. Think of it as a "bacon and eggs" breakfast. It can be baked as soon as it is assembled but is best when mixed a day before baking. The baked casserole may be made ahead and reheated, but it isn't as light.

6 to 8 slices bacon
2 to 3 tablespoons (⅓ stick) butter
¼ cup finely chopped shallots
10 slices white bread
2½ cups shredded Swiss cheese
9 large eggs, lightly beaten
3 cups milk
2 tablespoons Dijon mustard
1 teaspoon dried thyme
Salt
Freshly ground black pepper

Preheat the oven to 350°F. Lightly grease a 13x9x2-inch baking dish or two shallow 1½-quart casseroles.

In a skillet or microwave, cook the bacon until crisp. Drain it and let cool. Break the bacon into 1-inch pieces and put into a large zip-type plastic bag.

In a small skillet, melt the butter, add the shallots, and sauté. Set aside to cool slightly.

Trim the crusts from the bread slices and cut the slices into 1-inch pieces. Add to the plastic bag.

Add the cooled shallots and the cheese to the plastic bag and shake to combine.

In a large mixing bowl, whisk together the eggs, milk, mustard, and thyme, and salt and pepper to taste. Pour the egg mixture into the plastic bag and seal, carefully squeezing out the excess air. For safety, slide this bag, zipper end first, into a second zip-type plastic bag and seal. If possible, refrigerate overnight.

An hour before serving, pour the mixture into the baking dish or casseroles and spread evenly. Bake, covered with a lid or foil for 30 minutes. Uncover and bake another 30 minutes. May be refrigerated several days or frozen up to 3 months.

Brioche

MAKES 10

A brioche is a light and flavorful egg bread. Traditionally made in fluted brioche molds, it may be made in muffin cups or a loaf pan. I make this in a food processor, although it may be adapted to a stand mixer. It freezes well, if well wrapped, for up to three months, so you might want to make a double batch.

Since my son-in-law is French, I love keeping this on hand in the freezer for weekends when they drop by with the baby, Claire. He is always kind enough to say how much it resembles "the real thing." But it does excel at brunches and for weekend guests. Baked as a large brioche or loaf (see Tip), it makes wonderful French toast and sandwich bread.

1 package active dry
    yeast
⅓ cup sugar
¼ cup warm water (105°F.
    to 115°F.)
2⅓ cups bread flour
¾ cup (1½ sticks) butter,
    cool but not hard-
    chilled
3 large eggs

Glaze
1 egg yolk, beaten with 2
    tablespoons water

TIP

You can make one large brioche or loaf in a traditional brioche mold or loaf pan. Shape the dough as above, into one brioche, or shape as a regular loaf. Cook 30 minutes, or until the loaf registers 200°F. on an instant-read thermometer.

Preheat the oven to 375°F. Grease and flour 10 small fluted ⅓-cup brioche tins or one 3-cup brioche pan.

Dissolve the yeast and 2 teaspoons of the sugar in the warm water. In a food processor or mixer, combine the flour and the remaining sugar. Beat in the cool butter. Add the yeast mixture. Beat in the eggs, one at a time. Continue to beat until the dough is shiny and glossy and forms long slick strings that have an adhesive quality. (Usually if the food processor turns off automatically, the dough is ready.) Place the dough into an oiled plastic bag or oiled bowl and turn to coat. Seal or cover and let rise in a warm place until tripled, about 1 to 1½ hours.

Punch the dough down, recover, and place in the refrigerator for 6 hours or overnight. Take ¾ of the now spongy dough and, working quickly, form it into 10 balls to fill the greased brioche tins by two-thirds. Cut a ½-inch-deep cross in the center of each ball. With the remaining dough, form small pear-shaped knobs. Fit the pointed ends of the knobs into the center holes, making sure to press firmly in place. Let rise, uncovered, in a warm place until the dough has doubled, about 45 minutes to an hour, and place on a cookie sheet.

Brush the dough with the egg glaze. Bake on the middle rack of the oven until nicely browned, about 15 to 20 minutes. Let cool slightly before removing from the tins and then let cool completely on a rack. Keep in an airtight container for several days or store frozen for up to 3 months.

Three Simple Suppers

𝓔very person entertaining alone (or with a partner who is useless—I mean, a better guest than a host) needs menus that can be prepared without any stress and served without a helper. The following recipes can be the base of your own core menus. They are so good you can use them over and over and no one will object. They are expandable with the addition of a starter such as seviche or a soup; you should add your own munchies. The salads may be served before, with, or after the main course, depending on your timing and preference. Make notes about what works best for you. For instance, would you rather have the salad or starter on the table when your guests arrive, or do you like a longer hors d'oeuvre time, then serve the main course and salad together? There's no one way to do it!

The trick in single entertaining is preparation, aided by a simple menu. If you don't want your guests uncomfortably hungry because you are disorganized, prepare ahead. Do all the things we've mentioned before—get the ice, set the table, empty the dishwasher—to make yourself look serene. Don't go rushing out at the last minute to shop. Try to have it all organized ahead of time, so you will be calm. If there is only one of you to handle last-minute phone calls, disasters, and so on, you need more grace time and an honest drop-dead time. It's always helpful to have one friend who will help you clear and stay and talk to you as you wash dishes. Equally important is a good conversationalist who will keep the ball rolling while you are up and down with the wine, water, and food. Impromptu meals are another good way to begin to entertain as well. Guests at impromptu meals are usually good friends, so mistakes are forgivable at these meals if you want to use them as practice run-throughs for more extensive—or "important"—menus later.

There are some dangers in shopping at the last minute—there may be no Cornish hens, or they are all frozen, or no steaks available, just roasts, which take longer to cook. If you can't shop ahead, and the worst happens, be fearless: Cook a roast chicken or take your whole tenderloin and cut it into steaks, or your rib roast into boneless rib steaks (that will give you some nice ribs for use at a later time on the grill as well).

The munchies you serve should be your most comfortable favorite. My friend Carol Greer—an impeccable hostess—is perfectly happy serving a delicious store-bought spread from a jar with crackers or zucchini rounds. If you prefer making your own, see the list of munchie recipes on page 33. The breads and desserts range from very easy to somewhat challenging but are doable once you've tried them carefully. Purchase yours if you prefer and save the dessert making for another time.

And remember, if the finest restaurants in the world now serve pizza, so can you!

> *A little-known fact is that a table of five makes for wonderful conversation. The host can slip out to the kitchen knowing the guests will have one another to talk to or all four can talk together.*

> *For safety's sake—and to save your sanity—don't ever do an all-new menu at once. Take a dish you already know and love and substitute it in my menu. Or make one of the main dishes and add the best bread you can find and a store-bought dessert.*

My friend Molly Peterson once set a good example for me. As we walked into her lovely home, we could tell by the way our noses wrinkled that there was a problem with the shrimp she planned to serve. She asked me if I thought the seafood was bad. I did. We laughed, and she called out for pizza. Of all the meals we've shared, that is one we both most remember with affection. I remember how beautiful her home looked, and her charm and graciousness—and her apology and good cheer.

I have had enough kitchen disasters to learn that a little catastrophe needn't hurt anything. It can give you an opportunity to laugh. Friends worth having will forgive a mistake. The trick is to know when to admit your mistake and figure out how hard to work to fix it. Once I might have made myself miserable and neglected my guests trying to revive a dead entrée. If something catastrophic should happen now, I would make some pasta or order out. Accidents do happen. The trick is to not let them spoil the evening.

OTHER SIMPLE MENUS

Spinach and Mushroom Salad (page 265)
Vegetarian Lasagna (page 276) or
   Dudley's Lasagna (page 130)
Chocolate Roulade (page45)

Munchies or Tapenade Bread (page 254)
Onion Soup with Thyme Croûtes (page 262)
Simple Salad (page 60)
Raspberry-Pear Cobbler (page 280)

Roast Chicken (page 270)
Herbed Rice (page 265)
Snow Pea Salad (page 266),
Grilled Vegetables (page 264), or
   Last-Minute Roman-Style Spinach
   (page 265)
Cinnamon Ice Cream (page 284)

Quiche Lorraine (page 257)
Simple Salad (page 60)
Fresh Peaches or Pears in Creamy
   Caramel Sauce (page 285)

Steamed Mussels (page 258)
Simple Salad (page 60)
Brownie Truffles (page 282)

Beef with Celery and Walnuts
   (page 272)
Simple Salad (page 60)
Fruit Plate (page 76)

One-Pot Chicken (page 270)
Herbed Rice (page 265)
Soufflé Omelette with Jam (page 282)

Logistics for Three Simple Suppers

Here are three meals that can be prepared at the last minute if you have not had time to fix ahead. Although the breads and desserts would be doable by an experienced cook, less experienced hosts may prefer to purchase them, or make them ahead and freeze them.

When you adapt the time chart to your own schedule, remember there are three critical time frames: the arrival time of your guests, the amount of time you are going to spend welcoming your guests and schmoozing, and the time you want to sit down to dinner. A good kitchen timer with a clear and hardy signal is helpful to some. Always start with a preheated oven, and with the pans and dishes you will need for heating and serving, in addition to your set table, ready to be used. Make a place to set down hot dishes straight from the oven.

If you're entertaining without assistance, planning is essential. Figure out a table setting that works for you—your favorite place mats, napkins, which glasses—and use it for any of these meals. Set the plates on a base plate, or charger, on mats, or on a simple cloth, or if you have a beautiful table, leave the wood bare. Vary with flowers and centerpieces.

Menu 1

Munchies

Pear and Walnut Salad

Cornish Hens with Lime Spice Marinade

Green Beans with Mushrooms

Mock Potatoes Anna

French Bread (page44) or Focaccia★

Cinnamon–Orange Panna Cotta

This menu is designed for its simplicity and ease.

Grilled and roasted chickens are at the top of my personal favorites for company. But so many people are afraid of carving chickens that it is a good first step to start with Cornish hens, which can be served whole or easily split. There is nothing controversial in this meal, with a lot to like and nothing not to like. The menu is designed around the hens, with a salad starter, which will give you a breather if you have last minute things to do. The hens can be made ahead or done at the last minute. The dessert should definitely be made ahead.

When you are in the mood to vary this menu or serve more people, add the Simple Salad (page 60) as a side dish and the Shrimp and Fennel Risotto (page 43) as a starter.

Serving family-style is the easiest way to entertain, particularly if you don't have room in the kitchen to plate the hens individually. (I find I only have space to serve up one course. If I try to plate two courses, my kitchen is a jumble and I feel pressure at being away from my guests too long.) Do note, however, that all the recipes in this meal except the potatoes are good cold and this would make a lovely picnic, or summer meal, served cold or at room temperature.

Cooking Time Line

If you elect to use a store-bought item (or more than one), make sure it's on your shopping list and obviously you don't need to make it. Here's a timeline for preparing this menu in 4 hours, though much can be done ahead. It's not anywhere near 4 hours of cooking time: I've given you plenty of breathing room for all your preparations, including setting the table. A timer will be an invaluable help.

4 HOURS BEFORE

1. Prepare spice paste for the hens and marinate in refrigerator.
2. Make panna cotta.

2½ HOURS BEFORE

1. Make Mock Potatoes Anna.

2 HOURS BEFORE

1. Arrange clean lettuce on salad plates and chill.
2. Make cream cheese mixture for salad.

1½ HOURS BEFORE

1. Snap and cook green beans, cook mushrooms; leave together in pan to reheat.

2. Set table.
3. Dress and rest.

½ HOUR BEFORE

1. Set out munchies.
2. Start grilling hens.
3. Slice pears.
4. Set out ice, drinks.
5. Turn hens if necessary.
6. Serve pear salad.

AT SERVING TIME

1. Reheat bread, green beans, and Mock Potatoes Anna.

Pear and Walnut Salad

SERVES 8

This recipe can also be used as a light hors d'oeuvre, to dress up a cheese display, or to make a savory for a dessert party (see Variation).

4 ounces cream cheese, at room temperature
1½ to 2 tablespoons heavy cream
8 ounces blue cheese, crumbled
Juice of 1 lemon
1 cup water
4 ripe but still firm pears, unpeeled
Lettuce leaves, arugula, mixed greens, and so on, to line plates
½ cup toasted walnuts, roughly chopped

Beat the cream cheese with an electric mixer until soft. Beat in just enough cream to get a soft consistency. Gently fold in half of the crumbled blue cheese. This may be done in advance and refrigerated, but the mixture should be at room temperature when placing with the pears.

Mix the lemon juice and water in a nonreactive bowl or container. Cut the pears in half lengthwise and cut out the center core. Slice the halves lengthwise into wedges and put them in the lemon juice and water. You can leave the pears in the lemon water 3 to 4 hours. Drain and pat dry before using.

Line salad plates with the greens of choice (or none if you have high-contrast plates). Arrange 4 pear wedges on top and spoon a line of the blue cheese sauce down the center of the pears. Sprinkle the remaining blue cheese and the walnuts over all.

PEARS WITH WALNUT AND BLUE CHEESE DIP

Arrange as many pear wedges as desired on a tray. Increase the amount of cream to ½ cup for a thinner consistency. Finely chop the walnuts and fold them into the dip along with the remaining 4 ounces blue cheese. Pour the dip into a decorative container and place it in the center of the tray.

Cornish Hens with Lime Spice Marinade

SERVES 4

Cornish hens are one of the easiest things to cook. Built like a chicken, they are a step down in "degree of difficulty." Cornish hens are particularly nice for a seated dinner party. There is always some indecision about how much to serve. I never eat a whole hen, but my husband sometimes does. So for a seated dinner, I make one per person, but I keep the dream of leftovers in my mind. There is enough coating here for six hens. When oven space is a problem, I cook four, then put the final two in the oven, carefully setting the timer, when the guests arrive. Leftover Cornish hens can be served with salad and cheese for a nice lunch, or you can mix the meat with rice or couscous and serve hot or cold. The backbone is easily removed either by cutting straight down the middle or on either side with a knife or scissors. This allows the hen to lie flat on the grill and makes it easier for the diner to cut.

3 tablespoons lime juice
2 tablespoons olive oil
4 garlic cloves, chopped
2 whole scallions, finely chopped
Grated peel (no white attached) of 1 lime
1 tablespoon freshly ground black pepper
½ to 1 teaspoon cayenne pepper
1 teaspoon chili powder
1 teaspoon ground cumin
1 teaspoon dry mustard
½ teaspoon salt
½ teaspoon ground coriander
4 Cornish hens, backbones removed

Combine the lime juice, olive oil, garlic, scallions, lime peel, black pepper, cayenne, chili powder, cumin, dry mustard, salt, and coriander into a paste.

Flatten the hens by pressing heavily on the breast, cracking the bone. Spread the paste evenly over the hens. Cover with plastic wrap and then weigh them down, using cans on a plate for instance. Marinate in the refrigerator 24 hours if possible. (This flattening allows the hens to cook evenly.)

Place skin side next to heat and cook on a hot grill about 20 to 25 minutes per side, turning occasionally to prevent overbrowning, although a little dark flecking is pretty and tasty.

If roasting, preheat the oven to 400°F. Grease or spray a shallow roasting pan with nonstick spray. Place the hens side by side, but not touching, in the prepared pan. Cook the hens, uncovered, until a meat thermometer measures 170°F. and the juices run clear, about 45 minutes. If you are using two pans, rotate them periodically to allow even browning.

The hens may be cooked up to a day ahead and refrigerated. Reheat under the broiler or in a hot oven.

Split the hens completely and place them on a serving platter, piled up in a circular pattern at 15-degree angles.

Green Beans with Mushrooms

Green beans are an excellent foil for mushrooms as well as tomatoes, herbs, and other garnishes. They are easily made ahead and reheated in butter or oil on demand.

1 pound green beans,
   tipped and tailed,
   strings removed
3 tablespoons butter or
   oil
⅓ to ½ pound mush-
   rooms, sliced
2 tablespoons chopped
   fresh parsley or other
   herbs
Salt
Freshly ground black
   pepper

Bring enough water to cover the beans to a boil in a large pan. Add the green beans and let return to the boil. Boil, uncovered, until crisp-tender, 5 to 7 minutes. Drain the beans. This may be done several days ahead, and the beans kept refrigerated in a plastic bag or covered container.

Meanwhile, melt the butter in a skillet, add the mushrooms, and sauté until the mushrooms are soft. This may be done ahead several days and the mushrooms kept refrigerated in a plastic bag or covered container.

When ready to serve, add the beans to the mushrooms in a large skillet and heat through. Season to taste with herbs, salt, and pepper.

VARIATIONS

Use porcini, chanterelles, portobello, oyster, and other mushrooms, fresh or reconstituted, or a combination of all, if you like.

Substitute asparagus (page 155) for the green beans.

Mock Potatoes Anna

SERVES 6 TO 8

This is a delightful way to spruce up a meal. The potatoes alternate between crispness and softness, can be eaten with fingers or a fork, and can be shaped in rounds or hearts. The dish multiplies easily, each potato serving more than one person, when you have several, in a loaves-and-fishes way.

6 potatoes, peeled and
     sliced ⅛ to ¼ inch
     thick
6 to 9 tablespoons butter
     or oil
   Salt
   Freshly ground black
     pepper
3 to 6 tablespoons
     chopped fresh herbs
     (optional)

Preheat the broiler or oven to 500°F.

Arrange the thinly sliced potatoes on a well-greased or nonstick baking pan in overlapping wheels. Pat with butter or oil. Season well with salt and pepper. Place under broiler or in hot oven until deep golden brown. The potatoes may be prepared ahead to this point.

When ready to serve, turn carefully with a spatula, pushing together any parts that separate; brown quickly; remove to a serving plate; and sprinkle with the herbs, if using.

Cinnamon-Orange Panna Cotta

Panna cotta, Italian for cooked cream, is fast working its way up to being my favorite dessert. Ever so delicate, it slides down the throat, refreshing as it goes. A butter cookie, orange slice, or biscotti makes a lovely accompaniment.

2½ **cups heavy cream**
¼ **cup sugar, or more to taste**
2 **teaspoons orange extract**
½ **to 1 teaspoon ground cinnamon**
2 **teaspoons gelatin powder (1 package)**
¼ **cup cold water**

Oil or spray a 3½-cup glass pie dish with nonstick spray.

Heat 1 cup of the cream with the sugar until small bubbles form on the sides, 2 to 3 minutes. Remove from the heat and add the orange extract and cinnamon. Meanwhile, sprinkle the gelatin over the cold water in a small metal cup or pan and let it develop into a sponge. Melt the gelatin over gentle heat. Stir the dissolved gelatin into the warm cream, then stir in the remaining (cold) cream. Place over a pan of ice and stir until the mixture is chilled and nearly set. Pour into the prepared pie dish. Refrigerate 30 minutes or until completely set.

Gently pull the dessert away from the edge of the dish to "catch an air bubble," which will allow it to release from the dish. Put a very lightly oiled serving plate on the mold and turn over. Give the mold a shake to unmold the panna cotta onto the plate. (The oil will let you slide the panna cotta until it is centered.)

VARIATION

Substitute vanilla extract for the orange extract and omit the cinnamon.

TIP

After the main meal, the plated panna cotta can be moved from the refrigerator to a trivet so that it will not sweat; the dessert can be served with a wedge-shaped instrument such as a cake server or with two large spoons. Alternatively, put the dessert on the table and let everyone help themselves. I'm of the opinion that the panna cotta should not be served in the kitchen. It is prettier on the presentation plate than on individual plates.

Menu 2

Munchies

Simple Salad (page 60)

Shrimp and Fennel Risotto

French Bread★

Chocolate Roulade

Cooking Time Line

Here is a schedule for preparing this menu in 4 hours, assuming you have made the bread in advance or are using store-bought. (This includes time to dress and set the table. The menu doesn't require anywhere near 4 hours of cooking time.) If you are not cooking the risotto in advance, you certainly won't need 4 hours, but you will spend 30 to 45 minutes in the kitchen while your guests are there.

4 HOURS BEFORE

1. Make the roulade "sheet."
2. Whip cream for roulade and refrigerate.

3 HOURS BEFORE

1. Make risotto if guests can't join you in the kitchen.

2 HOURS BEFORE

1. Clean and prepare salad ingredients.
2. Set table.

1½ HOURS BEFORE

1. Finish roulade and refrigerate.

1 HOUR BEFORE

1. Dress.

30 MINUTES BEFORE

1. Set out drinks and munchies.

Shrimp and Fennel Risotto

SERVES 4 TO 6

This version is probably not traditionally Italian as Italians would not put cheese in the risotto if adding shrimp, and they usually add their heated stock slowly, cup by cup. It does save time to add most of the hot stock at once—a trick I learned from Lorenza de' Medici—but it still needs stirring and watching. I also prefer Parmigiano-Reggiano Parmesan whenever it is available. The risotto can be made ahead and reheated in the microwave. Substitute 3 cups sliced celery and 1 teaspoon roughly ground fennel seeds if no fresh fennel is available.

This recipe yields 8 cups, sufficient for a light meal for 4 or perhaps 6 or for a starter for 8.

6 to 10 tablespoons (¾ to 1¼ sticks) butter

3 small fennel bulbs or celery (1½ to 2 pounds), thinly sliced, to make about 3 cups

1 pound peeled and deveined shrimp

1 small onion, finely chopped

2 cups short- or medium-grain rice

½ cup dry white wine, regular or nonalcoholic

4 cups fresh or canned chicken stock or broth, heated

1 cup grated imported Parmesan cheese

8 sprigs fennel greens, chopped, or 1 teaspoon fennel seeds

Salt

Freshly ground black pepper

Heat 3 tablespoons of the butter in a 4-quart saucepan over low heat. Add the fennel bulbs and cook slowly until tender, about 25 minutes. Add the shrimp and cook over low heat until done, 3 to 5 minutes. Remove from the heat and set aside.

Melt 3 tablespoons butter in a large heavy skillet. Add the onion and cook over medium heat until tender, about 5 minutes. Add the rice and cook over low heat, stirring constantly, until translucent, adding more butter if needed.

Add ¼ cup of the wine, stirring constantly. Bring to the boil and add the remaining wine and 1½ cups of the hot chicken stock. Bring back to the boil and, stirring occasionally, cook until the liquid is nearly absorbed. Add 2 cups of the hot stock in ½ cup increments, each time cooking until the liquid is nearly absorbed. Continue until the rice is al dente, having a little firmness to it (15 to 20 minutes). Taste the rice and if it is still crunchy, add the rest of the stock and cook 5 minutes more until all the liquid is absorbed. Remove from the heat, add the cheese, fennel greens, shrimp, and remaining butter if desired, stirring with a fork, not a spoon. Season to taste with salt and pepper. Cover and let the rice rest for a few minutes before serving. The risotto may be made ahead several days or frozen up to 3 months. If so, reheat in the microwave or in a large nonstick skillet. Fluff with a fork before serving.

French Bread

This is the simplest bread to prepare, with its crisp crust making it crunchily close to traditional French bread. Many times I make the dough one day and refrigerate it in a plastic bag until the next day, then shape and let it rise the day I bake it. This gives it more flavor, as does a sourdough yeast. Slicing it on the diagonal makes a prettier presentation.

1 tablespoon cornmeal
2½ to 3½ cups bread flour
1 package quick-acting yeast
1 teaspoon salt
1½ teaspoons sugar
1 cup hot water (135°F.)

Glaze
1 egg, beaten, mixed with 1 tablespoon water

Preheat the oven to 400°F. Grease or spray a baking sheet with nonstick spray and sprinkle it with the cornmeal.

In a food processor or mixer, combine 2½ cups of the flour, the yeast, salt, and sugar. Add the hot water. Process or knead to make a soft dough like a baby's bottom, adding more of the remaining flour if needed. (Allow 1 minute in a food processor, 5 to 10 minutes in a mixer.) Place in an oiled plastic bag or oiled bowl and turn to coat. Cover or seal and let rise until doubled. Punch down. Shape into 2 long loaves. Place on the baking sheet and leave in a warm place until doubled, about 30 to 45 minutes.

Brush with the egg glaze. Slash the tops of the loaves with a sharp knife. Place on the middle rack of the oven with a small cake pan of boiling water on the bottom rack to help crisp the crust. Bake until brown and crisp, the bottoms sound hollow when tapped, and an instant-read thermometer registers 200°F., about 20 to 25 minutes. The bread freezes well and will keep, covered and at room temperature, a day or two. To refresh and recrisp from the freezer, put frozen into a hot oven until heated through and recrisped. For day-old bread, quickly run it under a light stream of tap water and reheat in a hot oven.

VARIATIONS

Toasted French bread

This makes a very nice toast, particularly brushed with basil oil or melted butter.

❧

Rusks of French bread

To make rusks of bread, slice thinly and place in a 200°F. oven until crisp but not brown, about 1 hour, depending on original freshness of bread—or use Melba toast.

Chocolate Roulade

SERVES 6 TO 8

This flat, flourless soufflé jelly roll is pretty indestructible. So indestructible, in fact, that I used to double the recipe for my restaurant. There are some caveats, however. You should expect it to crack like a log. If you want the smooth look, which I don't, roll it with the smooth side (inside) out. The size of pan is important: too large and it will be dry; too small and it will be too soft and too deep. When you double the recipe, be sure to stagger the pans in the oven so they don't overlap, or else switch places halfway through the baking, so you don't end up with the bottom one burned on the bottom and the top one burned on the top.

6 ounces semisweet
    chocolate bits
¼ cup water
5 large eggs, separated
1 cup sugar
1½ cups heavy cream
¼ cup confectioners'
    sugar
    Vanilla extract
    (optional)

Garnish
    Confectioners' sugar
    Chocolate buttons,
    caraque, or curls
    (page 136)(optional)

Preheat the oven to 350°F. Line a 10x15-inch jelly roll pan with baking parchment or wax paper. If using wax paper, oil the pan and the paper or spray it with nonstick spray.

Melt the chocolate with the water in a heavy pan over low heat, or microwave briefly to melt. Beat the egg yolks with the sugar until light. Beat the egg whites until they're in stiff but not rocky peaks. Fold the melted chocolate into the yolk mixture. Add a dollop of the whites to the yolks to soften, then fold the heavier chocolate mixture into the lighter whites until incorporated. Spread out evenly in the pan and bake until a toothpick inserted in the center comes out clean, about 15 minutes. Remove and let cool thoroughly.

Meanwhile, whip the cream with the confectioners' sugar and vanilla into stiff peaks, taking care not to overbeat.

Sprinkle another sheet of paper with confectioners' sugar. Flip the pan over on the paper and remove the pan. Tear off the baked-on paper in strips and throw away. Trim off any very dark or crisp edges. Spread enough of the whipping cream to totally cover the chocolate. Lift the paper and roll, as you would a jelly roll, starting from a short side and rolling from one end to the other lengthwise for 6 people, or starting with a long side and rolling horizontally to make a longer roll if serving more. Flip onto a platter with the last roll. Sprinkle with confectioners' sugar and pipe remaining cream in rosettes on cake. May be made ahead 3 days and refrigerated or frozen up to 3 months as a sheet or a filled roll, wrapped carefully. Defrost in the refrigerator.

To gild the lily, decorate with chocolate buttons, caraque, or curls (page 136).

Menu 3

Toasted Cheese Cutouts (page 215)

Orzo with Rice

Whole Baked Fish with Spinach and
Tomatoes

Sourdough Bread (page 55)

Grape Clafoutis

*W*hen dealing with people who are traveling on business, you never know how long they will be delayed at their last stop. So I have a few munchies ready—Toasted Cheese Cutouts, a bruschetta, caponata, or some such—to serve when they first come in. The orzo and the rice can each be cooked ahead, and the two tossed with butter or oil and reheated in the microwave. Everything else is ready to go—fish marinated, oven preheated, and the dessert finished. I wouldn't put the fish in until I was sure the diners were on their way.

Cooking Time Line

Here is a schedule for preparing this menu in 4 hours; it will go much more quickly after you've done the recipes a few times and if you have a food processor (or an assistant!) to help with all the chopping. You will also save time if you have the Toasted Cheese Cutouts (page 215) in the freezer or are substituting another munchie.

4 HOURS BEFORE

1. Chop all the ingredients for fish and marinate fish in refrigerator.
2. Cook vegetables for fish.

1½ HOURS BEFORE

1. Make cutouts, if using.
2. Set table.
3. Dress.

2½ HOURS BEFORE

1. Make clafoutis.

45 MINUTES BEFORE

1. Put fish and vegetables in oven.
2. Set out drinks.

2 HOURS BEFORE

1. Cook orzo; cook rice.

15 MINUTES BEFORE

1. Reheat rice and orzo, if necessary.
2. Broil cutouts.

Orzo with Rice

SERVES 6

Many people mistake orzo for a grain, but it really is a pasta shaped like rice. It's fun to mix it with rice for the variable texture. Rice and pasta may be made ahead and refrigerated several days or frozen, if well wrapped, although neither is as wonderful as when freshly made. Restaurants hold and reheat precooked rice in a colander over boiling water. This works for this recipe in addition to the two ways preferred below.

Salt
10 ounces orzo
1 cup long-grain rice
2 cups fresh or canned chicken stock or broth
Freshly ground black pepper
2 to 4 tablespoons butter

Bring a large pot of salted water to the boil and stir in the orzo. Reduce the heat and simmer until al dente, about 10 to 12 minutes, or cook according to package instructions. Drain and set aside.

Meanwhile, put the rice, stock, and salt to taste in a heavy 2- to 3-quart saucepan and bring to the boil. Cover, reduce the heat, and simmer until the liquid is absorbed and the rice is tender, about 15 minutes. The rice should be cooked to the point that when you pierce a grain the center will have a small dot of white. If the liquid has not been absorbed, cook another 2 to 4 minutes. Fluff with a fork and season with salt and pepper to taste.

When ready to reheat, melt the butter in a large saucepan. When it is hot, add the orzo and rice and toss together. Alternatively, toss the orzo and rice together in a microwaveproof bowl, dot with butter, cover with plastic wrap, and heat in the microwave about 2 minutes.

Whole Baked Fish with Spinach and Tomatoes

SERVES 4 TO 6

When people ask me what I serve special friends who also are PBS cooks, I remember this all-in-one fish dish. Martin Yan always arrives early, sometimes joined by Jeff Smith or others in town for an event, and we talk, compare notes, and swap stories until the wee hours. They love the whole fish, head and all, much as I do, with its Moroccan marinade chermoula.

Cilantro, a dominant herb, can be omitted for those who dislike it. The saffron can also be omitted for casual meals, but do use it when the meal is very special. To serve up to 6 people, use the lower end of the range given for the fish and vegetables; to serve up to 10, use the higher end of the range.

3 large onions, finely chopped
7 garlic cloves, finely chopped
½ teaspoon ground turmeric
1 teaspoon ground cumin
¼ cup finely chopped red bell pepper
½ teaspoon finely chopped hot red pepper (fresh or dried)
½ teaspoon saffron threads
½ cup finely chopped cilantro
¾ cup finely chopped fresh parsley
½ to ¾ cup olive oil
3 tablespoons lemon juice
Salt
Freshly ground black pepper
1 (3- to 5-pound) whole sea bass, sea trout, red snapper, or small salmon, cleaned, scaled, with head on

Preheat the oven to 425°F. Oil a pan deep enough to accommodate the fish and vegetables, preferably one you can serve from.

To make the chermoula, mix ½ cup of the onions, 3 teaspoons of the garlic, the turmeric, cumin, bell pepper, hot red pepper, saffron, 6 tablespoons each of the cilantro, parsley, olive oil, lemon juice, and salt and pepper to taste.

Rub the fish with the chermoula and refrigerate 2 hours or more in a sturdy plastic bag.

Heat 3 tablespoons of the oil in a large skillet. Add the remaining onions and garlic and cook until soft, about 5 minutes. Spread the drained spinach evenly in the bottom of the baking pan, stir in the onion and garlic mixture, and then top with the tomatoes. Evenly sprinkle over the vegetables the remaining cilantro, the thyme, the remaining parsley, the lemon peel, lemon juice, and salt and pepper to taste. You may assemble the dish to this point several hours in advance.

Place the fish on top of the vegetables and cover the body of the fish with the chermoula. Measure the thickness of the entire dish—fish plus vegetables. Cover with sturdy aluminum foil. Bake for 15 minutes per inch of thickness, approximately 45 minutes in all. (A cooked fish registers 140°F. on a thermometer inserted at the back, next to the bone.)

Serve in the baking dish or transfer carefully to a large platter. Leave the skin with its flavorful marinade on; cut down to the bone of the fish to serve. Pull up and remove the bone to serve the underside of the fish.

2 to 4 (10- to 12-ounce)
   packages frozen
   spinach, defrosted, or
   2 to 4 pounds fresh,
   blanched and
   squeezed lightly
2 to 3 tomatoes, peeled,
   seeded, and cut into
   ½-inch cubes
1 to 2 tablespoons finely
   chopped fresh thyme
   Grated peel (no white
   attached) and juice
   of 1 lemon

This is best served right away, but leftovers are quite tasty! Always refrigerate cooked fish promptly if you plan to serve it again.

VARIATION

If you can't find a whole fish, this will work with 4 to 6 fish steaks, such as salmon or swordfish, heating the vegetables through before you add the fish, and then cooking again until the fish steaks are cooked.

Grape Clafoutis

SERVES 4 TO 6

This delicious recipe is derived from the traditional French dish clafoutis, developed from leftover pancake batter poured over fruit and baked. That should give you some idea of how easy it is.

The range of quantities given for the grapes is the direct result of when we retested this recipe and accidentally used 3 pounds of grapes rather than 3 cups, the original amount. I thought 4 cups was ideal but Marion Sullivan, who was visiting for the week, and Kay Calvert, who typed this book, begged for the whole 3 pounds (about 6 cups, it turned out).

Hence the variation.

4 **to 6 cups seedless green or red grapes**
1 **cup sugar**
2 **egg yolks**
1 **egg**
½ **cup (1 stick) butter, melted and cooled**
1 **cup flour**
1 **teaspoon rum flavoring or 2 tablespoons rum**
¼ **teaspoon almond extract**
1 **cup milk**

Preheat the oven to 400°F. Heavily butter an 8- or 9-inch baking dish or pie pan.

Sprinkle the grapes with half the sugar, and let stand 30 minutes. For the batter, in a bowl or a food processor beat together the remaining sugar and egg yolks. Then beat in the egg. Gradually beat in the butter and then the flour. Finally, add the rum flavoring, almond extract, and milk. Beat until very smooth.

Pour one-third of the batter into the prepared pan. Spoon the grapes and their juice, if any, over the batter. Pour the remaining batter over the grapes. Bake the tart on the lower rack of the oven until a toothpick comes out clean, about 40 minutes. The texture should be soft and nearly custardy. Cool slightly and serve from the pan in wedges or squares. The tart may be prepared several days in advance and refrigerated or frozen up to 3 months. Serve it warm, reheated, or at room temperature.

VARIATION

There are many variations for this dish, which traditionally was done with cherries. Sliced peaches, strawberries, and raspberries are just a few of the fruits I use.

Paella and Friends for Ten

Sourdough Bread★

Gazpacho à la Mode

Paella

Simple Salad

Spanish Flan

Because I was briefly the chef of a restaurant in Majorca, Spain, one of the few "ethnic" meals I make regularly is this one. It's partly because of the memories and partly because everyone always loves it. Since all the dishes can be prepared ahead, this is a great meal to serve on the Saturday night of a guest weekend or just on your own deck at home.

Recently, my husband and I went from Bermuda to Italy on the *Royal Viking Sun*, where I gave a few cooking lessons and lectures on board. I thought everyone knew how to make paella and how good it was, but after the class these really well-traveled, sophisticated people oohed and ahhed and clamored for the recipe.

Then, when I finished teaching the gazpacho, I knew I had a hit menu on my hands. (They didn't even complain about the few eggs in the flan.)

Cooking Time Line

Remember, each day, check your preparations list for things like cleaning, shopping, setting table, drop-dead time, and so on. If you elect to use a store-bought item (or more than one), make sure it's on your shopping list (and obviously, then, you don't need to make it).

UP TO 3 MONTHS BEFORE

1. Make the bread and freeze.

UP TO 2 DAYS BEFORE

1. Make the gazpacho and salad dressing; refrigerate.
2. Make the paella and refrigerate.
3. Precook clams, shrimp, and mussels for 1 to 2 minutes in the oven and refrigerate.
4. Make the flan and refrigerate.
5. Prep the salad ingredients and accompaniments for the gazpacho; put in plastic bags and refrigerate.

The Day

UP TO 1 HOUR BEFORE

1. Pour the soup into the tureen; cover, keep refrigerated. Surround with garnishes.
2. Defrost bread and reheat.
3. Toss salad. Don't add dressing yet.
4. Start heating the paella.
5. Five minutes before serving the paella, add clams, shrimps, and mussels, pressing some into the hot rice. Sprinkle with chopped parsley.

SHOPPING TIP

Bread flour

Flours differ radically. Bread flour is higher in gluten (protein) than all-purpose. It gives a better rise and a nicer loaf to yeast breads. Less is required, too, so do buy bread flour if a recipe calls for it.

Sourdough Bread

1 LOAF

The new sourdough starter mix appeals to me for a couple of reasons. First, I don't have to try to keep a starter fed and happy all the time, a task with which I've never had much success. Second, I find the longer bread dough is left to grow, the more well-flavored the product. Although I sometimes use the quick-rise microwave method for rising dough when in a hurry, I really prefer to make my dough one day and bake it the next, as for this sourdough.

Having lived in England, I love a cool house at night. There, I would make the dough at night and leave it to rise overnight on the kitchen counter. Then I could shape and bake it the next day. My Sunbelt home here is too warm to let the dough rise overnight unrefrigerated—as the dough will overrise and collapse. Almost any bread dough can be refrigerated overnight and taste better, but the specific sourdough yeast has an additional burst of flavor.

**1 packet yeast with
ready-to-use
sourdough starter
1 cup warm water
(105°F. to 115°F.)
2½ to 3 cups bread flour
1 teaspoon salt**

Combine the contents of the starter and yeast packet with the water in a large bowl or in the food processor. Stir in 2½ cups of the flour and the salt. Knead with an electric mixer or food processor or on a floured board by hand until smooth and elastic like a baby's bottom, adding more flour if necessary.

Place the dough in an oiled or nonstick sprayed plastic bag or oiled bowl, turn to coat, and seal or cover. Let rise in a warm, draft-free place until doubled, 30 to 45 minutes.

Punch the dough down and shape it into a smooth round. Lightly oil baking sheet or spray with nonstick spray. Place the round on the sheet and lightly oil the top of the round or coat with nonstick spray. Cover loosely with plastic wrap and let rise 6 to 24 hours in the refrigerator. Remove the loaf and let stand, covered, 1 hour at room temperature.

Meanwhile, preheat the oven to 425°F. Make sure the oven is fully hot.

Uncover the loaf and lightly oil or coat with nonstick spray for a golden crust. Cut cross-hatch slashes ¼ inch deep across the top using a sharp knife or razor blade. Sprinkle with flour for a rustic look.

Bake in the middle of the hot oven until golden brown and an instant-read thermometer registers 190 to 200°F., or the bottom sounds hollow when rapped with a knuckle, about 30 to 35 minutes. Remove from the baking sheet and let cool on a wire rack. The bread may be kept frozen for up to 3 months if well wrapped.

ALTERNATIVE METHOD

Let the dough rise first overnight in the refrigerator. Knock down and shape into a smooth round and place on a prepared baking sheet. Let double—a bit more than an hour depending on the room. Proceed with preheated oven as above.

VARIATION

To serve with soup, slice about ½ inch thick and toast in a hot oven or under the broiler. Brush the slices with oil and sprinkle with grated Parmesan cheese.

Gazpacho à la Mode

SERVES 10 TO 12

Just as people enjoy building their own salad-bar salads, letting them add their own crunchy bits to a smooth soup can be enjoyable. The food processor makes this soup only a half hour project, so don't let the number of ingredients daunt you. The recipe doubles easily, so I frequently keep it in the refrigerator to use over a week. You can process it until smooth or keep it chunky—it's up to you.

I like a deep red gazpacho so I add tomato juice, but the traditional is pale pink. Since there are only a few months a year when good tomatoes are available, I sometimes compromise and use good canned plum tomatoes.

1 onion, cut up
2 to 3 garlic cloves
½ red or green bell pepper, seeded, deribbed, and quartered
1 medium cucumber, peeled and quartered
½ cup red wine vinegar
¼ cup bread crumbs
1¾ to 2 pounds very ripe tomatoes, peeled, seeded, and chopped or a 1-pound can Italian plum tomatoes, chopped
1½ quarts canned tomato juice, as needed, to make a total of 2 quarts with the tomatoes
Salt
Freshly ground black pepper

Purée the onion, garlic, bell pepper, and cucumber in a blender or food processor. Add the vinegar and the bread crumbs and process until smooth or until blended but still chunky. Add the chopped tomatoes and tomato juice and process until the mixture is as smooth as you want. Season to taste with salt and pepper. Serve well chilled, with the garnishes in separate bowls to be added at serving time. If you're in a hurry, stir ice cubes into the soup to chill it, if necessary, but be careful not to dilute it.

Without the garnishes added, this soup will last, covered, in the refrigerator a week or two. I keep it in a plastic pitcher for quick pouring.

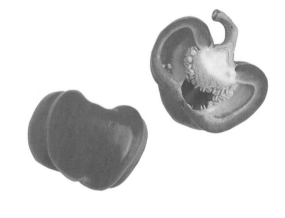

Garnishes

- 1 onion, finely chopped
- 1 tomato, yellow or red, preferably half of each
- 1 red, green, or yellow bell pepper, cored, seeded, and chopped, preferably half of two kinds
- 1 cup bread cubes, fried in 3 tablespoons olive oil or homemade croutons (right)
- ½ unpeeled cucumber, chopped
- 1 cup sour cream or plain nonfat yogurt

HOMEMADE CROUTONS

Cut French bread—leftovers are fine—into cubes, leaving the crust on. Toss the cubes with herbed olive oil or melted butter and then with salt and pepper. (It's the salt and pepper that really makes the difference.) Bake the croutons at 325°F. until baked through, about 5 minutes. Turn them if necessary. Keep an eye on them, because the size of the cubes ultimately determines how long they bake. Let cool to room temperature and store in an airtight container for about a week or freeze for up to a month. Refresh the croutons in a 300°F. oven for a couple of minutes before using.

VARIATIONS

Roast Tomato Gazpacho

Roast halved tomatoes at 450°F. until soft and charred at the edges, about 15 minutes. Remove the skin and substitute for the fresh or canned tomatoes. Can be served hot or cold.

ð

Provide side dishes of shrimp, crab meat, lobster, or other tiny seafood morsels to make a "meal soup."

ð

Yellow Gazpacho

Substitute yellow tomatoes for the tomatoes, yellow peppers for the peppers, and white wine vinegar for the red wine vinegar. Garnish with same ingredients, but use a mixture of colors for the tomatoes and peppers or all yellow.

Paella

Paella is a traditional Spanish dish made in a flat-bottomed pan that looks like a shallow wok. It is different every time you eat it in Spain. This version is as much like the paella we ate in Majorca, when I was chef of a restaurant, as I can get it with the ingredients available in my Atlanta grocery store. Vary it according to what's available in your area. The variation in the amount of saffron is to take into account the strength of the saffron as well as the cost.

The right size paella pan is tricky. If your pan (I use an enamel-lined one or a wok) is too small, reserve and cook some of the seafood separately and pile it on top when serving. If you think there will be a guest averse to shellfish or pork, reserve a portion before you add them.

½ **pound dried Spanish pork chorizo, good red Italian-style pepperoni, or dried salami**
2 **pounds large shrimp (16 to 20 per pound)**
3 **pounds chicken thighs or wing drumettes**
Salt
Freshly ground black pepper
¼ **to ½ cup olive oil**
1 **to 3 tablespoons saffron threads**

Preheat the oven to 400°F.

Skin the sausage and slice it into ⅛-inch rounds. If desired, peel the shrimp, leaving the tails intact, or remove only the legs and leave the shells on. Set the sausage and shrimp aside.

Dry the chicken pieces and season with salt and pepper. Heat ¼ cup of the olive oil in a paella pan, large heavy-bottomed casserole, or large ovenproof skillet until very hot. Add the chicken pieces, skin side down, and brown on 1 side, about 3 minutes. Turn and brown the second side, another 3 minutes. Remove the chicken and set aside.

Meanwhile, soak the saffron threads in the lemon juice and a little of the chicken broth.

SHOPPING TIP

Saffron

Saffron is the stigmas of a crocus, and since it is very costly to gather, it is very expensive. It may be hard to find at your local grocery store. Be sure to ask for it, because it is frequently locked up. Indian grocery stores usually have some, as do specialty gourmet shops.

The numerous brands of saffron vary considerably in quality. Since the deeper the color the better the saffron, some brands have inferior ingredients added to intensify color but have little flavor. Get the best product you can afford and make notes on how you felt about the flavor; you may want to switch brands.

The strength varies considerably with the quality, with Spanish being stronger than Indian and some others. If saffron is too expensive or not available, try substituting turmeric. It gives an interesting color and a flavor different from that of saffron, but it is still quite nice.

1 tablespoon lemon
   juice
2 cups fresh or canned
   chicken broth
½ pound lean boneless
   pork (such as
   shoulder or loin),
   cut into 1-inch
   cubes
1 large onion, finely
   chopped
3 to 5 garlic cloves,
   finely chopped
1 large fresh or canned
   tomato, peeled,
   seeded, and chopped
1 tablespoon paprika
2½ cups rice, preferably
   imported short-grain
   rice such as Arborio
   or Valenciano
½ red bell pepper,
   seeded, deribbed,
   and finely chopped
½ green bell pepper,
   seeded, deribbed,
   and finely chopped
½ cup fresh or frozen
   green peas, thawed
1 pound red snapper,
   flounder, sea bass, or
   orange roughy, cut
   into 1-inch cubes
1 or 2 lobster tails,
   shelled and cut into
   1-inch medallions
   (optional)
1 to 1½ pounds mussels
   (see Box page 258)
   or clams in the shell
   or ½ pound sea
   scallops (optional)
2 tablespoons chopped
   parsley

If necessary, add more oil to the pan. Add the pork cubes and sauté briefly, turning to brown on all sides, about 5 minutes. Remove and set aside. Add the onion and garlic to the oil, and cook until soft, about 7 minutes. Add the tomato and paprika. Cook, stirring, until most of the juice evaporates. Add the rice, salt to taste, and the saffron with its soaking liquid. Cook, stirring, 1 minute. Mix the remaining chicken broth with enough water to make 5 cups and bring to a boil in a separate pan or in the microwave. Pour it onto the rice mixture. Bring back to the boil quickly, stirring constantly. Cook 5 minutes, stirring.

Remove from the heat and arrange the chicken, sausage, pork, and bell peppers in and over the rice. Bake in the middle of the oven for 40 minutes. (The dish can be made to this point and refrigerated up to 2 days. When ready to proceed, reheat in a 400°F. oven until heated through, 20 to 30 minutes, then continue.)

Scatter the peas, fish, lobster, and shrimp over the top. Return to the oven and cook until the fish is almost cooked but not dry, about 5 more minutes.

Add the mussels, clams, and/or scallops. Return to the oven and cook until the liquid has evaporated, 5 minutes more. Remove from the oven and let rest 5 to 10 minutes draped with a towel. Sprinkle the parsley over the paella.

VARIATIONS

Serve chilled on a bed of lettuce as a main course salad. It's wonderful! Add more salt and pepper when serving chilled.

To save time when making the paella, the clams, shrimp, and mussels can be precooked in a 400°F. oven for 1 to 2 minutes, then refrigerated. Add to the paella a few minutes before removing from the oven, pushing some into the rice, and top the paella with the rest.

Simple Salad

A combination of different lettuces makes an interesting plate of flavors, colors, and textures. Try red leaf, Boston, Bibb, and romaine. Years ago I never added anything to a lettuce salad except herbs and a simple vinaigrette. Oh, maybe some green onions—but bell pepper? I considered such things sacrilege. But I got over it and found that, on occasion, I enjoyed the contrast with the light greens. There are now salad mixes of small lettuces sold by the scoop or in bags, prewashed, which are a perfectly fine accompaniment to many meals and are frequently less expensive than doing it yourself from several varieties. One trick is to put the vinaigrette in the bottom of the bowl, add 2 large salad implements, crossed to form a rack, then top with the lettuce and salad ingredients. When ready to serve, pull out the implements and the lettuce falls into the dressing, ready to be tossed.

6 to 8 cups lettuce, torn into bite-sized pieces

3 scallions, green part only, sliced crosswise

2 tablespoons chopped fresh thyme, oregano, or basil

4 to 6 tablespoons Basic Vinaigrette (below)

1 green bell pepper, seeded, deribbed, and thinly sliced (optional)

1 avocado, sliced (optional)

2½ cups arugula (optional)

In a large salad bowl, toss together the lettuce, scallion greens, green pepper, avocado, if using, and arugula, if using. Add the herbs. Add enough Basic Vinaigrette to barely coat the lettuce.

BASIC VINAIGRETTE

MAKES 1 CUP

I have used this recipe, or one very like it, as a basic salad dressing for years. It lends itself to many variations, depending on my mood or on what's on hand.

In a medium bowl, whisk the vinegar, mustard, and garlic together. Whisk in the oil in a slow, steady stream until thick and creamy. Season to taste with salt, pepper, and sugar. (A pinch of sugar can help tame the acidity.)

¼ cup red wine vinegar

1 teaspoon Dijon mustard

1 garlic clove, very finely chopped

¾ cup vegetable oil

Salt

Freshly ground black pepper

Sugar (optional)

VARIATION

Use red leaf lettuce, sliced red onion, and red bell pepper.

Spanish Flan

This smooth, sweet, and lightly rich dessert is perfect after the paella or any substantial meal. For a variation, this traditional Spanish crème caramel recipe is given a Mexican flair with a touch of cinnamon. Ramekins are usually thicker and better insulated than glass ovenproof custard cups. These are best done a day ahead.

1¾ cups sugar
¾ cup water
6 large eggs
¼ teaspoon vanilla extract
⅛ teaspoon salt
1 quart milk

VARIATION

Add 1 to 2 teaspoons cinnamon with the vanilla.

Measure your cups, as you should fill them nearly to the brim. Cut circles from baking parchment to fit the top of the ramekins.

Preheat the oven to 325°F. and put ten ½-cup ramekins or ovenproof custard cups in the oven to preheat.

Dissolve 1 cup of the sugar in ½ cup of the water in a 1-quart heavy pan over low heat without boiling, occasionally brushing the sides of the pan with a wet brush. When completely dissolved, turn up the heat and boil until the liquid turns amber, about 20 to 30 minutes. Continue to brush sugar crystals from the sides of the pan. Carefully add the remaining ¼ cup of water to the saucepan, to avoid splattering. Bring back to a boil and stir until the caramel is completely dissolved and smooth.

Using heavy oven mitts, pour the caramel sauce into the hot cups one by one, carefully but quickly tilting the cups of hot caramel to coat the bottoms evenly. Allow to cool slightly.

In a mixing bowl, lightly beat together the remaining ¾ cup of sugar and the eggs, vanilla, and salt. Stir in the milk. Ladle the mixture into the caramel-lined custard cups.

Put a kitchen towel in the bottom of a roasting pan to insulate. Place the cups on top, and add enough hot water to the pan to reach halfway up the sides of the cups. Cover each cup with a baking-parchment circle to prevent a skin from forming. Bake in the center of the oven until they set, 20 to 30 minutes, adding hot water to the roasting pan as necessary if the water boils out.

Remove the custard cups from the water bath, remove their paper, and let them cool at room temperature, and then cover them well and place them in the refrigerator to chill for at least 2 hours or up to 2 days.

To serve, run a small thin knife between the custard and the cup. Place a small plate over the custard cup. Flip the plate and the custard cup over, and gently lift the cup. Let the caramel sauce drizzle from the cup over the custard.

Moroccan Dinner

Lentil Soup with Harissa

Chicken B'stilla

Grilled Moroccan Lamb

Grilled Herbed Zucchini

Olive Bread

Pita Bread★

Fruit Plate

It was a cold, wet, and dreary December day when we arrived in Casablanca. We hadn't reckoned on the rain, and the streets no more welcomed it than we did. The water dripped off our faces and pooled under our feet as we ran to the car rental agency to pick up our car. David, my favorite former husband, had words with the rental clerk who wanted a little under-the-table baksheesh in addition to the fee we had been quoted—after all, it was his last car and it was a rainy day.

Finally, we were in the car and determined to make our first day in Morocco a glorious one after such a bad beginning. And so we drove to Marrakech. We sat in the lobby of the Hotel Mal-muna and marveled at its ceilings, envying the glamorous personages who waltzed through the lobby in gorgeous leather coats and striking clothes. We ate a meal full of exotic flavors and exquisite taste, we toured mosques, open-mouthed at their beauty, wandered through the market, and reluctantly made the long trek back to Casablanca and our Russian cruise ship. I brought with me a set of skewers and a brass Moroccan "picnic basket." I have them still, tarnished but capable of bringing up memories of the Casbah and my day in Morocco. I intend to go back, but in the meantime, I can at least make my own Morocco and share it with my friends.

Whenever I serve this menu, I'm asked for the recipes. They are so good! As a bonus, there is nothing difficult in this menu (although the b'stilla may appear to be) and the total time spent in preparation should be less than four hours, spread over a few days if possible.

An exotic menu can enable you to create a fantasy world for the duration of the meal. This is one such menu. But if you really don't want all that, any of this menu's components would make a casual meal with flair and panache.

If you're thinking of having a theme party, don't feel you have to develop all new recipes. Take one of your core menus and play with changing the names of the dishes to fit the occasion. One of my favorite theme parties was the losers' party put on by "the food group"—my gourmet group, if you will, for lack of a better definition. We were all politically active. Jimmy Bently had been insurance commissioner, Betty Talmadge had run for Congress as well as having been the wife of a governor and senator and daughter-in-law of a governor. Dick Williams wrote a political column for the paper, and his wife Becky Chase was a top national television reporter. So it was natural that when we had a gubernatorial election, we decided to honor the losers, for we had all been losers ourselves at one time or another. Besides, the losers were particularly colorful and plentiful that year—Jack Watson had been in the Carter White House and Billy Lovett was a handsome maverick.

We draped the house in black and put a black wreath on the door. Jimmy typed up the menu in advance, reprinting it for the guests. We each chose a dish we liked to cook and he made up names for them. A few items were added for their cachet. For instance, pickled pigs feet became "The Agony of De-feat"; my carrot cake was decorated like a hat and called "Hat in the Ring" Cake. We served "Sacked" Wine and Old Crow, "Whipped" Potatoes, and Crow Balls. It was a marvelous party, and everyone who attended loved it. So much so that the next day the party was written up on the front page of the Atlanta Constitution. Pretty good for a party just serving foods we could easily make!

This menu, which has two main courses, is designed to serve sixteen, but if you omit the lamb or the b'stilla, the meal would do nicely for eight. I'd serve the zucchini with the b'stilla if I omitted the lamb. Another way to handle small numbers would be to halve all the recipes, making two smaller b'stillas and reserving one for another time. The lamb would halve easily, uncooked, or it could all be cooked and half of it frozen for another time.

This meal would also work for a tailgate or regular picnic. Most of the food can be kept at room temperature for a few hours, with the soup in a thermos and the b'stilla kept well chilled in a cooler.

Cooking Time Line

Remember, each day, check your preparations list for things like cleaning, cleaning grill, shopping, setting table, drop-dead time, and so on. If you elect to use a store-bought item (or more than one), make sure it's on your shopping list (and obviously, then, you don't need to make it).

UP TO 3 MONTHS BEFORE

1. Make the soup, harissa, and bread; freeze.

UP TO 1 MONTH BEFORE

1. Make the b'stilla and freeze.

UP TO 2 DAYS BEFORE

1. Prepare the zucchini; grill and chill. (Or just prepare and grill at the same time as the lamb.)

UP TO 1 DAY BEFORE

1. Remove the soup, harissa, and b'stilla from freezer.
2. Marinate the lamb (or freeze in marinade up to 6 months; thaw in the refrigerator 36 hours).

3. Prepare the pineapple and oranges; refrigerate separately.

The Day

UP TO 45 MINUTES BEFORE

1. Start heating the soup.

30 MINUTES BEFORE

1. Start heating the b'stilla.
2. Finish the Fruit Plate.
3. Grill the lamb; heat the zucchini.

Serve either at the dining room table or as a buffet, or, to reap the full atmospheric benefits of this exotic menu, at a coffee table with plump pillows on the floor for your guests. Add any artifacts you can find in an import store or can borrow.

Before and after the meal, bring out a large silver tea or coffee pot of warm water, a large bowl, and towels. Pour some water over your guests' outstretched hands over the bowl and offer them a towel. (At the end of the evening, sprinkle their hands with rose water or orange flower water if they'll cooperate.)

Try at least the first two courses with no silverware. Pull the b'stilla apart with your hands or cut it with pizza scissors and then eat it with your hands. Slice the lamb in the kitchen, put it on a large platter or tray, and surround it with the couscous, chermoula, and grilled vegetables. Couscous is supposed to be eaten with the fingers—you may have to lead the way. The dessert is also fingers only.

Lentil Soup with Harissa

MAKES 10 CUPS

Unadorned, this makes a pleasant everyday soup on its own. With the harissa, a spicy Moroccan condiment, you have a fashionable soup. It's more of a broth with lentils than a thick lentil soup, so it can be served in a cup, as it was served to me in a Moroccan restaurant. To make it richer in flavor, use both the butter and the olive oil. Or if you prefer, reduce or omit the fat and use a nonstick pan. A store-bought lentil soup can be zipped up with the addition of harissa. If you prefer a thicker soup, which would necessitate a spoon for eating, mash some or all of the lentils. This recipe halves very easily for a smaller group.

2 tablespoons butter
2 tablespoons olive oil
2 medium onions, chopped (½ to 2 cups)
1½ cups lentils, preferably red
10 to 12 cups fresh or canned chicken stock or broth, preferably fresh
¼ teaspoon freshly ground black pepper
½ teaspoon cayenne pepper
    Salt
    Harissa (page 70)

Pick through the lentils for any stones.

Melt the butter and olive oil in an 8-quart stockpot. Add the onions and sauté until light golden brown, about 8 minutes. Add the lentils, stock, black pepper, cayenne pepper, and salt to taste. Bring to the boil, reduce the heat, and simmer, covered, until the lentils are soft, about 30 to 45 minutes. Serve the broth, then scoop up some of the lentils into each bowl or cup. To be on the safe side, do not add the harissa to the soup, but pass a bowl of it separately so each person can season to taste— and remember to warn them that it is fiery hot.

This soup can be made 4 days ahead and refrigerated, or kept frozen for up to 3 months.

SHOPPING TIP

Chicken broth

Chicken stock, or broth, is available in most grocery stores. I prefer the canned type that is not condensed. It is less salty and has a lighter flavor. Stock cubes and granules are also available but are usually more highly seasoned. I use them for emergencies.

Chicken B'stilla

My son-in-law's family lived in Morocco, so in addition to my own love of the cuisine, I have his input as well. This dish is a variation of a pigeon b'stilla served to me, Audrey, and my friend Barbara St. Amand when we were his mother's guests in a Moroccan restaurant in Paris. With its crisp crust, it is rich, and a little goes a long way. We ate with our hands, but forks are allowed, too.

I had novices test this recipe to prove that it is quite achievable in the home kitchen. The recipe can—and should—be made over several days: Clarify all the butter at one time. Marinate the chicken with the chermoula one day, cook it the next, and organize the ingredients for the next day. The total effort will take less than two hours. Take care to notice the amounts called for in the recipe steps, as many items are used in more than one place. You may choose to omit the butter that is added when cooking the chicken, but it does enhance the dish.

Chermoula
- **1 large onion, finely chopped**
- **4 garlic cloves, finely chopped**
- **1 teaspoon finely chopped ginger**
- **¼ cup finely chopped fresh parsley**
- **3 tablespoons finely chopped cilantro**
- **½ teaspoon saffron threads**
- **1 teaspoon freshly ground black pepper**
- **1½ teaspoons coarse salt**
- **6 tablespoons olive oil**

Preheat the oven to 425°F.

Make the chermoula: In a large bowl, combine the onion, garlic, ginger, parsley, cilantro, saffron, pepper, salt, and olive oil.

Rub the chicken all over with the chermoula and place in a large plastic bag or covered bowl in the refrigerator for at least 2 hours but preferably overnight.

Place the chicken and chermoula in a large casserole. Add 3 cups water or more if necessary to cover the chicken, ½ cup clarified butter, and the ½ teaspoon saffron. Sprinkle with ¼ cup of the confectioners' sugar. Cover the casserole, bring to the boil, reduce the heat, and simmer until the chicken is cooked, up to 35 minutes (for boneless breasts), 60 minutes for bone-in pieces.

Remove the cooked chicken to a plate, let cool, and tear or cut into bite-sized pieces. Bring the cooking broth to the boil and reduce to 4 cups if necessary. Add the eggs and lemon juice to the broth. Stir with a wooden spoon over low heat, constantly scraping the bottom, until the eggs are in large soft curds like scrambled eggs. Remove from the heat and set aside.

Place the ground almonds, ¼ cup of the confectioners' sugar, 4 tablespoons of the orange-flower water, and the cinnamon in a bowl and mix well. Set aside.

In a small pan, heat together over low heat the 4 tablespoons melted butter (not the clarified butter) and the remaining 3 tablespoons of the orange-flower water. Set aside.

Chicken filling

- 2 (3-pound) chickens, cut up, OR
- 3 pounds boneless, skinless chicken meat from the breast
- 3 cups water, or more if necessary
- 1 cup clarified butter OR ½ cup smen and ½ cup clarified butter (page 71)
- ½ teaspoon saffron
- ¾ cup confectioners' sugar, plus some for serving
- 8 large eggs, well beaten
- ¼ cup lemon juice
- 3 cups ground almonds
- 7 tablespoons orange-flower water
- 1 to 2 teaspoons ground cinnamon
- 4 tablespoons (½ stick) butter, melted, plus 1 tablespoon
- One 16-ounce package phyllo dough (18 to 24 sheets)
- 1 egg yolk, beaten with a little water

TIP

Leftover phyllo dessert: Butter the sheets of phyllo, fill with slices of soft fruit (such as peaches or cooked apples), sprinkle with sugar as desired, and seasoning such as cinnamon. Gather up the edges and twist. Bake at 425°F. for 20 minutes, or until brown and crisp.

Assemble: Brush a 12-inch tart pan with a removable bottom or a 14-inch round pan with the remaining 1 tablespoon melted butter. Unwrap and open the phyllo and cover with a damp, but not wet, light tea towel. Remove 1 sheet of phyllo dough and place on the bottom of the pan. Brush starting at the edges with some of the clarified butter. Add another sheet of phyllo dough at a 45-degree angle to the first and again brush with clarified butter. Continue layering and brushing with clarified butter until you have 10 sheets of phyllo, making sure you turn each sheet 45 degrees, so that when finished it looks almost like the petals of a two-layered flower.

Spread half the almond mixture over the center of the phyllo, leaving a ½-inch space around the edge. Top with 2 more phyllo sheets, brushing each with clarified butter. Sprinkle evenly with two-thirds of the butter-and-orange-flower mixture.

Cover with 2 more phyllo sheets, brushing each with clarified butter, and sprinkle with 2 tablespoons of the remaining confectioners' sugar. Arrange the chicken on the phyllo and top with the egg mixture. If there is too much egg mixture for the pastry, reserve the extra in the refrigerator.

Cover the chicken and eggs with 2 more buttered phyllo sheets, place the remaining almond mixture on top, sprinkle with the remaining 2 tablespoons orange-flower mixture, then sprinkle with the remaining 2 tablespoons confectioners' sugar.

Turn up the overlapping phyllo sheets and seal them together with some of the egg yolk. Place 2 more buttered sheets of phyllo on top and gently turn the overhanging edges under to form a smooth top. Brush the top with butter and then with the remaining egg yolk to form a glaze.

Bake at 425°F. until the pastry is golden brown, about 20 minutes. To remove from the pan, run a knife along the edge of the pan, lift with a spatula, and slide onto a large round platter. When slightly cool, sprinkle with confectioners' sugar to serve. Cut with a large scissors or a pizza cutter. If you have reserved extra egg mixture and the b'stilla is dry, reheat the egg mixture gently and pass as a sauce.

The b'stilla can be made ahead two days and refrigerated, or frozen in a sturdy sealed container for a month and reheated. Freeze the extra sauce as well. Defrost overnight in the refrigerator and reheat carefully at 350°F., until hot through, about 30 minutes.

Harissa

Harissa is searingly hot, so warn your guests before they load up on it. It is more authentic—and tastes better—when you grind your own coriander and cumin seeds. If you use already ground spices, cut back on the amount since a tablespoon of ground coriander, for instance, is made from more than a tablespoon of whole coriander seeds. A small electric coffee mill or food processor is a big help for grinding the seeds.

2 cups hot fresh or dried chile peppers
6 garlic cloves, chopped
¼ cup coarse salt
⅓ cup coriander seeds
¼ cup cumin seeds
¼ cup lemon juice
8 to 10 tablespoons olive oil

Remove the seeds from the peppers and discard. If using dried, place the peppers in a bowl and cover with hot water. Let the peppers soak until softened, about 30 minutes.

Drain the peppers if necessary. Place the garlic, peppers, and the salt in a food processor bowl and purée. Alternatively, place in a mortar and pestle and pound until smooth.

Place the coriander seeds and cumin seeds in a pepper mill or coffee grinder or use a mortar and pestle or rolling pin and grind to a powder. Add the coriander, cumin, and lemon juice to the mixture in the food processor and process until well blended. With the food processor running, add enough olive oil to reach a medium-thin consistency. Place in a sealed jar. This will keep almost indefinitely in the refrigerator.

Clarified Butter/Smen

Smen is a Middle Eastern butter sauce that is aged for years much as balsamic vinegar is. A primary ingredient is the herb za'ator, but I can rarely find it, so I use thyme or herbes de Provence.

Clarified butter is butter that has been separated to remove the milk solids and salt. I use it primarily for dunking seafood and for brushing phyllo. If you wish to avoid clarifying butter, you may use soft, room-temperature butter for brushing the phyllo.

1 pound (4 sticks) unsalted butter

1 tablespoon coarse salt (if making smen)

¼ teaspoon za'ator, thyme, or herbes de Provence (if making smen)

To clarify the butter, bring it to the boil in the microwave or over low heat without browning. Set it in the refrigerator for an hour or so, until the butter has separated. Remove any salt on the top with a spoon. The middle layer is the clarified butter, and the bottom layer is the milk solids.

If making smen, put the salt and herbs into a cheesecloth-lined strainer set over a bowl and spoon the clear liquid into it. Strain the liquid again into a sterilized jar. Refrigerate until needed. It will last 6 months.

SHOPPING TIP

Herbes de Provence, which is available packaged in gourmet shops, is a blend of dried thyme, bay leaf, rosemary, basil, and savory. You can substitute any of those herbs or a mixture in any proportions, though the flavor of the finished dish will, of course, be affected.

Grilled Moroccan Lamb

Like many who have lived in England, I am a fan of Robert Carrier, whose book on Moroccan food, now out of print, is a favorite of mine. This recipe is adapted from one he uses for a haunch of camel, flavoring it with another version of chermoula.

Lamb takes well to grilling, so I'm sure your guests will enjoy it as much as I do, served hot or cold or sliced and wrapped in a soft bread like pita for a picnic.

Our modern American lamb is generally rather large (though smaller, of course, than camel). Should you be fortunate enough to find Australian, New Zealand, or small U.S. farm-raised lamb, cut the amount of chermoula in half. Bone in or bone out, one way or the other, you pay for the bone, so why not pluck up your courage, buy the leg with the bone in, and remove it yourself?

1 leg of lamb, 4 to 6 pounds whole or 2½ to 4 pounds boned
2 large onions, finely chopped
5 garlic cloves, finely chopped
1 cup chopped fresh parsley
½ cup chopped cilantro
1 tablespoon ground cumin
1 teaspoon ground cinnamon
1 teaspoon finely chopped fresh ginger
1 teaspoon ground saffron threads
½ teaspoon cayenne pepper
½ cup olive oil
10 tablespoons honey
½ cup lemon or lime juice
2 cups raisins
6 cups cooked couscous, prepared according to package directions

Preheat the broiler or grill.

If you have purchased a whole leg of a lamb, use the instructions opposite to bone the meat. Open the boned leg of lamb out with the skin side down.

Make the chermoula: Mix the onion, garlic, parsley, cilantro, cumin, cinnamon, ginger, saffron, cayenne, olive oil, honey, lemon juice, and raisins together.

Rub the chermoula well into both sides of the lamb. Place the lamb and the rest of the chermoula in a large plastic bag or pan and let sit for at least 2 hours at room temperature or overnight in the refrigerator.

Remove the lamb from the chermoula, brushing off any raisins that adhere to the meat, and reserving with the chermoula, and grill or broil 6 inches from the heat source, 15 to 20 minutes per side for medium-rare. This may be done a day or two in advance, if necessary, then refrigerated and reheated, taking care not to overheat.

Heat the reserved chermoula in a saucepan or the microwave until it comes to the boil. Slice the lamb, place it on a platter, and surround with the couscous. Spoon the chermoula over the lamb and couscous.

Boning a Leg of Lamb

Most butchers will perform the boning of the lamb for you, but the cost per pound will be several dollars higher. The boning is not too difficult to manage by yourself, the price will be less per pound, and the bones and trimmings can be turned into a good sauce or stock. These instructions for boning will enable you to try it and then make your own decision about whether it is worth paying extra to have your butcher bone it for you. You will find that after you have boned one leg, the second boning is much easier. Don't be afraid of "damaging the meat," as the boned meat can be rolled and any small loose pieces tucked inside so they won't be wasted.

To butterfly the leg of lamb, lay the leg on a board with the less fatty side facing up. Using a sharp knife, trim off the purple inspection stamp and all but a thin layer of fat. Using a small sharp flexible knife, find the hip bone, if any, or wide part of the bone. Cut through the meat to the bone. Cut around the bone, working your way down from the "hip" to the "knee," then down the shank of the leg, until it is free of bone. Feel all over for any small pieces of gristle, fat, or musk gland. The first time you do it, the job will seem very intimidating and terrifying. Even so, with a sharp knife it will only take you 10 to 15 minutes. You really can't ruin the meat, because it can be sewn together with unwaxed dental twine, or even pushed together on the pan.

NOTE

Freezing meat coated with the chermoula is a convenient way to impart flavor that involves little or no extra effort on your part and allows you to bone and butterfly the meat and prepare the chermoula ahead of time. Instead of allowing it to sit for 2 hours at room temperature, seal the container and freeze for up to 6 months. Defrost in the refrigerator overnight, then complete the recipe by grilling or broiling.

Grilled Herbed Zucchini

SERVES 4 TO 6

Zucchini is an incredibly versatile vegetable that is universally popular. It takes well to grilling in long fingers, with herbs on each side adding flavor. The zucchini may be prepared ahead and reheated in the microwave if grilling space is short.

**2 to 3 medium zucchini
   (1½ to 2 pounds),
   cleaned, ends
   trimmed**
**6 tablespoons olive oil
   Salt
   Freshly ground black
   pepper**
**½ cup chopped fresh
   herbs, such as thyme,
   parsley, and/or
   marjoram**

Preheat the grill or broiler. If using the broiler, cover the broiler pan with aluminum foil.

Slice the zucchini lengthwise into quarters and brush with the oil. Place on the hot grill or in a broiler pan and put the pan 6 inches from the heat. Cook until just starting to brown, about 2 to 5 minutes. Turn and cook the other side. Remove from the heat and arrange on a serving platter. Sprinkle with salt, pepper, and herbs.

SHOPPING TIP

Zucchini

Big zucchini tend to be pulpy and often have a bitter taste. Smaller ones are more likely to be tender and sweet, to say nothing of the fact that they are easier to handle and look better on the plate. Choose zucchini with a shiny, firm, unblemished skin.

Olive Bread

I make bread every day, since it is so easy using the food processor. Here, I added olives to a basic bread recipe. You can also add herbs or other ingredients if you like. If you use the steel blade in your food processor, you don't need to chop the olives. If you're making the dough in a mixer or by hand, however, chop the olives before mixing them in.

2½ to 3 cups bread flour
1 package quick-acting yeast
1 teaspoon sugar
1 teaspoon salt
1 cup very warm water (135°F.)
½ cup Kalamata or Niçoise olives, pitted and finely chopped
1½ tablespoons olive oil

Preheat the oven to 350°F.

Place 2½ cups of the flour, the yeast, sugar, and salt in the bowl of a food processor and pulse until thoroughly mixed. Add the warm water and process to form a soft dough, adding more flour as necessary. It will take about 1 minute to knead in the food processor or 10 minutes in the mixer or by hand. Mix the olives in the olive oil and knead into the dough on a floured board until combined with the dough.

Form the dough into a round and place on an ungreased baking pan. Cover and leave in a warm place until doubled in size, about 1 hour.

Bake until an instant-read thermometer reads 200°F., 25 to 30 minutes.

SHOPPING TIP

Kalamata olives are brine-cured Greek olives that are very well flavored. Niçoise olives are very small and equally well flavored, but quite different. Because of their size, they are hard to pit. There are many other lesser known varieties of flavorful black olives on the market, and you may want to experiment with them.

TIP

To pit olives, there are many gadgets around, but the easiest way is to smack them with a flat surface such as a board or the wide side of a knife blade.

For a marbled olive bread, add the olive oil with the water and then process the whole, pitted olives into the dough by pulsing the food processor 5 to 7 times. Be careful not to overmix.

Fruit Plate

SERVES 8 TO 10

An easy finish to any rich meal, this treatment invites any fresh fruits of the season—melons and strawberries are particularly nice when I can get them.

1 **pineapple, peeled and sliced, slices cut in half**

3 **navel oranges, peeled, all white pith and membrane removed and sliced**

3 **apples, cored, cut in wedges, and sprinkled with lemon juice**

1 **bunch grapes, washed**

1 **tablespoon orange-flower water**

1 **to 2 cups fresh or dried pitted dates and figs**

Arrange the pineapple slice halves, the orange slices, the apple wedges, and the grapes around a platter. Sprinkle with the orange-flower water. Mound the fresh or dried dates and figs in the center.

SHOPPING TIP

Orange flower water

My Atlanta supermarket is very good about ordering what I need. In Oxford, however, I get this from a shop, Marie's, that specializes in Middle Eastern delicacies. Like rose water, it has a short shelf life and should be kept refrigerated. Brands vary in quality and flavor, so experiment with different ones.

This incredibly beautiful, spectacular menu tastes as good as it looks. I use this menu for special occasions, relishing its knock-'em-dead aspects. To prove how easy it is, I've even asked my guests to pour the soup and cut the roast—always with excellent results. Amazingly, it is also an adaptable menu that works outside as well as inside, can be toted to symphony in the park, or can be served on the finest china with sparkling crystal and polished silver in a chandeliered dining room.

Cooking Time Line

Remember, each day, check your preparations list for things like cleaning, shopping, setting table, drop-dead time, and so on. If you elect to use a store-bought item (or more than one), make sure it's on your shopping list (and obviously, then, you don't need to make it).

UP TO 3 MONTHS BEFORE

1. Buy the pork roast; have the butcher make it a crown roast if desired; freeze.
2. Make the bread, torte, and pepper-tomato soup purées (omit final addition of stock); freeze.

2 DAYS BEFORE

1. Move the pork from the freezer to the refrigerator to thaw.

UP TO 1 DAY BEFORE

1. Remove the bread, torte, and soup purées from freezer to thaw.
2. Cook the Brussels sprouts and refrigerate.

The Day

UP TO 3 HOURS BEFORE

1. Cook the roast and potatoes.
2. Thin the soup purées to the desired consistency.
3. Arrange the cheese and fruit platter; cover.

UP TO 1 HOUR BEFORE

1. If serving the roast hot, reheat it and the potatoes.
2. Pour the soup into bowls—enlist help if necessary—and put them on the table.
3. Cut the torte and chill. Whip the cream and refrigerate.
4. Heat the bread.

AT SERVING

1. Put the pork roast on the platter (remove strings) with the potatoes and sprouts. Top the bones with cherry tomatoes or Brussels sprouts.

Tricolored Soup

This edible mosaic, which is surprisingly easy to make, changes with every spoonful. The yellow tomatoes and peppers may be available only seasonally. We substituted green tomatoes for the yellow when we couldn't get them. If green tomatoes are hard to find in your local grocery, use one cup chopped, uncooked tomatillos. Each tomato should yield one cup of fruit after roasting and peeling, and each pepper should yield about ⅓ to ½ cup. The peppers are so flavorful that sometimes I don't even season the soup with extra salt.

Although it looks like you'll have a gracious plenty of soup, the sieve takes away a lot of volume. Be sure to measure your soup bowls before you start to be sure they will hold the right capacity. A wide, shallow bowl is best to show off the soup. Leftovers are equally spectacular, so I plan a special lunch the next day. Amazingly, this soup is good hot, room temperature, or cold.

1½ tablespoons olive oil
2 to 3 garlic cloves, chopped
3 pounds tomatoes, equal amounts of red, yellow, and green
3 pounds bell peppers, equal amounts of red, yellow, and green
Drop or two of red, green, and yellow food coloring
4 cups fresh or canned chicken stock or broth
Salt
Freshly ground black pepper
Sugar (optional)

Garnish (optional)
⅓ cup plain yogurt, drained
Edible flowers or herb leaves

Preheat the broiler.

In a heavy saucepan, heat the olive oil. Add the garlic and cook until soft, about 1 minute. Set aside.

To broil the tomatoes, cut off the stems and place them in an oiled roasting pan. Put the tomatoes 6 inches from the heat, and broil until the skin is cracked and charred, about 15 to 20 minutes. When cool enough to handle, peel the skin off. Broil and peel the peppers (page 167).

Purée each color tomato separately with its matching bell pepper and one-third of the garlic. Strain each purée into a 2-cup container, preferably with a handle and spout such as a glass measuring pitcher. Mix in food coloring carefully, one drop at a time, if needed or desired. Add ¾ cup chicken broth to each cup of purée and mix in. To test the consistency, spoon a small amount of each on a saucer or a small plate and see if they stay separate. If so, viscosity is equal. If not, boil the thin-

ner one(s) to reduce or add additional stock to the thicker one(s). Taste and adjust the seasoning with salt, pepper, and sugar, as desired. The soups may be refrigerated at this point up to 2 days or frozen up to 3 months.

To serve, whisk each soup to make sure they have the same consistency. Pour ¼ cup of each two soups into a bowl, followed quickly by ¼ cup of the third. Alternatively, cut a strip of cardboard (like a shirt cardboard) and fold in half to form a "V" that fits the bottom of your bowl and divides the bowl into three parts. Have one person hold the cardboard while you pour two soups and they pour one simultaneously. Remove the form. Garnish with yogurt and flowers if desired.

NOTE

To serve 12 to 16, make 3 recipes, 1 all red, 1 yellow, and 1 green.

When I was trained at the London Cordon Bleu, I do not remember us ever using a dye, and with the exception of Easter eggs, I avoided such a practice for a long time, particularly in my restaurants.

Then, in the height of the nouvelle cuisine craze, I went to France to study with Michel Guerard, the famous guru of nouvelle cuisine, at the spa Eugénie-les-Bains, in a small town a few hours from Bordeaux. I showed up for the class, but he didn't. Since I was the only student registered, he had split. I was, however, welcomed by the kitchen staff. I worked in the kitchen the better part of a week, and the staff showed me a great deal. I loved it.

One day, one of the young chefs was cooking something exotic I had seen on the menu the night before. It had been a particularly beautiful red at dinner that night, but it didn't look that pretty to me in the kitchen as we were puréeing it. So I watched carefully to see how he was going to get that color. I turned my back, he went into a side room, and the next thing I knew, the dish was a vibrant red. Hmmm. I suspected then, as I do now, a bit of food coloring.

All this is by way of saying that if you want a dish to be a spectacular color, like the Tricolored Soup, there is nothing wrong with edible dyes. I'm reminded again of Julia Child, who, when I was wearing a costume jewelry necklace one night, effusively complimented me on it. I stammered, as I always do around her, as I am so admiring of her, and proceeded to tell her it wasn't "real," and that I had bought it on sale, and I went on and on prattling away about how little it cost. Finally she said, "My dear, don't ever apologize that way. Say instead, 'Oh, yes, thank you. The Maharishi gave it to me when I was in India!'" So when someone comments on how beautiful the color contrast is, don't tell everything you know. Sit back and say, "Yes, it is beautiful, isn't it?"

Crown Roast of Pork

A crown roast is one of the most impressive presentations there is, once you have mastered it. They are rarely seen in a restaurant, so they retain an aura of specialness. Once you have made your first crown roast (which may take an hour or so the first time), you will see how easy they are and will buy rib roasts on sale to shape into crown roasts yourself and pull out of the freezer all year long for a dazzling main course. Traditionally, crown roasts are made from lamb or pork. Beef crown roasts are, of course, larger and even more visually spectacular. All three animals are similar in their rib and backbone configuration. Just bear in mind the differences in size.

Customarily, crown roasts are made by taking the center 6 ribs of two animals matched in size, joining them together, and turning them to shape a crown. If the vertebrae have been removed (usually sliced off by the butcher, or "chined"), the roast will have a smooth exterior. If the vertebrae are left on, it will be necessary to cut between each vertebra with a knife before cooking to facilitate easy carving later.

I used to put paper frills on the bone ends, but now I like them plain or topped with hollowed cherry tomatoes or Brussels sprouts.

1 **crown pork roast (see Box, page 82), stuffed with an aluminum foil ball**
3 **tablespoons fresh rosemary**
3 **garlic cloves, finely chopped**
2½ **pounds small new potatoes**

Garnish (optional)
   Cherry tomatoes, hollowed and drained, OR Brussels sprouts, blanched and hollowed, OR paper frills for the end of each rib

Preheat the oven to 350°F. Cover the exposed bones of the roast with aluminum foil to prevent burning.

Rub the roast with rosemary and garlic and place it in a shallow sided pan with sides sufficient to catch its juices. Roast until an instant-read thermometer registers 160°F. when inserted in the middle of the meat, about 20 minutes per pound (about 2 hours for a large roast). Add the potatoes to the roasting pan about 30 minutes before the roast should be done. Stir them occasionally so they brown all over. (If you wish to "extend" the roast, roast some of the loin simultaneously.)

When ready to serve, remove the strings from the roast, place it on a platter, and surround with sliced meat from one loin and the potatoes. Place the cherry tomatoes, Brussels sprouts, or frills on the bone ends if desired, or use the vegetables to fill and surround the roast. You can also fill the center with other vegetables, wild rice, or another filling. Degrease the juices in the pan and pour into a serving boat. Serve the roast and juices warm, at room temperature, or cold. Slice between each rib at the table and serve.

The crown roast can be carved at the table, but if you wish you can slice between the chops in the kitchen and "reassemble" the roast on the serving platter, so that each chop can then be easily removed at the table.

I must point out that these chops are a lot of fun to eat with your fingers. At least consider it—even with your good china.

How to Prepare a Crown Roast

There are two ways to make a crown roast. I am giving you the more spectacular and expensive way first, and the less expensive, fun way second. I'd practice in reverse order, serving the fun way for family and close friends. Preparing it will give you an understanding of what you need from the butcher if you ever decide to have him prepare it for you, and what is entailed in preparing it. Your first crown roast may take you an hour. There is something about handling such a large piece of meat that is intimidating. The second time, you will have more courage, and by the third time you will find it takes less than half an hour of your time, plus the roasting time. Then when people compliment you, you will say, "It's so easy—let me show you how!"

It would be wonderful if the average butcher could prepare a crown roast for you. If so, the trimmings, which you have paid for, may be stuffed inside the crown. Remove them, because they will shrink during cooking and cause a sloped roast. They can be used for a pâté or sausage.

Since the average butcher in the places I live has never made a crown roast, take these detailed instructions with you to the store when you go to purchase your meat. (I find that during the summer and fall there are one or two sale periods for pork. That is when I go to buy my sides of pork.) A side of pork, from the sirloin to the top rib, contains a nice sirloin roast for later, the tenderloin (usually smaller than those sold as tenderloins), and 13 ribs. Buy a whole side. For a majestic presentation, you will need two sides, preferably opposite sides from the same pig so they match in size when they are united in the crown.

Ask the butcher to slice just the backbone (also called the vertebrae or chine bone) off of each side. It should be sliced leaving all the ribs attached to the meat. (Recently a butcher sliced off the ribs as well as the backbone, necessitating returning to the butcher and getting another piece of meat, so supervise the process if you can.) I find it helpful to use my own body structure as a mental guide, as we are built somewhat the same way, although I understand the comparison is less than flattering.

The purpose of slicing off the backbone is to enable you to slide a knife between each rib easily when serving. (If the backbone is not removed, you must hack away at the bones prior to forming the crown, by hammering a knife between the vertebrae). There is an alternative presentation: Have the butcher saw between the individual vertebrae but leave the backbone on. If you have a good butcher, that's fine, as it does make a splashier presentation, but you may find the butcher has sliced into the meat more than you wish.

To proceed, remove the bottom (loin) roast and set aside for another time. If you are serving a crowd and the crown is your centerpiece, cook this roast separately, slice it, and put the slices around the crown. This technique works for a buffet and is good for second helpings.

"French" the bones of the ribs on the remaining section: Cut down along each side of each bone to the fleshy part of the meat, and then cut across to detach the trimmings between the ribs and reserve for another use. Scrape the exposed bones until they are clean of meat and sinew. The bones form the crown.

To make the crown from two sides of one pig, turn the meat so the rib ends point outward to look like a crown, and match the two sides. You may need to remove one or two of the tiny ribs, the shoulder bone where it is tucked into the meat, and perhaps one or two of the larger rib bones and their meat, in order for both sides to come together into a crown. Take care to have pieces of meat on the outside of the end ribs, so that the meat will adhere when cooking; bones in the way will prevent this.

Now that you have determined that your roast will look like a crown, lay the meat out flat and trim off any excess fat. Turn the sides again with the tops of the ribs pointing outward and join

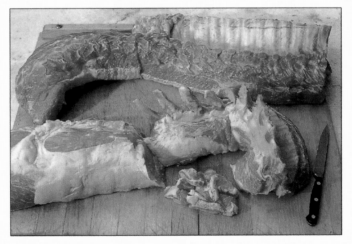

the flesh on either end of the roasts. You should have approximately 8 to 10 ribs per side, making 16 to 20 ribs joined together. Sew the meat together with a trussing needle and twine or wax-free dental floss. Alternatively, tie the ribs together and wrap several lengths of twine around the "belly" (lower part) of the roast. If the meat does not sit up straight, slice a little flesh judiciously off the bottom. Make a thick ball of aluminum foil and put it into the center to help hold the shape.

To make the family-style roast, using only one long loin, turn the ribs to form the crown, removing more flesh in order to shape the crown. There will be a greater variation in the size of the bones, but still it's snazzy for the family. Save the removed meat for a stir-fry.

FORK MEALS

It might mean a quiche with a close friend eaten off laps while curled on the sofa or an elegant all-dessert "midnight supper": What distinguishes fork meals is—yes—they require only a fork to eat them.

Fork meals allow you flexibility in decor and number of servings as well as remove the rigidity of seating assignments. They ensure more ease, both in serving and eating. But while a fork supper may sound more casual than a "sit-down dinner," such meals need a bit more planning because of their requirements. Before deciding to have a fork meal, you should have studied your venue (page 8) to determine that a supper using only a fork, plate, and napkin is your best option, based on the following criteria, and then, most important, plan your menu accordingly.

    ❦ You do not have enough places for all your guests to sit at a table, where they can wield a knife and fork, and they must eat on their laps or

    ❦ It is physically and socially appropriate for most of the group to stand and eat or

    ❦ You want your guests to be able to circulate among themselves rather than be stationary as at a fixed-place sitting at a table.

Although fork suppers are designed to allow eating standing up, as well as sitting on a chair or sofa, it's nice to have enough seating so that those who really want to sit down, especially the frail and elderly, can do so and will have a place to put their drink. Usually I encourage those guests to serve themselves first as an informal way to ensure their getting a seat. People normally don't sit down long at this kind of occasion. They like the opportunity to mix and mingle.

Fork Salad
Summer Lunch

Parmesan Coins

Curried Shrimp and
Rice Salad

or

Chicken Salad Provençale

Roberta's Tomatoes and
Cucumbers

Mint Crescent Rolls★

Summer Fruits in Bubbly★

or

Melon Basket

This is the kindest of menus to the host: salads that can all be done ahead and refrigerated. I was invited to a luncheon in honor of my friend Carol Lynn's high school graduation. I remember it as the first time anyone treated me like a grown-up in a social setting. The hostess's ease and grace were so magical, I even remember the punch (a ginger ale punch) with its ice cream. Only now do I appreciate the kindness of that hostess.

This menu also adapts to serving as a supper before the theater or even a late-night supper. A supper is not as extensive or heavy a meal as dinner. To make it more substantial do both the Curried Shrimp and Rice Salad and the Chicken Salad Provençale. Store-bought ice cream bonbons add a nice touch if you aren't making your own ice cream.

Cooking Time Line

Remember, each day, check your preparations list for things like cleaning, shopping, setting table, drop-dead time, and so on. If you elect to use a store-bought item (or more than one), make sure it's on your shopping list (and obviously, then, you don't need to make it).

UP TO 3 MONTHS BEFORE

1. Make the rolls and Parmesan Coins; freeze.

UP TO 2 DAYS BEFORE

1. Prepare the cucumbers and salads (this can be spread over a couple of days); refrigerate.

UP TO 1 DAY BEFORE

1. Carve the melon, cut out the melon balls or cubes, and refrigerate in an airtight container.
2. Prepare the tomatoes.
3. Remove the rolls and Parmesan Coins from the freezer and leave to thaw.

The Day

UP TO 1 HOUR BEFORE

1. Combine the tomatoes and cucumbers and set out.
2. Arrange the salads on platters and set out.
3. Prepare the fruits for dessert and refrigerate.

SERVICE

1. When the main course is cleared, dish up the dessert and garnish it.

Parmesan Coins

MAKES ABOUT 100

These luscious wafer-thin coins add a note of luxury wherever they are served. Keep the roll of dough wrapped in plastic wrap or a freezer bag in your freezer and cut off thin rounds and bake whenever you need a few, or roll the dough ⅛ inch thick and cut out fanciful cookie shapes.

The amount of salt is dependent on your cheese—if it is very salty, you will need none.

1 garlic clove
1 to 1½ cups all-purpose flour
¾ cup grated imported Parmesan cheese
¼ pound (1 stick) unsalted butter, at room temperature
¼ to ½ teaspoon salt (optional)
Dash of hot sauce

VARIATION

Substitute 1½ cups grated cheddar cheese for the Parmesan and up to ¼ teaspoon cayenne pepper for the hot sauce.

Preheat the oven to 350°F.

Finely chop the garlic in the bowl of a food processor. Add 1 cup of the flour, the cheese, the butter, salt if needed, and hot sauce. Process until the mixture forms a ball of dough, adding more flour if needed. (If you don't have a food processor, crush the garlic clove, add the butter, beat with a mixer until light, and then beat in 1 cup of the flour, the cheese, and the hot sauce, adding more flour as necessary.)

Divide the dough in two. Place one piece in a heavy sandwich-sized plastic bag and roll it into a 1-inch tube. Repeat with the remaining dough. Place in the freezer until firm, 20 minutes or longer, or keep frozen for up to 3 months. When ready to use, sliver off tiny pieces, or slice ⅛ inch thick. (The dough may need to sit at room temperature for a few minutes to facilitate cutting without crumbling.) Place the disks on a nonstick baking pan and bake until dappled with pale brown, about 8 to 10 minutes, checking to be sure they are not browning on the bottom. Store in an airtight container or freeze up to 3 months if not for immediate use.

Curried Shrimp and Rice Salad

SERVES 4 TO 6

A rice-and-mayonnaise base welcomes all sorts of variations. You can substitute chicken or other meats—or reserve a portion without shrimp—if some of your guests can't eat shellfish, or even use broccoli or eggplant for vegetarians.

Shrimp can be used whole or cut into two or three pieces before adding. The smaller the shrimp or chicken pieces, the more they stretch the dish to serve more people. There's no reason why you can't purchase your shrimp cooked if your store does as good a job as mine does.

The frozen peas need no further cooking. Just defrost and add to the rice vinaigrette.

Accompany the dish with as many of the condiments as you like. The more you add, the more flavor and fun! You can toss the leftover condiments with the leftover salad for an exotic meal the next day, never to be duplicated.

2 **cups long-grain rice**
2 **tablespoons white wine vinegar**
1½ **teaspoons Dijon mustard**
Salt
Freshly ground white pepper
¾ **cup vegetable oil**
1 **cup plain yogurt, drained, or mayonnaise or a combination**
2 **tablespoons curry powder**
1 **teaspoon sugar**
1 **teaspoon Worcestershire sauce**
2 **scallions sliced (white and green parts)**
2 **Granny Smith apples, peel on, cored and roughly chopped**
1 **to 2 stalks celery (sliced on the diagonal)**
2 **pounds medium (31 to 35 count) shrimp, cooked, peeled, and deveined**

Bring a large pot of salted water to the boil. Slowly stir in the rice and simmer until tender, about 15 minutes. (Test it by tasting or by breaking it with a thumbnail. It should have a small opaque dot in the center when it's done.) Drain well. This will give you 8 cups of rice.

In a large bowl, whisk together the vinegar and mustard and salt and pepper to taste. Slowly whisk in the oil. Add the hot rice to the vinaigrette and stir in with a fork. Let cool to room temperature. The rice can be dressed several days ahead and refrigerated.

Meanwhile, stir together the drained yogurt, curry powder, sugar, and Worcestershire, and ¼ cup of the scallions to the

**1 (10- to 12-ounce)
package frozen green
peas, defrosted and
drained**

Condiments
**1 cup toasted coconut
1 cup chopped roasted
peanuts
1 cup dried currants or
raisins
1 cup cooked and
crumbled bacon
1 cup mango chutney**

Garnish
**Lettuce, kale, or
watercress**

TIP

*Press the rice and peas into a
ring mold sprayed with nonstick spray before chilling for
several hours or overnight.
Turn the mold upside down
on a plate and give it a firm
smack to get it out.*

yogurt mixture. Add the apples, celery, and shrimp. Combine with the rice. Season with a little salt and white pepper and more curry powder if you like. Refrigerate, covered, for several hours or up to 2 days to develop the taste. Taste before serving and season with more salt and pepper if necessary.

Just before serving, add the defrosted peas to the rice and spread the salad in a wide serving dish. Make a well in the center of the rice and pile in the shrimp mixture. Top with the remaining tablespoon of scallions. Serve at room temperature or cold, as you prefer. Surround the platter with bowls of condiments and tuck lettuce under the outside of the rice.

SHOPPING TIP

Shrimp are readily available already cooked, peeled, and deveined at fish stores and better supermarkets. They are more expensive purchased this way, but if you can afford to, make it easy on yourself and buy them prepared.

Chicken Salad Provençale

This wonderfully tasty version of chicken salad is low in fat, which is always good news, and the watercress adds a piquant flavor. Although the recipe calls for serving the salad on a platter, you could very well put it on individual plates ahead of time.

1 onion, sliced
1 shallot, sliced
1 carrot, peeled and
    coarsely sliced
    Handful of celery
    leaves
¼ teaspoon thyme
1 bay leaf
8 parsley stems
1 teaspoon black
    peppercorns
3 whole cloves
2 teaspoons salt
4 whole chicken breasts,
    on the bone
½ cup olive oil
3 tablespoons chopped
    fresh oregano
2 cups green beans, tops
    and tails removed,
    cut into 2-inch
    pieces
3 tablespoons lemon
    juice
½ cup imported brine-
    cured black olives,
    pitted
2 tablespoons capers,
    drained
2 cups halved cherry
    tomatoes
    Salt
    Freshly ground black
    pepper
3 bunches watercress
    (see Note)
    Toasted pita triangles

Bring 1 quart of water to the boil in a heavy pan. Add the onion, shallot, carrot, celery leaves, thyme, bay leaf, parsley stems, peppercorns, cloves, and salt. Allow the water to simmer uncovered for 20 minutes. Add the chicken breasts, cover, and simmer another 20 minutes. Remove from the heat and let the chicken breasts cool in the liquid. Remove the skin and bones from the chicken breasts and cut the meat into bite-sized pieces. Place in a large bowl and toss with the olive oil and oregano. Cover the bowl and allow it to stand at room temperature 1 hour.

While the chicken is marinating, plunge the green beans into a large pot of boiling water. Let the green beans cook for 3 minutes, and then drain them and refresh under cold water (to stop the cooking and retain the color). Drain them and dry on paper towels or tea towels.

Gently stir the lemon juice, olives, capers, tomatoes, and green beans into the chicken. Season to taste with salt and pepper.

Arrange the watercress on a large serving platter. Mound the chicken salad in the center and surround with pita triangles. Pass additional triangles on the side.

NOTE

All recipes for watercress seem to call for "the leaves and tender stems." For years I wondered exactly what this meant, until finally one day I made an executive decision on the subject and put the matter to rest permanently. It simply means everything above the rubber band that holds each bunch together. I hope this saves you some worry.

Roberta's Tomatoes and Cucumbers

Once when I was visiting my friend Roberta Salma, in California, she needed to stretch a meal for some extra guests. "No problem" was the response, as she added this perfectly simple tomato recipe to dinner. As so often happens with simple, fresh dishes, they become the stars of the meal. The salt brings out the liquid in the tomatoes, making a wonderful tomato juice. The vinegar is unnecessary if the tomatoes are ripe.

2 pounds ripe tomatoes, cut into ½-inch cubes
1 to 2 teaspoons salt
Freshly ground black pepper
½ cup finely chopped fresh parsley
Up to ¼ cup red wine vinegar, if needed
2 pounds cucumbers, cut into ½-inch cubes

Sprinkle the tomatoes well with the salt and pepper and toss with the parsley. Cover and leave 1 hour or up to 2 days. Taste and add vinegar if necessary.

Sprinkle the cucumbers with salt and let sit in a colander 30 minutes. Rinse well and drain. Stir into the tomatoes. Pour into a serving bowl.

Mint Crescent Rolls

The slight bit of whole wheat in these rolls gives them an attractive touch of color, but you can also use all white bread flour. Although the kneaded dough is slightly stickier than a regular dough, each piece picks up more flour as it is rolled out into a thin circle on a floured board. If you don't have fresh mint, substitute basil (my favorite), thyme, and/or marjoram. If you can't get fresh herbs, move on to another recipe.

To speed up the rising time, you can use quick-acting yeast—just add the water at 135°F., and let the dough sit only 20 minutes before shaping. Alternatively, let the dough sit, covered, in the refrigerator overnight and shape it and let it double the next day.

1 package active dry
  yeast
2 tablespoons sugar
¼ cup warm water
  (105°F. to 115°F.)
½ cup milk
4 tablespoons (½ stick)
  butter, melted
1 teaspoon salt
2 large eggs, lightly
  beaten
½ cup whole-wheat flour
2 to 3½ cups bread flour

Herb Butter
1 tablespoon chopped
  fresh mint OR basil,
  thyme, and/or
  marjoram
5 tablespoons (⅝ stick)
  butter, at room
  temperature
⅓ cup grated imported
  Parmesan cheese

Glaze
1 large egg, beaten with
  1 teaspoon water

Preheat the oven to 350°F. Grease 2 baking sheets.

In a food processor or mixer bowl, dissolve the yeast and 1 tablespoon of the sugar in the warm water. Add the remaining sugar and the milk, butter, salt, eggs, and whole-wheat flour and knead with the steel blade or mixer until blended. Add the bread flour, ½ cup at a time, to make a smooth but still loose and slightly sticky dough. Place in an oiled plastic bag or oiled bowl, covered, and let rise in a warm place until doubled.

Punch the dough down and divide into 3 equal pieces. (You can weigh them to be sure they are equal.) On a floured board, roll out each piece, one at a time, to make a circle 10 inches in diameter. Mix the mint, butter, and Parmesan cheese. Spread one-third of the herb butter over each circle, then cut each circle into 8 triangles, like a pizza. Roll each triangle up from the side opposite the point to the point. Pull the ends in to make a crescent shape. Place on the greased baking sheets. Let rise until doubled, about 45 minutes.

Brush the rolls with the glaze. Bake on the middle rack of the oven until golden, about 15 minutes, or until an instant-read thermometer inserted in the center of the rolls registers 200°F.

The rolls can be kept frozen for up to 3 months.

Summer Fruits in Bubbly

SERVES 6

Choose a sweet pink champagne or a sweet nonalcoholic champagne or ginger ale for this breezy summer dessert. It is beautifully (and easily) served in large red wine goblets. Nectarines don't have to be peeled and, when fully ripe, are as juicy and wonderful as peaches. Especially late in the summer, nectarines get sweeter. If you have other varieties of mint than spearmint, do try them. Orange mint, peppermint, chocolate mint, or lemon balm adds a lovely touch.

2 pints red raspberries or strawberries, hulled, halved (quartered if large), and lightly crushed

3 ripe nectarines, cut in slivers

2 to 3 tablespoons lemon juice

1 bottle pink champagne or nonalcoholic sparkling wine OR 1 liter ginger ale

Fresh mint or lemon balm leaves for garnish

Place the raspberries, nectarines, and lemon juice in a bowl and toss gently to combine. Cover and refrigerate for 1 hour to allow the flavors to blend.

To serve, spoon the fruit into 6 large glasses or glass dessert bowls. Add enough champagne or ginger ale to each glass to just cover the fruit. Garnish with mint and serve.

VARIATION

Substitute 1 pint Mango Sorbet (page 170) balls for some of the fruit and lemon juice.

With a melon baller or small spoon, scoop the sorbet into small balls several hours before the party or the night before. Place them on a foil-lined cookie sheet and put them back in the freezer. Cover tightly with plastic wrap until firmly frozen. Pile them in a chilled glass bowl and serve with toothpicks. Or bring out a bottle of chilled champagne and the bowl of sorbet when you are ready to serve dessert. Open the champagne, spoon a ball of sorbet and some fruit into each wineglass, and finish it off with champagne. The guest picks up a wineglass, plate, and spoon. A lovely, fresh, sparkling dessert.

How to Make a Melon Basket

Pick as pretty a melon as you can. Set the melon vertically or horizontally, depending on the look you want for your table. Level the bottom if it wobbles by slicing off a little. Make a pattern, lay it over the melon, and cut, making sure to leave a handle. Scoop out the meat and reserve for another time or make into melon balls and serve. This may be used to hold the mango sorbet balls or either of the melon salads in this book.

Soup Party

Parmesan Coins (page 89)

Stilton and Apple or
Pear Soup with Onions

Fresh Garlic Soup

Minestrone

Salad of Baby Greens

Sourdough Bread (page 55)

Whole-Wheat Bread Pudding with
Dried Cranberries

*S*oup is one of the most versatile of all our foods, as are the ways to serve it. Hot, it warms and energizes. Cold, it refreshes as it whets the appetite. Room temperature, it accommodates itself to the meal and season. In fact, it is easily added to almost any meal, or can be a meal in itself!

Here are some ideas on ways to serve it. Juggle the recipes for the soups here and in the rest of the book and come up with your own combinations.

Serve two to three smooth soups—such as the Stilton and Apple (page 100) or Tricolored Soup (page 79)—in antique demitasse cups before the opera or an elegant repast; tote soups to the game in a thermos to serve in mugs as the core of a tailgate meal; offer two or three or make a giant batch of one for New Year's or Halloween.

One time, I had an autographing party for Mimi Sheraton, who had written a fabulous chicken soup book. She was adamant everyone taste her soup. She came down from New York ready to work, and we cooked soup all day. For some of us, cooking together is relaxing and fun, and so it was that day. I've known Mimi for years, but the memory I treasure the most is of how beautiful she looked, flushed and happy, as she finished her soups. We served three of her soups to over a hundred people, in little paper cups. To tell the truth, I had thought the whole idea, including the paper cups, a bad one, but I went along with it to please her. It worked so well, I've now had many soup parties but for smaller groups using real cups or bowls.

There are a variety of things beside the Parmesan Coins (page 89) that work on a soup plate to add a bit of crunch—Toast Points (page 177), croûtes (page 262), even asparagus tips. I like to serve a green salad after all the soups are eaten, or as a side dish to eat between soups. The bread pudding, hearty and filling, is the perfect finish lest there be even the slightest possibility that my guests might leave hungry!

Jack and I are blessed in more ways than we can count. But particularly, we are blessed in our friends and family. We came together after I had been divorced nearly twenty years from my favorite former husband, who is still a dear friend. It might seem that Jack and I would have had to start forming all new friends at a rather late stage of life. No such thing. Although we hadn't known each other, or even known *of* each other, before my friend Carol Muldawer fixed us up, we soon found we had many, many friends in common. Perhaps it is because we are Southern, and the South is, in fact, a very small place.

One of those acquaintances was Father Austin Ford, a priest who ran a church in a very impoverished section of Atlanta. A kind spirit with a rapier wit, he drew many people we knew around him. We found our Oxford, Mississippi, friends Dennis and Barbara Phillips were very fond of Austin and that, through them, he had met out dear friends Steve and Marie Nygren. Since Dennis and Barbara were coming to visit us in Atlanta, we determined to get everyone together at the Nygrens' farm outside Atlanta.

It was one of those magical days. When the weather was cool enough to walk and warm enough to walk easily. When the rabbits had baby rabbits, the pigs had little pigs, and the Nygren children introduced us to all the horses, turkeys, and other animals on the farm. We sat and swung on slatted love seats, facing each other across the long porch, our conversation interrupted only occasionally by a persistent animal's monologue.

When it came time to eat, Marie had everything ready in a jiffy. The children had helped her set the long table, and we sat down to a splendid meal. Marie included this garlic soup from Lynne Rossetto Kasper's *The Splendid Table.* Marie had simmered the broth all the day before. It was indeed a splendid table, and although I've made adjustments so you can use the same broth recipe in making your turkey stock for Thanksgiving ahead of time, I think you'll like the final product and relish it as much as we did then.

The garlic soup brings many occasions to mind, for it is now a repeat star in the cuisine of our house.

Cooking Time Line

Remember, each day, check your preparations list for things like cleaning, shopping, setting the table, drop-dead time, and so on. If you elect to use a store-bought item (or more than one), make sure it's on your shopping list (and obviously, then, you don't need to make it).

UP TO 3 MONTHS BEFORE

1. Make the Parmesan Coins, the soups (without cheese; add last), bread, and bread pudding; freeze.

UP TO 1 DAY BEFORE

1. Remove the Parmesan Coins, soups, bread, and bread pudding from the freezer.
2. Make the vinaigrette.

The Day

UP TO 1 HOUR BEFORE

1. Heat the soups and bread. Remember to add cheese.
2. Set out the Parmesan Coins.

AT SERVING TIME

1, Toss the salad with the dressing.
2. Start heating the bread pudding.

ALL THE OTHER SOUPS

Cold Soups
Cold Borscht (page 260)
Gazpacho à la Mode (page 56)

Hot Soups
Fresh Garlic Soup (page 101)
Herbed Tomato Soup   (page 261)
Lentil Soup with Harissa   (page 67)
Minestrone (page 102)

Onion Soup with Thyme Croûtes (page 262)
Stilton and Apple or Pear Soup with Onions
    (page 100)
Wild Mushroom and Wild Rice Soup
    (page 244)

Hot or Cold Soups
Cream of Carrot Soup (page 124)
Tricolored Soup (page 79)

Stilton and Apple or Pear Soup with Onions

SERVES 6 TO 8

My friend Jane Mullen brought this to an impromptu dinner party one night. We all loved it. Since then, I've found it a marvelously adaptable soup. I use either apples or pears, I omit the garlic if it doesn't suit my mood, and I add cooked Italian sausage pieces when I need to stretch the menu. The soup is good hot, at room temperature, or cold. It freezes and reheats well. When I serve it in demitasse cups or mugs with no spoon, I process it in a food processor until smooth.

4 tablespoons (½ stick) butter
4 large yellow onions, sliced
1 large red onion, sliced
1 whole head of garlic, papery outside layer removed
4 apples (preferably 3 Fuji and 1 Granny Smith) or 4 pears (Bosc or other cooking pear) peeled, cored, and thickly sliced
6 cups fresh or canned chicken stock or broth
3 ounces Stilton cheese, crumbled
Salt
Freshly ground black pepper

Garnish
Fresh thyme or rosemary, chopped

Melt 2 tablespoons of the butter in a large, heavy pot. You may need two pans for browning the onions. Add the onions, and cook over medium-low heat, stirring occasionally, until caramelized—light brown in color and soft in texture—about 30 minutes.

Meanwhile, microwave the unpeeled head of garlic for 1 minute on high until soft. If not soft, microwave 1 to 2 minutes longer. Allow to cool, then peel.

When the onions are caramelized, add the garlic and the sliced apples. Stir in the stock or broth, bring to the boil, reduce the heat, and cook over low heat until soft, 40 to 50 minutes. Add the crumbled cheese and heat until melted. Season to taste with salt and pepper. Garnish with fresh herbs. Serve hot, room temperature, or cold.

Fresh Garlic Soup

This beautiful, tawny-brown soup, rich in flavor, is perfect to start a meal. Some of its richness comes from sage, a strong yet subtle herb when fresh, pungent and aggressive when dried. It doesn't need cold weather. I once served it in August to raves. The secret is the broth, which will take a while to prepare but may be made several months in advance and frozen. Always taste the stock before you get started—if it is not strong enough in flavor, bring it to the boil and reduce it. If it is too rich, dilute it with a little chicken broth or water. This soup is adapted from a recipe in Lynne Rossetto Kasper's book The Splendid Table.

2 large heads garlic, papery outer layer removed

¼ cup extra-virgin olive oil

6 shallots or 2 medium onions, finely chopped

6 fresh sage leaves or ½ teaspoon dried

3½ cups Quick Turkey Stock or Broth (page 263)

Salt

Freshly ground black pepper

⅔ cup plus 3 tablespoons shredded imported Parmesan cheese

Croûtes

4 to 6 (½-inch-thick) slices long Italian bread

2 tablespoons olive oil

3 to 5 tablespoons grated imported Parmesan

Put the whole garlic heads in the microwave and cook until soft, 1½ to 2 minutes on high, checking every minute or so. Alternatively, separate the unpeeled cloves and cook in boiling water for 10 minutes. Let cool until cool enough to handle, then peel and remove the stem end of each clove.

Meanwhile, in a 2-quart saucepan, heat ¼ cup of the olive oil, add the shallots, and cook until soft, about 7 minutes. Add the cooked garlic, the sage, and the turkey broth. Bring to the boil over medium-high heat. Partly cover and cook 5 minutes. Remove the lid, reduce the heat, and simmer another 5 minutes.

Remove the sage leaves and discard. Let the soup cool slightly and purée it in a blender or food processor, processing the solids first and adding liquid as necessary. Season to taste with salt and pepper. Sprinkle the soup with ⅔ cup of the Parmesan.

For the croûtes, preheat the broiler. Put the slices of bread on a baking sheet and toast them under the preheated broiler until crisp and golden, 2 to 5 minutes. Turn, brush the other side of the bread with olive oil, top with ½ tablespoon Parmesan on each slice, and put back under broiler until brown, about 1 to 2 minutes. Cut the croûtes to fit the cup or bowl, put one in each cup, and top with soup. You can also pass the croûtes separately.

Minestrone

SERVES 8 TO 10

To me minestrone is a multicultural answer to summer meals, when the vegetable stands are offering produce that abounds with flavor. My own minestrone varies each time I make it, as should yours. I always make enough to freeze for future meals. Parmigiano-Reggiano makes an enormous difference in this dish.

½ pound dried white beans, such as cannellini or Great Northern, picked over

2 tablespoons olive oil

¼ pound lean slab bacon, finely chopped

¼ pound salt pork, roughly chopped

2 tablespoons chopped fresh parsley

3 tablespoons chopped fresh basil

1 teaspoon chopped fresh oregano or marjoram

⅛ teaspoon chopped or crushed red chile pepper, fresh or dried

1 medium leek, white part only, halved lengthwise and sliced

1 celery stalk, sliced on the diagonal

2 tablespoons finely chopped garlic

½ pound Swiss chard, coarsely chopped (optional)

One 14½-ounce can Italian peeled tomatoes, coarsely chopped

2 quarts fresh or canned chicken stock or water

1 medium carrot, peeled and sliced crosswise ¼ inch thick

½ pound Savoy cabbage, shredded

1 medium zucchini, halved lengthwise and the halves sliced on the diagonal

6 to 8 ounces spaghetti, broken

Salt

½ pound fresh spinach (optional)

1 cup grated imported Parmesan cheese

Freshly ground black pepper

Place the beans in a large bowl, and pour in enough cold water to cover by 2 inches. Let soak overnight. (Alternatively, place the beans in a large saucepan with cold water to cover, bring to the boil, boil for 2 minutes, and then let sit for 1 hour before proceeding. If you use this quick-soak method, you may need to cook the beans an extra 30 minutes.) Drain and rinse well.

In a large pot, heat 1 tablespoon of the olive oil over moderate heat. Add the bacon and salt pork and cook until the fat is rendered, 7 to 8 minutes, adding more oil if necessary. Add the parsley, basil, oregano, and chile pepper. Cook, stirring occasionally, for 2 minutes. Add the leek, celery, and garlic. Cover and cook over low heat until soft, about 5 minutes.

Stir in the chard, if using, and the drained beans, tomatoes, and stock. Bring to the boil over high heat. Reduce the heat to moderately low, cover, and simmer for 30 minutes. Stir in the carrot and cabbage, cover, and cook until tender, about 30 minutes. Stir in the zucchini, pasta, and salt to taste and bring to the boil. Cook 10 to 15 minutes longer, until the pasta is done. If using spinach, add a few minutes after the pasta. Serve in bowls with a sprinkling of Parmesan and black pepper. (The soup will keep for up to 1 week, covered and refrigerated, or it may be frozen for up to 3 months. Reheat before serving.)

FORK MEALS

Salad of Baby Greens

SERVES 6 TO 8

There are many variations of packaged salad greens now for sale in the grocery store, which I find easier than buying whole heads and bunches of everything and mixing my own. I have a particular affection for arugula, which is sold as an herb in my store, so I add a bunch or so.

1 pound mixed baby greens, washed and dried

1 bunch arugula, washed and dried

½ cup Basic Vinaigrette (page 60)

1 to 2 tablespoons chopped fresh basil, thyme, or oregano (optional)

Toss the greens and arugula with the vinaigrette and herbs, if using, just before serving.

Hospitality is universal and timeless, but manners reflect the culture and historical moment that produced them. Some that were once de rigueur now seem somewhere between quaint and bizarre. In the South, for instance, we were brought up with the rule that a lady never asked for anything directly, lest it imply that the man in her life was not all he should be, for a true gentleman could anticipate a woman's every need and desire. So in the days of Southern colonels, a lady would just rattle her ice and a young lieutenant would bring her a drink. Were her glass empty, she would murmur to her beau, "Bubba, honey, if I had any ice in my glass, I'd rattle it." So, too, at the table, rather than ask to be passed the peas, one would turn to one's neighbor and say, "Wouldn't you like some peas?" After accepting some, that person would say, "Wouldn't *you* like some peas?" And you could then put peas on your plate without further demurring. Cookbook author Claudia Roden talks of being brought up in a society where she was trained that you should turn down food or drink when it was first offered, and that it would then be vigorously offered again, at which point you could accept. When she came to America, she found it was never offered a second time.

Whole-Wheat Bread Pudding with Dried Cranberries

SERVES 8 TO 10

The whole-wheat bread gives this warm dessert a hint of nutty texture unusual for bread pudding. It's very homey and satisfying. It's delicious straight out of the oven, but provides an equally enjoyable dessert for several days. Of course you could use Basic Crème Fraîche (page 254) in place of the yogurt, but it seems a shame to destroy the illusion of a meal brimming with the promise of healthy living. Just don't mention the cream.

12 slices whole-wheat bread
 2 cups milk
1½ cups heavy cream
 3 tablespoons butter, melted
 4 large eggs, lightly beaten
1½ cups sugar
 1 tablespoon vanilla extract
 2 teaspoons ground cinnamon
 1 cup dried cranberries, soaked in 2 cups water for 2 hours and drained, liquid reserved
    Grated peel (no white attached) of 2 oranges
 1 cup chopped pecans
 1 cup lemon yogurt for serving

Preheat the oven to 375°F. Butter a 13x9x2-inch baking dish.

Tear the bread with or without crusts into 1-inch pieces and place them in a very large bowl. In a 2-quart measuring cup, combine the milk, cream, butter, eggs, sugar, vanilla, cinnamon, and cranberries. Pour over the cubed bread and lightly toss. Pour the mixture into the baking dish and bake for 30 minutes.

While the pudding is baking, in a small saucepan, boil down the cranberry soaking liquid and the orange peel until it measures ½ cup and is thick and syrupy, about 10 minutes. Add the pecans and pour over the partly baked pudding. Continue baking 30 minutes longer, or until set, about 1 hour total. It's best hot, but still very good cold or at room temperature. Serve with a dollop of lemon yogurt.

You may refrigerate the pudding several days, or keep it frozen for up to 3 months, reheating it for 20 minutes at 350°F. or in the microwave until warm.

Special Barbecue

Baby Artichoke and New Potato Salad

Ginger-Soy Ribs

Spicy Grilled Butterflied Chicken

Grilled Portobello Mushrooms

Lexington Sauce

Karen's Summer Slaw

Wild Rice, Snow Pea, and Pineapple Salad

Quick Asian Ratatouille

Ginger-Lime Zebra Cake

The word *barbecue* conjures up different things to different people. In Texas and the rest of the Southwest, you'd think beef. In the South, it more probably would be pork. There are all sorts of contraptions for barbecuing, from kitchen grill pans to giant-sized covered grills to simple briquette containers. Or no contraption at all—just a pit with a whole beef buried in it as I saw in Montana or a whole pig racked over it as we do in the South. So instructions on cooking barbecue must be very broad. Each circumstance requires a little adjustment and a little different planning.

At the casual barbecue for my high school reunion in Virginia, we served "pulled" pork on buns, with barbecue sauce on the side. I thought it pulled-off-the-bones perfect and very traditional, but my friend Pat Colarco, who has lived in California since graduating, expected ribs. One family's "one and only proper way" is rank heresy to another, so please be tolerant.

For years a group of us (called "the food group") gave regular barbecues in Lovejoy, Georgia. There, we'd dig a "six-pack pit," meaning two men would finish a six-pack while digging it, and we'd wire a pig of about 100 pounds onto a rack. We would solemnly bless it the night before, and then let it cook slowly all night, while we talked and told tall tales. The next day, usually the Fourth of July, the pig would be cut up and laid out on a long table. Another table would be laden with homemade cakes, brought by the guests.

Before tackling a whole pig, you might start with these tasty Ginger-Soy Ribs or Spicy Grilled Butterflied Chicken. Portobello mushrooms are "meaty" enough to stand up to grilling, and they provide a vegetarian option. All three can be cooked on the grill or in the oven, and all can be made ahead and reheated.

Whether you choose to emphasize the all-American barbecue aspect of this meal, or the Asian flavors aspect, you'll have a popular, tasty menu and a good time.

Cooking Time Line

Remember, each day, check your preparations list for things like cleaning, cleaning grill, shopping, setting the table, drop-dead time, and so on. If you elect to use a store-bought item (or more than one), make sure it's on your shopping list (and obviously, then, you don't need to make it).

UP TO 3 MONTHS BEFORE

1. Make the cake and freeze it. (The cake must be made at least 6 hours in advance and refrigerated.)

UP TO 1 WEEK BEFORE

1. Make the Lexington Sauce and potato salad; refrigerate.

UP TO 2 DAYS BEFORE

1. Make the ratatouille and refrigerate.

UP TO 1 DAY BEFORE

1. Marinate the chicken and ribs. (The ribs can be cooked ahead and simply reheated on The Day.)
2. Make slaw and refrigerate.

The Day

1 HOUR BEFORE

1. Put the chicken on the grill.
2. Remove the slaw from the refrigerator.

30 MINUTES BEFORE

1. Put the ribs on the grill.

Paper towels are great for handling really messy foods. For a bit of pizzazz, however, use hot, damp mismatched cotton napkins or tea towels. Layer them in a pie dish with slices of lemon and pour a little hot water from a teakettle over them. Or dampen them all and place them in the microwave for 1 to 2 minutes. Take great care to avoid burning yourself or others. Sometimes I move them to a shallow silver bowl, other times to a pottery dish. Either way, guests are delighted to see them.

Baby Artichoke and New Potato Salad

Several years ago, I went to see artichokes growing in California, and I was amazed to see that they varied enormously in size on each plant. For lunch that day, I had a cooking lesson with Biba, the talented TV cook and author. She taught us how to use those little artichokes some people call hearts but are really the small artichokes on the artichoke plant. I didn't get her recipe written down, but here's mine. If using bottled artichoke hearts, taste the marinade. If you like it, all or part may be substituted for the oil in the recipe. If not, drain before proceeding. You may keep the salad in a covered container in the refrigerator a week or so. I even use it for snacks. It may be eaten with a toothpick or skewer as well as a fork. If no small potatoes can be found, halve or quarter them.

2 pounds small new potatoes (1 to 2 inches in diameter)
2 pounds trimmed whole baby artichokes, cooked, fresh, or bottled
1 or 2 medium red onions, thinly sliced
4 to 5 garlic cloves, crushed with 2 teaspoons salt
3 tablespoons chopped fresh parsley, thyme, and/or oregano
¼ cup red wine vinegar
½ cup extra-virgin olive oil
Salt
Freshly ground black pepper

Bring a large pot of water to the boil. Add the potatoes and cook until done, about 15 minutes. Remove the potatoes to a colander and drain thoroughly.

In a large bowl, toss together the potatoes, artichokes, onions, garlic, parsley, vinegar, and olive oil. Taste for seasoning and add salt and pepper as needed. Serve at room temperature or chilled.

SHOPPING TIP

New potatoes

What is a new potato exactly? It is technically any newly picked potato of any size with a skin so tender it can be scraped off. For my recipes, look for small, immature, unblemished, firm potatoes about double the size of a silver dollar. They weight about 10 to a pound. Uniform size is desirable so they will all cook at the same rate. I like to buy red new potatoes because I find them pleasing to the eye and I like their sweet tender taste, but white potatoes are perfectly acceptable. I've become enamored of the variety called Yukon Gold, which are becoming more widely available. If you see them, buy them.

Ginger-Soy Ribs

SERVES 6

Baby back ribs—the smallest ribs from the pork back rib section—are good as finger food because they are more tender, don't become gummy-sticky, and are small enough to be held in one hand. When purchasing, plan on 1 to 1½ pounds of ribs per person for a main course, ¼ to ½ pound for an appetizer of the baby backs.

An ooh-ahh technique, which I learned from Charleston restaurateur Louis Osteen, is to serve only meaty ribs by a trick of careful slicing. The trick is to slice right next to the bone on the first and third ribs, leaving the meat on either side of the middle, or second, rib. Alternate down the rack, throwing away every other bone.

¼ cup soy sauce
2 cups rice wine vinegar
½ cup hoisin sauce
¼ cup vegetable oil
4 teaspoons toasted sesame oil
1 to 2 teaspoons hot red pepper flakes
4 garlic cloves
¼ cup finely chopped fresh ginger
2 tablespoons sugar
6 to 9 pounds baby back ribs

Heat the grill or grease a large pan with nonstick spray.

In the bowl of the food processor, combine the soy sauce, vinegar, hoisin sauce, vegetable oil, sesame oil, pepper flakes, garlic, ginger, and sugar. Process until well blended. Place in a zip-type 1- to 2-gallon plastic bag. Add the ribs to the mixture and seal. Shake to thoroughly coat. Marinate 30 minutes to overnight.

Remove the ribs from the marinade and place on the prepared grill or the baking pan. Pour the marinade into a small saucepan. Grill or broil the ribs, turning halfway through the cooking, until spotted with black and gold, done but slightly pink, 10 to 12 minutes. Arrange the ribs on a serving platter or tray.

Bring the sauce to the boil, cook 5 minutes, and then pour over the ribs.

The ribs may be done in advance and reheated.

Spicy Grilled Butterflied Chicken

This is very similar to a recipe I learned from a Texas cooking school teacher and restaurateur, Mary Nell Reck. Splitting the chicken down the backbone encourages it to cook more evenly.

1 **chicken, about 2½ to 3 pounds**
Juice of 1½ lemons
2 **garlic cloves**
1 **tablespoon salt**
1 **tablespoon freshly ground black pepper**
2 **teaspoons ground cayenne pepper**
1 **tablespoon paprika**
2 **tablespoons unsalted butter, melted**

Prepare the grill.

Split and butterfly the chickens by cutting down the backbone and opening the chicken, leaving the breast attached. Squeeze lemon juice over the chicken. Mix together the garlic, salt, black pepper, cayenne, and paprika and add to the melted butter. Pour over the chicken. If possible, let the chicken sit overnight, uncovered, in the refrigerator to let the paste harden.

Place the chicken, breast side up, on the grill. Cover the grill and cook the chicken until crisp and done throughout, about 50 minutes. Or preheat the oven to 350°F. and bake the chicken until done, about 50 minutes. Don't turn it. If the skin is not crispy, place the chicken under the broiler to crisp the skin and brown, watching carefully so that it doesn't burn.

Grilled Portobello Mushrooms

SERVES 4 TO 6

Portobello mushrooms (a large variety of the cremini mushroom) are now grown all over the United States. Although they can be small or very large, depending on their age, I prefer the burger-sized ones.

Grilled portobello mushrooms are so flavorful and satisfying they can be served as a main course. Placed on a bun, they can be served to your vegetarian guests as a substitute for hamburger, equally juicy and delicious.

If you decide to cook more than needed, use them as an accompaniment for lamb, beef, and chicken or slice and serve in a quesadilla or over pasta. There are many uses!

4 to 6 medium-sized portobello mushrooms, each about 4 inches across
Salt
6 garlic cloves, finely chopped
4 to 6 tablespoons olive oil
Freshly ground black pepper
Fresh herbs of your choice (optional)

Preheat the broiler.

Clean the mushrooms with a damp paper towel that has been dipped in salt. Remove the stems and reserve for another use.

Put the garlic, olive oil, and salt and pepper to taste in a plastic bag. Add the mushrooms, seal, turn to distribute the seasonings, and allow to marinate for 1 hour.

Place the mushrooms, top side up, on a broiler pan and grill 4 minutes. Turn the mushrooms and cook 4 minutes more. The mushrooms should be well cooked on the outside but creamy and tender on the inside. Sprinkle with fresh herbs if desired.

VARIATIONS

For Portobello Bruschetta, chop the reserved stems and sauté in butter. Toss with garlic, green onions, rosemary, parsley, and lime juice. If there are leftover grilled portobellos, slice them and toss with the rest. Serve on toasted bread.

Grilled asparagus and portobello mushrooms

Brush 1 pound thin trimmed asparagus with oil, add to the hot grill with the mushrooms, and cook, turning, until crisp-tender, about 5 minutes. Serve whole, or cut both mushrooms and asparagus on the diagonal and serve as a side dish.

Lexington Sauce

Lexington, North Carolina, reputedly has seventeen barbecue restaurants per capita and more are being added! Every one of them insists its recipe is secret and the best, the very best. People drive to Lexington from all over to taste barbecue, so save this sauce for your local barbecue contest—and add a few secrets of your own!

3 tablespoons sugar
1 cup apple cider
   vinegar
⅔ cup ketchup
½ cup water
⅛ teaspoon cayenne
   pepper
¾ teaspoon salt
   Freshly ground black
   pepper
   Dash of hot sauce

Mix together the sugar and vinegar in a small nonaluminum pan and heat until the sugar dissolves. Add the ketchup, water, cayenne, salt, pepper, and hot sauce. Simmer 10 minutes, stirring occasionally. If the sauce is too thick for your taste, add more water; if too thin, boil it down a bit more. Serve over pork barbecue with grated cabbage or cole slaw.

Karen's Summer Slaw

This recipe is a versatile and colorful side dish and is great served as a main course. Karen, who gave me this recipe, always tries to make her recipes have a dual purpose—as a main dish as well as a side dish, for instance.

4 cups sliced green
   cabbage
2 cups sliced red
   cabbage
2 carrots, cut into 2-
   inch-long thin strips
1 medium sweet onion,
   thinly sliced
1 medium beet, steamed
   (crisp-tender) and
   cut into thin strips
   (optional)
½ cup dried blueberries
   or cranberries
   (optional)
1 to 2 garlic cloves,
   finely chopped
½ tablespoon chopped
   fresh basil
½ tablespoon chopped
   fresh dill
½ teaspoon cayenne
   pepper
1 tablespoon fresh
   orange juice
2 to 3 tablespoons sugar
1 teaspoon Dijon
   mustard
¼ cup red or white wine
   vinegar
½ cup olive or vegetable
   oil
1 teaspoon finely
   chopped orange peel
   (no white attached)

Mix together the cabbages, carrots, onion, beet, and dried berries, if using, and set aside.

Make the dressing: In a separate bowl, mix the garlic, basil, dill, cayenne, orange juice, sugar, mustard, and vinegar. Whisk in the oil gradually. When thoroughly mixed, toss the dressing with the vegetables. The slaw may be refrigerated if making ahead, but remember to remove it from the refrigerator at least 1 hour before serving. This slaw is better served at room temperature. Toss again right before serving and garnish with the orange peel.

VARIATION

For an Asian flavor, Karen uses ⅓ cup chopped scallions in place of the sweet onion, 2 to 3 tablespoons soy sauce in place of the same amount of vinegar, 2 to 3 teaspoons toasted sesame oil, 1 (11-ounce) can mandarin oranges (drained), and 1 tablespoon black and white toasted sesame seeds.

Wild Rice, Snow Pea, and Pineapple Salad

SERVES 4 TO 6

This salad is particularly refreshing with lamb. If snow peas are out of season, asparagus can be substituted.

1 cup wild rice
1 pound snow peas, strings removed, cut diagonally OR asparagus, cut in 2-inch pieces

Vinaigrette
⅔ cup olive oil
⅓ cup vinegar
  Salt
  Freshly ground black pepper
2 teaspoons Dijon mustard

3 to 4 slices fresh or canned pineapple, cut into 1½-inch pieces, with juice
2 to 3 heaping tablespoons finely chopped fresh mint or lemon balm (optional)
1 small head Bibb or butter lettuce (optional)

Rinse the wild rice under cold running water and add to 4 cups boiling water. Cover and simmer until cracked and puffed, 50 to 55 minutes. Place the snow peas in boiling water to cover and boil 2 minutes. Drain. Rinse with cold water to refresh (to stop the cooking and set the color). Drain again.

Make the vinaigrette by mixing together the olive oil, vinegar, salt, pepper, and mustard. Combine the vinaigrette with the cooked rice, pineapple, and herbs, if using. Mix in the snow peas just before serving. Serve warm or chill and serve cold on the lettuce, if you like. The salad can be made several days in advance sans the peas.

SHOPPING TIP

A packaged mixture of long-grain rice and wild rice is available. The wild rice has been partially cooked, enabling it to be cooked with the long-grain rice and have both done in 25 minutes. This is a good substitute for plain wild rice.

TIP

Wild rice

Wild rice is actually a grass, not a rice. It should be rinsed thoroughly before cooking. One cup of raw wild rice will yield about 3½ to 4 cups cooked. Cooked wild rice can be refrigerated, covered, for up to 10 days, and it freezes very well. If using in a recipe that calls for it to be reheated, add a little hot water and reheat in a heavy saucepan or in the microwave.

Quick Asian Ratatouille

SERVES 6 TO 8

Ratatouille, the French vegetable dish, takes on a new personality when seasoned with Asian flavors. This version is particularly good with grilled poultry or meat.

2 medium eggplant, cut
   into cubes
   Salt
3 tablespoons oil
2 garlic cloves, peeled
   and chopped
1 tablespoon finely
   chopped fresh ginger
3 scallions, chopped
2 bell peppers (red or
   green), cored,
   seeded, and cut into
   1-inch chunks
3 zucchini, sliced
2 tomatoes, cut in
   wedges or ½ cup
   canned tomato sauce
½ cup sliced mushrooms
1 to 2 teaspoons hot
   sauce
2 tablespoons teriyaki
   sauce
2 tablespoons red wine
   vinegar
2 teaspoons sugar
1 teaspoon chopped
   fresh lemongrass
   (optional)
½ cup fresh or canned
   chicken broth or
   stock

Sprinkle the eggplant with salt, and let stand in a colander for 30 minutes to drain. Rinse, drain, and pat dry with paper towels. Heat the oil in a large skillet or wok. Add the eggplant, and cook over high heat, tossing until soft and brown, about 8 minutes. Add the garlic, ginger, scallions, bell peppers, zucchini, tomatoes, and mushrooms. Cook over high heat, tossing, for 2 minutes. Add the hot sauce, teriyaki sauce, vinegar, sugar, lemongrass if using, and chicken broth. Bring to the boil, and boil until the liquid is absorbed, about 5 minutes. The ratatouille will keep 2 to 3 days in the refrigerator.

VARIATION

Ratatouille

For a standard ratatouille, delete the ginger, scallions, zucchini, hot sauce, teriyaki sauce, vinegar, and lemongrass. Cook 1 sliced onion with the eggplant, and then add the garlic, bell peppers, tomatoes, and mushrooms. Stir in ¼ cup chopped herbs and simmer until soft, about 1 hour. Stir in another ¼ cup chopped herbs and salt and pepper to taste.

Ginger-Lime Zebra Cake

SERVES 4

This is an exotically flavored variation on the "back-of-the-package" chocolate cookie and whipped cream cake that I learned about from Sally Young, my former apprentice cook, who made it with her dad when she was a child.

½ cup heavy cream
1 cup Lime Butter
    (opposite)
1 (9-ounce) package
    large thin Swedish-
    style gingersnaps

Garnish
    Candied ginger,
    chopped

Whip cream just until it forms soft peaks.

Gently fold together the lime butter and the whipped cream. Spread ½ tablespoon of the whipped cream mixture on each gingersnap. Stack them together to make a 14-inch log and lay it on its side on a serving platter. Frost the log with the remaining whipped cream. Chill 4 to 6 hours, or cover with plastic wrap and freeze. If frozen, thaw in refrigerator 1 hour before serving. To serve, garnish with the candied ginger and slice the roll at a 45-degree angle. Keep refrigerated until serving.

VARIATIONS

To make Dr. Bob's Zebra Cake, whip 2 cups heavy cream and mix with 1 teaspoon orange extract. Spread on chocolate wafers, form into a log, and ice with the whipped cream mixture. Garnish with chocolate curls.

Spread gingersnaps with apricot jam and stack together. Ice with whipped cream lightly flavored with orange extract and fresh orange zest. Garnish with finely chopped orange peel and candied ginger.

Making Chocolate Curls

In one hand, hold a block of chocolate wrapped in several paper towels so you don't melt the chocolate. Hold a sharp potato peeler against the upper edge of the chocolate and draw the blade slowly toward you, shaving the chocolate in thin, curling strips.

Lime Butter

Lime butter is rich, fattening, sinful, and wonderful with a lovely taste of lime. Its high acid content allows it to keep indefinitely in the refrigerator. Thin it with heavy cream or use as is to fill puff pastry or cream puffs. It also makes an excellent hostess gift, jarred with a bow on top.

1 cup sugar
¼ pound (1 stick) unsalted butter
3 large eggs, lightly beaten
2 tablespoons all-purpose flour
Grated peel (no white attached) of 3 limes
Juice of 3 limes

Place the sugar, butter, eggs, flour, lime peel, and lime juice in a heavy saucepan. Cook, stirring, over low heat, without boiling, until thick. Remove from the heat and let cool. Use as a sauce or icing. Will keep almost indefinitely covered in the refrigerator.

SHOPPING TIP

Lemons/limes

Thick-skinned lemons and limes are much easier to peel, but on the other hand, you get more juice from thin-skinned ones. You can find dried peels, but they are nowhere near as nice as the fresh and are for absolute emergencies. Lemon and lime juice substitutes vary widely in quality; some are quite acceptable. If you aren't using fresh juice, buy the best substitute you can find.

Supper Buffet for Six to Thirty

Cream of Carrot Soup

Parmesan Coins (page 89)

Lemon Couscous

Roberta's Tomatoes and
Cucumbers (page 93)

Citrus Fruit and Feta Salad

Quick-Rising Cumin-Fennel Bread★

Bobotie with Vegetables

or

Dudley's Lasagna

Chocolate Delirium Torte

I first served this menu for a buffet to welcome a new member of my husband's journalism department faculty at Ole Miss. As a newlywed, I particularly wanted the party to be successful. The budget was necessarily modest and the dinner hour early, as it was a "school night."

I'd been out of town, and my husband, sometimes an absentminded professor, issued the invitations, forgetting to include an RSVP! Although we made follow-up phone calls, it was hit or miss, leaving me unsure about how many guests would attend. I estimated to the best of my ability that it would be between twenty and thirty-five. (Ultimately, nearly thirty showed up.)

Because we'd recently completed a kitchen renovation and lacked room for a sit-down affair for more than twenty guests, I settled on a casual, gather-in-the-kitchen type meal; that's the room where many great gatherings converge anyway. The challenge was familiar: Guests needed to be able to maneuver with food and drinks while standing up. A knife and fork would be too unwieldy, so the fork would be the only eating utensil. I wanted to serve something they wouldn't have had before, yet something that would not intimidate. I did not want speculation on how much money we had spent.

The faculty was ethnically diverse, and the guests required some flexibility on our part: One couple told us they would be unable to attend unless they could bring their pre-teens. This increased the menu challenges. The bobotie (bah-BOO-tee)—a delicious curried tagine or casserole of meat, custard, and vegetables—was unusual enough to be interesting to a well-traveled crowd, yet was enough like meat loaf to seem familiar. I made three. I also served chicken wings cut into finger-food-sized drumettes. I decided to cook plenty of pasta (this time in the form of couscous, an easy-to-prepare, tiny Moroccan-style pasta) to fill up the picky eaters. Those who wanted to could make a meal of the chicken and couscous or the couscous and salad while the rest of us feasted on bobotie. I've decided a soup first course is a good alternative, so I am suggesting the Cream of Carrot Soup to give a fresh feel and color to the menu. Another alternative would be puréed Stilton and Apple or Pear Soup with Onions (page 100). Either one can be served in cups, not requiring a spoon.

At the end of the party, I had thoroughly enjoyed meeting everyone and felt the party had had just the tone I wanted—relaxed, convivial, and not at all pretentious. Everything was done ahead of time, so I had plenty of time to enjoy the group and the party. Everyone proclaimed the bobotie wonderful, but much to my surprise we only ate one and a half of the three I'd made. ("Better too much than too little" is one of the most important rules of entertaining.) With the leftovers, I was ready the next night for an impromptu dinner party when an out-of-town friend called unexpectedly, and this time six of us ate one bobotie. Which goes to show that there is no accurate way to gauge appetites or the difference in what people eat standing up versus sitting down.

Cooking Time Line

Remember, each day, check your preparations list for things like cleaning, shopping, setting the table, drop-dead time, and so on. If you elect to use a store-bought item (or more than one), make sure it's on your shopping list (and obviously, then, you don't need to make it).

UP TO 3 MONTHS BEFORE

1. Make the soup, Parmesan Coins, bobotie, bread, and torte and freeze, well wrapped.

UP TO 3 DAYS BEFORE

1. Prepare the couscous and fruit for the salad; refrigerate.

NIGHT BEFORE

1. Prepare the tomatoes and the cucumbers (don't combine), cover, and refrigerate.
2. Remove the soup and bobotie from freezer and thaw in the refrigerator.
3. Remove the bread and torte from freezer and let thaw at room temperature.

The Day

UP TO 1 HOUR BEFORE

1. Combine the tomatoes and cucumbers and set out.
2. Slice the bread and place on a platter or in a basket. Cover well.
3. Set out the Parmesan Coins.

30 MINUTES BEFORE

1. Heat the bobotie.
2. Heat the soup if serving hot or pour into a tureen if serving cold.
3. Toss the salad and prepare the dressing.
4. Put the couscous in a microwave-safe serving bowl and put it in microwave.

SERVICE

1. Pour the custard on the bobotie and return it to the oven.
2. Set the microwave to wait 20 minutes and then heat the couscous for 5 minutes.
3. Start the coffee.
4. Start serving the soup.

LEFTOVERS

At any time a host may invite guests to take something home with them. And it is certainly a nice gesture to send something special to a guest's ailing family member or to a friend who was unable to attend for any reason.

If guests bring food, they are welcome to their leftovers. If a guest wants to leave his or her remaining food, remove it from the dish, wash the dish well, and return it immediately. To store in their dish, with plans to return it at a later date, means inviting trouble when it gets lost, or broken, or forgotten.

Cream of Carrot Soup

This smooth, adaptable soup can be served hot or cold, and it accommodates to new trends, just as a basic black dress or a white plate can be dressed up or down.

Heat the butter in a large, heavy pot until foaming. Add the carrots and onion, cover, and cook over low heat until soft but not brown, about 10 minutes. Stir in the garlic and stock, bring to the boil, reduce the heat, cover, and simmer until the vegetables are very soft, about 30 minutes. Remove the solids with a slotted spoon and purée them in batches in a food processor or blender until very smooth, adding cooking liquid as needed. If you want a silky-smooth soup, force the purée through a fine-mesh sieve. Stir the purée into the cooking liquid. This may be done ahead and refrigerated for several days or frozen for up to 3 months. If serving hot, bring just to the boil, add the cream or yogurt, and warm through but do not boil. If serving cold, whisk in cream or yogurt but do not heat. Season to taste with sugar and white pepper. The soup may be made ahead to this point also, but it needs careful reheating. Pour into a soup tureen or individual bowls and sprinkle some chopped herbs over the top.

2 tablespoons butter
5 to 6 medium carrots, sliced
1 onion, thinly sliced
1 garlic clove, finely chopped
4 cups fresh or canned chicken stock or broth
¾ cup heavy cream or plain yogurt
1½ tablespoons sugar, or to taste
Freshly ground white pepper
Finely chopped cilantro, chives, parsley, thyme, lemongrass greens, or herb of your choice, for garnish

VARIATION

Add ½ cup orange juice in place of the cream and 1 to 2 tablespoons grated orange rind.

Lemon Couscous

Here is couscous at its best—simple, fast, and very good. Not only is it the quickest starch to prepare, it does most of the work itself off the heat! I add the seasonings, peel, juice, and couscous to the serving bowl, pour the hot water over it, and cover with plastic wrap. When it's ready, I add the onion and basil and fluff it up—no pan to wash. What luxury!

1½ **cups water or fresh or canned chicken stock or broth**
½ **teaspoon salt**
½ **teaspoon freshly ground black pepper**
Grated peel (no white attached) of 2 lemons
Juice of 2 lemons
1 **cup quick-cooking couscous**
4 **whole scallions, sliced**
1 **tablespoon finely chopped fresh basil**

In a medium saucepan, bring the water or stock to the boil with the salt, pepper, lemon peel, and lemon juice. Stir in the couscous, cover, and remove from the heat. Let stand 5 minutes. Just before serving, add the scallions and basil and fluff the couscous with a fork.

VARIATION

For Basic Couscous, don't use the lemon peel, lemon juice, scallions, and basil. Simply heat the liquid, salt, and pepper to a boil, stir in the couscous, cover, and let stand off the heat for 5 minutes. Fluff with a fork and serve.

Citrus Fruit and Feta Salad

SERVES 6 TO 8

This is so, so refreshing and pretty and healthy-feeling too! In my grocery store you can buy prepared fruit in plastic containers when in a rush. This convenience certainly makes the salad even easier, although more expensive.

1 orange
3 to 5 cups washed and torn red leaf and Boston lettuces
⅓ cup roughly chopped fresh parsley
½ cup red seedless grapes, halved
1 red grapefruit, peeled and sectioned (all pith and membranes removed)
½ large red onion, halved, thinly sliced, and separated into pieces
¼ cup (1 ounce) feta cheese, crumbled

Dressing
2 tablespoons fresh orange juice
1 to 2 tablespoons fresh lime juice
1½ teaspoons coarse-grain mustard
1 garlic clove, chopped
1½ teaspoons grated fresh ginger
½ teaspoon honey
¼ teaspoon hot sauce
¼ cup olive oil
Salt

Grate the peel from the orange without including any of the white and set aside for the dressing. Finish peeling the orange and break it into sections. Remove all the pith and membranes.

In a large bowl, toss together the lettuces, parsley, grapes, grapefruit, orange sections, and red onion. Sprinkle with the crumbled feta cheese.

In a small bowl, whisk together the orange and lime juices, mustard, garlic, ginger, honey, grated orange peel, and hot sauce. Whisk in the olive oil and season to taste with salt. Serve with the salad, or add a small portion to the salad, toss, and serve the rest on the side.

TIP

To quickly peel citrus, cut off a slice at the top and bottom. Then cut down vertically and peel off the skin.

Quick-Rising Cumin-Fennel Bread

MAKES 1 LOAF

This savory bread is wonderful with rich soups and hearty dishes. It calls for quick-acting yeast and uses the microwave to speed up the rising of the dough. If you prefer, you can use regular yeast, leave the dough in the refrigerator one or two days to rise, and bake it the day you serve it, following the directions on the yeast package.

Cornmeal, for dusting pan
2½ to 3 cups bread flour, as needed
1 package quick-acting yeast
1 teaspoon sugar
½ tablespoon salt
¼ teaspoon ground cumin
¾ tablespoon fennel seeds
1 cup hot water (135°F.)
¼ cup olive oil

Glaze
1 egg, beaten with 1 teaspoon water

Preheat the oven to 425°F. Grease or spray a large baking sheet with nonstick spray. Sprinkle with the cornmeal.

In a food processor with the steel blade attached, or in a mixer, mix together 2½ cups of the flour and the yeast, sugar, salt, cumin, and fennel seeds. Add the water and olive oil and knead until the dough bounces back when you touch it and feels like a baby's bottom, about 10 minutes. To let the dough rise in the microwave, form it into a ball. With your thumbs, punch a hole to form into a doughnut shape and place the dough in a microwave-safe mixing bowl. Cover loosely with a damp tea towel and place in the microwave. Place an 8-ounce glass of water in the back of the microwave. Lower the microwave to 10 percent power or the next-to-lowest setting. Heat for 3 minutes. Let rest for 3 minutes. Repeat. Finally, heat for 3 minutes and let rest for 6 minutes, or until doubled in bulk.

To let rise without the microwave, place in an oiled plastic bag in a warm place until double, about 1 hour.

Punch the dough down and shape into a round loaf. Place the loaf on the prepared baking sheet. With a sharp knife, scissors, or razor blade, slash a shallow (¼-inch) X into the top of the loaf. Let the loaf rise until doubled in bulk. Brush with the glaze. Bake until it sounds hollow when tapped on the bottom, 20 to 30 minutes. An instant-read thermometer should register 200°F. Remove to a rack to cool. The cooled loaf may be kept tightly covered 2 days or frozen for up to 3 months.

EQUIPMENT

Gourmet cookware stores now sell the Baker's "razor slash," which is a very handy gadget for slashing bread to decorate its top. I've used scissors or a knife for years, but I do now enjoy my razor slash.

Bobotie with Vegetables

SERVES 6 TO 10

My friend Barbara Ensrud first encountered this dish (pronounced bah-BOO-tee), minus the vegetables, in South Africa. I think the spices make it more Mediterranean, or perhaps North African, in flavor. With the vegetables, it is similar to that perennial favorite, moussaka. Without the custard or vegetables, it becomes my "Mediterranean meat loaf," and I sometimes serve it that way. Whatever way you serve this dish, it is always a crowd pleaser—hearty, with flavors that are intriguing but not too hot and spicy.

The quantities can easily be multiplied to serve more, so when I am on a weekend cooking spree, I prepare two or three "meat loaves" and freeze them. When I'm ready to make the bobotie, I defrost the loaf and vegetables and heat them in my enamel paella pan, a tagine, or other oven-to-table dish. I push a few holes in the meat with a large fork or the end of a wooden spoon, and then I add the custard and bake for 15 to 20 minutes more.

The whole dish freezes well, too, but it is best when completed a day ahead and reheated. It can be made the day of the event, but it requires about an hour of assembling and organizational cooking, plus the actual cooking time of the meat loaf and the custard. I hope you will avoid the stress and cook the whole thing ahead.

2 medium-sized eggplant (about 1 to 1½ pounds), peeled
6 zucchini (about 2 pounds)
Salt
6 to 8 tablespoons vegetable oil
2 medium onions, finely chopped
6 large garlic cloves, finely chopped
1 tablespoon curry powder, preferably Madras
1 tablespoon saffron threads
Juice of 2 lemons (about ½ cup)
½ cup bread crumbs
Grated peel (no white attached) of 1 lemon (see Tip)
2 large eggs, lightly beaten
Freshly ground black pepper

Preheat the oven to 350°F. Spray a 12-inch round or 10x14-inch oval, 3-inch-deep oven-to-table baking dish with nonstick spray, or lightly grease.

Slice the eggplant and zucchini into ⅛-inch-thick rounds. Cut an X across the surface of the eggplant slices, sprinkle with salt, and place in a colander to drain for 30 minutes. Rinse the eggplant well, squeeze it, and dry with paper towels.

Heat 2 tablespoons of the oil in a skillet, add the eggplant and zucchini, and cook until tender, 4 to 5 minutes, working in batches. Remove from the pan and set aside on paper towels to drain.

Heat the remaining 4 tablespoons oil in the skillet. Add the onions and sauté until golden brown, about 10 minutes. Add the garlic and curry powder and continue to cook over low heat for 2 to 3 minutes. Remove from the heat and let the skillet cool slightly. Meanwhile, soak the saffron in the lemon juice. When the onions have cooled, add the bread crumbs, lemon peel, lightly beaten eggs, saffron, and lemon juice, pepper, chili powder, cumin, cinnamon, raisins, ground meat, and 2 teaspoons salt. Thoroughly mix the ingredients. To taste for seasoning, sauté a tablespoonful in a small pan or the microwave until brown. Add salt, pepper, or other seasonings to the raw mixture as needed.

2 teaspoons chili powder
**1 teaspoon ground
cumin**
**¼ to ½ teaspoon ground
cinnamon**
½ cup seedless raisins
**2 pounds lean, coarsely
ground beef or lamb**
2 large eggs
2 cups milk

Spread the eggplant and zucchini rounds over the bottom of the prepared baking dish and then cover with the meat mixture, patting it out evenly. Bake 1 to 1½ hours, depending on the size of pan, until the meat is brown and registers 160°F. on an instant-read thermometer. Remove from the oven. Skim or pour off the fat, leaving the juices in the pan. Using a large meat fork or the end of a wooden spoon, poke several holes in the meat loaf. The dish can be prepared to this point and refrigerated several days or frozen; thaw if necessary, let the dish come to room temperature, and reheat before proceeding.

Beat the remaining 2 eggs and the milk and pour over the baked meat. If it does not quite cover, you can mix up another ½ cup milk with 1 egg and pour over. Return to the oven until the custard is set and the top is browned, an additional 15 to 20 minutes. If serving later, allow to cool, cover with aluminum foil, record the date, and store in the freezer.

If you have frozen the entire dish, remove the bobotie from the freezer 36 hours before serving and let it defrost in the refrigerator. If not thoroughly defrosted 4 hours before the party, defrost in the microwave or a 300°F. oven, checking frequently. When ready to serve, preheat the oven to 350°F. and reheat the bobotie for about 45 minutes, depending on the size and shape of the pan.

TIPS

Cutting an X in the eggplant allows the salt to penetrate and aids in pulling out the excess liquid, which can be bitter and some find hard to digest. The salt must be rinsed off and the vegetables dried before browning.

To get the peel from a lemon, rub it on a small grater, removing just the yellow part. The white is bitter, so don't include any. There is also a little hand zester with little holes and sharp surfaces, and finally, a knife or potato peeler can be used to remove, then chop.

For a slightly lower-calorie alternative, instead of frying the sliced eggplant and zucchini, spray them with nonstick cooking spray and broil until browned and tender.

Dudley's Lasagna

Single people have to eat, and entertain too. This is one of three recipes Dudley Clendenin does to perfection. His only flaw is that he waits to start it until everyone arrives, as if for moral support. I hope you will make it a day ahead or at least early in the day. You may make your own sauce, using the one in the Vegetarian Lasagna (page 276), or you can use store-bought, as Dudley does—and I do.

1 (8-ounce) package lasagna

2 pounds lean ground beef

1 onion, chopped

4 garlic cloves, chopped

1½ tablespoons dried or fresh thyme

2 tablespoons chopped fresh oregano

1½ teaspoons fennel seeds

1 teaspoon hot red pepper flakes

1 teaspoon salt
Lots of freshly ground black pepper

4 cups Vegetarian Lasagna Sauce (page 276) or 2 (15½-ounce) jars spaghetti sauce

2 cups (15 ounces) ricotta cheese or cream-style cottage cheese

12 ounces mozzarella cheese, shredded

¼ to ½ cup grated imported Parmesan cheese

Preheat the oven to 375°F. Grease a 12x8x1½-inch baking dish.

Cook the lasagna noodles in a large quantity of boiling salted water for 9 to 10 minutes. Drain and set aside. In a skillet, brown the ground beef, remove, and set aside, leaving 1 to 2 tablespoons of the fat. Add the onions and garlic, cooking until soft and opaque, 5 to 7 minutes. Add the thyme, oregano, fennel seeds, pepper flakes, salt, pepper, and lasagna sauce.

In the prepared dish, layer in this order: a thin layer of the sauce to prevent browning, pasta, sauce, ricotta, and mozzarella. Repeat, starting with the pasta, for all the layers. Bake for 20 minutes. Sprinkle with the Parmesan. The lasagna can be made ahead to this point. When ready to serve, return to the oven for 10 minutes or until heated through. (It may take up to 45 minutes if cold from the refrigerator.)

The lasagna may be refrigerated for up to 3 days, or kept frozen for up to 3 months

---

SHOPPING TIP

Ground beef

The most flavorful ground beef is chuck. It is also usually the cheapest as well as the fattiest, so you can see that it has some pros and cons. Ground round or ground sirloin can also be used in dishes calling for ground beef, as well as ground lamb or veal or a combination of the two. Each will also exude a different amount of fat and juices, and shrink accordingly. I prefer ground chuck, but the others will work in most dishes.

Chocolate Delirium Torte

SERVES 8

This is a very rich, delicate, melt-in-your-mouth torte, hence it is the source of many fantasies—and yes, even delirium. The only reason this dessert needs to be baked is to cook the eggs. Wrapping the pan with foil may seem complicated, but it is very easy, and you will make this torte over and over. It is most easily handled when it is very cold. I put mine in the freezer for a day before removing it from the pan.

12 ounces semisweet chocolate, in chips or small pieces
½ pound (2 sticks) unsalted butter, cut into 1-inch pieces
6 eggs

Garnish
1 vanilla bean or 1 teaspoon vanilla extract
1 cup heavy cream
3 tablespoons sugar
Edible flowers, berries, or chocolate curls
8 mint leaves

Preheat the oven to 350°F. Grease or spray a 9- or 10-inch tart pan with removable bottom with nonstick spray and wrap the outside and bottom with aluminum foil so the bottom is water tight. If you have no tart pan, line the bottom and sides of a 9-inch pie plate with parchment paper or very smoothly with aluminum foil.

Melt the chocolate and butter in the microwave or in a heavy pan over very low heat, stirring with a rubber spatula or wooden spoon until completely melted. Set aside.

Lightly beat the eggs and stir them into the melted chocolate mixture. Pour the chocolate mixture into the tart pan, cover with foil, and set it in a heavy roasting pan. Pour hot tap water into the roasting pan halfway up the sides of the tart pan to create a bain-marie and place it in the preheated oven for 30 to 35 minutes. Remove the pan from the oven and uncover it. The torte will be a soft batter that will solidify when cold. Let it cool to room temperature on a wire rack, and then cover it with plastic wrap. Refrigerate or freeze at least 2 hours.

Release the sides of tart pan. You can freeze the well-wrapped torte at this point for up to 3 months.

To make the whipped cream garnish, split a vanilla bean with a paring knife and scrape the seeds into a cold mixer bowl with the heavy cream and sugar. Start on low speed, slowly increase the speed, and beat on high speed until firm but be careful not to let it separate. If using vanilla extract instead of the bean, beat it in at the end. Refrigerate. (The tiny brown flecks, the seeds of a vanilla bean, give the whipped cream a "homemade" look.)

When ready to serve, cut the still cold or even frozen torte into 8 pieces with a hot, wet non-serrated knife. (Clean the knife in hot water after each cut.) The torte will defrost rapidly and is best moved when frozen.

Place 1 heaping tablespoon of whipped cream on the torte. Place 1 wedge of frozen torte on a plate. Garnish with edible flowers, fresh berries, or chocolate curls.

All-Desserts Buffet

CHOCOLATE STATION

Semisweet Chocolate Pie in
Cocoa Pastry Crust

Chocolate Delirium Torte
(page 131)

Chocolate Roulade
(page 45)

FRUIT STATION

Cold Lemon Soufflé

Star-Spangled Cranberry-
Apple Pie

Strawberries with
Balsamic Vinegar

COOKIE STATION

Anise Cookies

Chocolate and Almond
Biscotti

Lemon–White Chocolate–
Pistachio Cookies

RUSTIC DESSERTS

Spanish Flan (page 61)

Grape Clafoutis (page 52)

here are times when a full-blown dinner—or even a cocktail party—can't be worked into the schedule or the budget. For those of us not into deprivation, a dessert party is the answer.

The first time I heard of a dessert party, and the first time I heard of using a variety of tables for a party rather than one long one, was from one of my students at Rich's who became known as the "chocolate man"—he loved chocolate and making chocolate curls (page 118). He and his wife would have annual after-symphony or after-theater dessert parties, always making a couple of chocolate desserts, a lemon mousse, and meringues or tarts. (When they moved to Virginia, they lost their recipes and called back for copies so they could continue their tradition, making their march on a new town.) For their parties, they set up three individual card tables and small tables around their home—one for chocolate, one for fruit, and one for coffee and dessert wine, with cookies for dipping, and meringues.

Now even hotels have "stations" for parties—pasta stations, omelet stations, and particularly dessert stations. Plan on each guest eating one small slice of each of the tortes and pies, a spoonful or two of the mousse, and four of the cookies.

Cohosting

ohosting can be disastrous or delightful. Much of the outcome depends on communication and consensus.

Sometimes cohosts are surprised equally to discover they have been tapped by a third person to entertain for a charity function or a special occasion for mutual friends.

The most important element, which can lead to success or failure, is an understanding between cohosts of the Who, Why, What, Where, and When, and several Hows. It's not necessarily easy to agree—in fact, friendships and business relationships can break down over these negotiations—but it's essential to discuss all of these elements.

Once you mutually have decided on the details, put your combined ideas in an informal note. (Getting it in writing avoids misunderstandings and saves friendships.) Compromise where you can, but if you and your cohost truly are unable to reach an agreement, tactfully suggest hosting the party by yourself or withdrawing.

Caveat: If the dinner is at your house, be sure to insist on preparing the main course. Then, if for any reason your cohost has a problem, the evening won't be a disaster. I would urge you to do so even if you're just lending your house and are not responsible for the cooking. I was a guest at a party recently where the main course never arrived. The host was not responsible for any of the food, but that's who you blame if you're hungry.

Cooking Time Line

Remember, each day, check your preparations list for things like cleaning, shopping, setting table, drop-dead time, and so on. If you elect to use a store-bought item (or more than one), make sure it's on your shopping list.

UP TO 3 MONTHS BEFORE

1. Make chocolate pie, chocolate torte, chocolate decorations, Chocolate Roulade, Star-Spangled Cranberry-Apple Pie, biscotti, and cookies; freeze.

UP TO 2 DAYS BEFORE

1. Remove roulade from freezer.
2. Cook Grape Clafoutis; refrigerate.
3. Chill beverages.

AT LEAST 1 DAY BEFORE

1. Make the Cold Lemon Soufflé and the Spanish Flan.

UP TO 1 DAY BEFORE

1. Remove pies, torte, biscotti, cookies, roulade, and chocolate decorations from freezer.
2. Roll Anise Cookies in sugar.

3. Lay out the cookies and wrap them well.
4. Fill roulade and refrigerate.

The Day

UP TO 1 HOUR BEFORE

1. Warm Star-Spangled Cranberry-Apple Pie and Grape Clafoutis if desired.

AT LEAST 30 MINUTES BEFORE

1. Prepare strawberries.
2. Set out pies, torte, mousse, and flan.
3. Start the coffee, tea, if needed.

Setting the Scene

A dessert party is easily accommodated to a variety of serving locations and styles: a marble console, a beautiful antique mahogany table, a hand-painted table, a cheap table draped with inexpensive saris from an import store and set up in the corner. Set out plates, forks, or spoons, and napkins at each location. You need not set out the full complement of plates at each station as long as you have a plan for putting out more if needed. Wine, coffee, and tea can be set on the table of cookies and pick-up desserts that can be eaten out of hand or from a plate.

Alternatively, set the desserts out on a long buffet or table with coffee and tea in the kitchen, and set small tables with the silver, napkins, wine and water glasses.

Chocolate Decorations

These garnishes are among the easiest things to prepare. I always keep semisweet chocolate on hand just for emergencies.

6 ounces semisweet chocolate or milk chocolate

Melt the chocolate in a medium microwaveproof bowl on high 1 minute, stir, and put back into the microwave for 30 seconds more if necessary.

Chocolate Designs

Lay out a sheet of wax paper or parchment paper. Draw a design on the paper with a pencil—a butterfly, spell out a name, make circles, or whatever. Turn over the paper. Make a paper cone or use a plastic squeeze bottle, and fill partially with the melted chocolate. Snip off the tip of the cone and follow your design. Allow to harden at room temperature or freeze. Remove when hard, place in an airtight container, and freeze until needed.

Instead of making designs, you can spread out the melted chocolate on the paper. When it is hard, cut circles with a biscuit cutter or tiny corer, or other shapes with a sharp cookie cutter. Alternatively, cut squares or triangles. Put in an airtight container and freeze until needed.

Use as decoration, or serve as chocolate pennies or triangles with coffee.

Chocolate Candies

Buy some inexpensive candy molds. Spray them with nonstick spray. Fill the molds with melted chocolate. Scrape off any excess. Put the molds in the freezer or refrigerator. When they are hard, pop out and blush when everyone says how wonderful they are.

Chocolate Cups

Cut four 6-inch squares of wax paper or parchment paper. Spread the melted chocolate out thinly and evenly on the squares to about 1 inch from the edge each. Place over the back of the bottom an overturned custard cup, with the paper next to the cup, and shape. Place the custard cups on a tray and put in the freezer until the chocolate hardens. Remove the chocolate and paper from the custard cups and carefully peel off the paper. Fill with berries, chocolate truffles, chocolate pennies, chocolate mousse, etc.

TIP

To whip cream more easily, chill the bowl and beaters, and keep the cream cold until starting to beat. Or you can "whip" the cream in the food processor. (I use the steel blade to get a thickly whipped cream.) Either way, if the cream starts to separate, stop whipping and put it through a strainer. If you wind up with butter, drain off the whey, call it sweet butter, and serve it as a novelty.

NATHALIE DUPREE'S COMFORTABLE ENTERTAINING

136

Semisweet Chocolate Pie in Cocoa Pastry Crust

MAKES 2 (11-INCH) PIES

This rich chocolate pie is sure to be a crowd pleaser—it certainly pleased my dad. It can be served as is or garnished with chocolate coins, curls, or other decorations, or with a dollop of whipped cream.

Pastry
2 cups all-purpose flour
½ teaspoon salt
2 tablespoons cocoa powder
½ pound (2 sticks) cold unsalted butter, cut into 1-inch pieces
¼ cup ice water

Filling
1 pound semisweet chocolate
1 cup water
2 cups sugar
1 pound (4 sticks) butter, at room temperature
8 large eggs
2 tablespoons vanilla extract

Optional garnish
Whipped cream
Chocolate decorations (page 136)

Preheat the oven to 375°F.

Put the flour, salt, and cocoa powder in a bowl or the food processor and cut in the butter with 2 knives, a pastry blender, or the knife blade of the processor until the mixture resembles coarse meal. Add just enough water so that the pieces of dough can be pulled together in a ball by hand. Do not overwork or let come to a ball in the processor.

Divide the dough into 2 pieces and form each half into a disk. Wrap in plastic wrap and refrigerate 30 minutes or up to 2 days. Remove the pastry from the refrigerator. When the dough is malleable, lightly flour a board, or wax paper, and roll out one ball of dough into a circle about ⅛ inch thick. Carefully lay the dough in a tart pan with a removable bottom. Gently ease the dough into the pan and press onto the sides. Be careful not to stretch the dough. Refrigerate or freeze for 10 minutes or longer. Fill with crumpled wax paper extended to the edges and top of the crust and fill with pastry weights or dried beans. Make another pie shell with the rest of the dough. Bake both shells until just set, about 15 minutes. Remove from the oven and remove the paper and weights. Let the pie shells cool. (The beans can be used over and over as pie weights.)

To make the filling, melt the chocolate with the 1 cup water and the sugar over low heat. Place the melted chocolate in the bowl of an electric mixer and beat in the butter. Beat in the eggs, one by one, scraping down the sides of the bowl occasionally. Add the vanilla and mix well.

Evenly divide the chocolate mixture between the shells. Bake until the filling is set, 20 to 25 minutes. Let cool on a rack. The tarts may be made ahead several days or frozen, with or without the garnish, for up to 3 months. Pipe cream, if using, shortly before serving and garnish with the optional decorations.

Cold Lemon Soufflé

This recipe is a challenge for the novice cook, but if you have the time a day in advance, it is well worth the effort, because it is so dazzling and memorable. It's really a mousse, but it becomes a cold soufflé when you use a collar on a soufflé dish to make it extend above the sides of the dish. I was working in New York City writing the restaurant guide for the New York Convention and Visitors Bureau when I ate my first serving of this wonderful dish at the Copenhagen Restaurant. It was incredibly tender and delicious. But be warned: I have tried this recipe with dehydrated egg whites and without yolks and it's not the same. So if you are concerned about using raw eggs, do another dessert.

2 packages unflavored gelatin
¼ cup cold water
3 eggs, separated
1½ cups sugar
½ cup fresh lemon juice
Lemon peel (no white attached) of 4 lemons, grated or finely chopped
2 cups heavy cream

Garnish
Thin lemon slices (optional)
1 cup heavy cream, stiffly whipped (optional)
Candied violets or other edible flowers (optional)

Oil a 1½- to 2-quart soufflé dish, bowl, or pretty mold or spray with nonstick spray. To make it look like a soufflé, wrap a horizontally doubled strip of wax paper that has been oiled or sprayed with nonstick spray around the top of a soufflé dish and secure it in place with string, tape, or a rubber band to make a collar that increases the height of the dish.

Sprinkle the gelatin over the cold water in a small pan. When the gelatin is absorbed like a sponge, heat over low heat, stirring occasionally, until it is completely dissolved.

Meanwhile, beat the egg yolks until they become light, about 4 minutes. Add the sugar and lemon juice and continue beating until the sugar is dissolved, 5 to 8 minutes, and the mixture is thick and light in color. (You may want to place the

A prerequisite for the Advanced Certificate at the London Cordon Bleu was culinary business experience. My friend Diane Uslaener and I started a dessert business called "Just Desserts," which we delivered via taxi to our customers, who were primarily our friends. Our first customer ordered the Cold Lemon Soufflé. Imagine our chagrin when she reported a hair in it. We examined it microscopically—only to find it was a hair from the pastry brush I used to brush lemon peel from the grater. To prevent this problem, place a piece of plastic wrap over the rough grating surface. It miraculously keeps the rind from clinging to the sharp edges of the grater and removes the need to brush the grater with a pastry brush.

Gelatin is attracted to cold, so it will go to the bottom and sides of your dish unless stirred or whisked frequently. If it does not get stirred enough and forms lumps, the mixture can be strained and the lumps melted over low heat and added back into the mixture, stirring continually, until set. Some volume will be lost, but it will still taste delicious.

If you make this in a dish larger than 2-quart, the finished dish won't look like a soufflé, as the mixture won't extend above the edge of the dish to mimic a hot soufflé. It will still taste fabulous. Consider buying a smaller dish or serve in a decorative bowl as a mousse.

With care, this may be turned out and served free-standing. Run a hot knife around the dish and with your hands pull the mixture away from the sides to catch an air bubble, which will release the soufflé. Oil a plate, place it on top of the mousse, invert the whole thing, and give a good shake. Decorate as desired, above.

Although it is fun to candy your own flowers, candied violets may be purchased at gourmet stores.

bowl in a pan of very hot water to speed the process.) Add the melted gelatin and the lemon peel. Put this mixture in the refrigerator or freezer and whisk it from time to time until it is cold throughout and reaches the consistency of very softly whipped cream. Or you can place the bowl with the mixture over ice and stir continually until it reaches the same consistency. Whip the 2 cups cream to soft peaks and fold it into the chilled mixture.

Whip the egg whites until stiff but not dry. Stir 1 spoonful into the lemon mixture to lighten it. Then fold the lemon mixture into the egg whites. Spoon into the oiled dish and smooth the top. Put in the refrigerator until it sets, 3 to 5 hours.

Remove the collar if using and garnish with lemon slices, whipped cream, candied violets, or other edible flowers, if desired.

Star-Spangled Cranberry-Apple Pie

SERVES 8

This is an open-faced fruit pie that can be made with a variety of crusts. An old-fashioned Southern pie crust, its crust made flaky by using a soft-wheat flour and a light hand, works wonderfully. The traditional French pâte brisée works well, as would the nut crust of a German Linzertorte. I must confess that because of my busy working schedule, I often buy crusts at the grocery store, roll them out, put them in my own pie dish, hand crimp the edges, and then freeze (or refreeze) before baking. Whichever you select, use an extra pie crust, or reserve some pieces of the one you made, to make the stars for the top decoration.

2 (9-inch deep-dish) pie
    crusts (page 279)
6 tablespoons (¾ stick)
    unsalted butter
2 cups firmly packed
    light-brown sugar
¾ teaspoon cinnamon
½ teaspoon freshly
    grated nutmeg
1 teaspoon finely
    chopped fresh ginger
2 large unpeeled Red
    Delicious apples
    (about 1 pound),
    cored and sliced
2 medium unpeeled
    Granny Smith apples
    (about ¾ pound),
    cored and sliced
12 ounces cranberries (1
    package), picked
    over and washed

Garnish
1 cup heavy cream,
    whipped with sugar
    or 1 quart vanilla or
    cinnamon ice cream

Preheat the oven to 375°F.

Prebake 1 pie crust. Roll out the second and cut out a dozen small (1½- to 2-inch) stars. Chill 30 minutes or longer if possible. Place them on a baking sheet and bake until golden brown. Reserve. (This can be done while you are prebaking the pie crust.)

Melt the butter in a large skillet. Add the brown sugar, cinnamon, nutmeg, ginger, apples, and cranberries and gently stir to mix well and let the sugar dissolve. Cook over medium-low heat, stirring occasionally, until the cranberries have popped and the fruit is tender but the apples still have some body.

Remove the fruit with a slotted spoon and reserve. Bring the juices to the boil, reduce the heat, and simmer until they reduce and become thick and jammy, about 8 minutes. Stir the fruit into the juices. Taste to be sure it is sweet enough, adding more sugar if necessary. If it is runny, boil down until the juices are reduced. The filling may be made ahead to this point several days or frozen for up to 3 months. When ready to use, reheat. Spoon the filling into the prebaked shell. Decorate the top with the stars. Serve with whipped cream or ice cream.

NOTE

If the pie has been made ahead and allowed to cool, reheat it in a 325°F. oven until it is warm through, about 10 minutes. This pie freezes well. Place it in the freezer, freeze thoroughly, and then wrap with foil. Let thaw in the refrigerator overnight and reheat.

Strawberries with Balsamic Vinegar

SERVES 4

This is one of those easy, delicious little recipes that act as "standbys." The technique is at its best when used with u-pick or really good store-bought strawberries, but it even brings the regular grocery-store type up to a new level. Everything should be balanced—the goal is to increase the strawberries' flavor, but sort of mysteriously.

1 pint strawberries
1½ teaspoons balsamic vinegar
2 tablespoons light brown sugar
⅛ teaspoon freshly ground black pepper
½ cup lemon yogurt or heavy cream (optional)

Wash the strawberries and dry them on paper towels. If the strawberries are small, remove the green caps. Cut large strawberries in half or quarters. Put the strawberries in a large bowl. Sprinkle the balsamic vinegar, brown sugar, and pepper over the top, toss gently, and allow to stand 30 minutes at room temperature.

Spoon the berries and their juices into a beautiful glass bowl, into stemmed goblets, or as my friend Shirley does, into a wide-mouthed cylindrical vase. If desired, top with a little lemon yogurt, just enough for contrast, and pass the rest.

SHOPPING TIP

Strawberries

Flavorful strawberries have a heady perfume. At the very least, they should have fresh green caps. If not, they are going over the hill. If there is a noticeable amount of white flesh at the top of the berry, it was picked before substantial ripening could take place.

Balsamic vinegar

The really good variety is aged and is extremely expensive and mellow. Add it carefully to taste, because it has a stronger flavor than the grocery-store variety. To intensify the flavor of an inexpensive vinegar, bring it to a boil and reduce it by ¼ to ½.

Anise Cookies

These tiny morsels can be served with a berry dessert or other "soft" dessert that needs a crisp companion, or they can be tucked on a saucer next to a cup of tea or coffee for the "I never eat dessert, but . . ." crowd. They are lovely for weddings and holiday gifts.

½ **pound (2 sticks) unsalted butter, at room temperature**
⅔ **cup confectioners' sugar**
2 **teaspoons anise extract**
2 **teaspoons finely chopped lemon peel (no white attached)**
2 **teaspoons finely chopped orange peel (no white attached)**
1 **cup all-purpose flour**
¾ **cup whole-wheat flour**
½ **cup cornstarch**
2 **teaspoons crushed anise seeds**
1 **cup finely chopped pecans**

Coating
1 **cup sifted confectioners' sugar**

Preheat the oven to 325°F.

In a mixer bowl, beat the butter and confectioners' sugar until light. Add the anise extract and the lemon and orange peel. Sift together the all-purpose flour, whole-wheat flour, and cornstarch and add to the butter mixture. Mix at low speed until almost combined. Add the anise seeds and nuts and mix until combined.

Shape into balls the diameter of a nickel and place on an ungreased baking sheet. Bake until the bottoms are lightly browned, 20 to 25 minutes. Transfer to a wire rack to cool for 5 minutes. Roll the cookies in the sifted confectioners' sugar and let them finish cooling completely on a rack. Roll again in confectioners' sugar and store in an airtight container several days, or up to 3 months in the freezer. Roll again in confectioners' sugar before serving.

Chocolate and Almond Biscotti

MAKES 24

These twice-baked Italian cookies are perfect for dunking in coffee or nibbling anytime. I adore them and have to keep them in the freezer so I won't eat them all myself!

%2½ cups all-purpose flour
1 cup sugar
2 teaspoons baking powder
2 large eggs
2 large egg whites
2 teaspoons vanilla extract
3 tablespoons unsweetened cocoa powder
1 tablespoon instant coffee granules
5 teaspoons boiling water
1 cup whole almonds, toasted
1 teaspoon almond extract
1 cup chocolate chips
2 tablespoons unsalted butter

NOTE

If you only have cake flour or other soft wheat all-purpose flour available, you will need an extra ½ cup or so of flour to reduce the stickiness and make the dough manageable.

Preheat the oven to 325°F. Lightly grease a large cookie sheet and set aside.

In a large bowl, stir together 2¼ cups of the flour, the sugar, and the baking powder. In a small bowl, mix together the eggs, egg whites, and vanilla. Add the egg mixture to the dry ingredients and stir until it becomes a smooth dough.

In a small bowl, combine the cocoa, instant coffee, and boiling water. Add the cocoa mixture, almonds, and almond extract to the bowl of dough and mix until blended. Refrigerate the dough until firm, about 30 minutes.

Place the dough on a work surface floured with the ¼ cup remaining flour and pat into a thin 6x12-inch rectangle. Place on the prepared cookie sheet.

Bake until firm, 20 to 25 minutes. Transfer to a wire rack and let cool 5 minutes. Reduce the oven temperature to 300°F. Using a serrated knife, cut the dough into ½-inch-thick slices. Stand the slices upright on the baking sheet and return to the oven for 25 to 30 minutes, until crisp and dry. Let cool completely on wire racks.

Melt the chocolate chips with the butter in a small saucepan over low heat. Using a pastry brush, paint melted chocolate onto 1 end of the biscotti. Place on wax paper until the chocolate hardens. The cookies may be stored in airtight containers or frozen for up to 3 months.

Lemon–White Chocolate–Pistachio Cookies

MAKES 50 TO 60 COOKIES

White chocolate and pistachios make an irresistible combination. These cookies are equally good made with orange peel instead of the lemon peel.

2¼ cups all-purpose flour
1 teaspoon baking soda
¾ teaspoon salt
½ pound (2 sticks) unsalted butter
1 cup firmly packed light-brown sugar
½ cup granulated sugar
2 large eggs, at room temperature
1 teaspoon vanilla extract
1 tablespoon grated lemon peel (no white attached)
1 cup white chocolate chips or chunks
1 cup coarsely chopped unsalted pistachios

Preheat the oven to 350°F.

Sift the flour, baking soda, and salt onto a sheet of wax paper, and set aside.

In the large bowl of an electric mixer, beat the butter and both sugars together until light. Add the eggs, vanilla, and lemon peel and blend well. With the mixer at low speed, add the flour mixture and continue mixing until well blended. Stir in the white chocolate and nuts.

Drop the cookies by rounded teaspoonfuls 2 inches apart onto an ungreased baking sheet. Bake 10 to 15 minutes, or until lightly browned. The cookies should look slightly underdone when removed from the oven. Allow to cool slightly on the pan before removing to a wire rack to cool completely.

VARIATION

Divide the dough in half and add lemon peel to one half and orange peel to the other half.

TIPS

If you sift the dry ingredients onto wax paper, it makes it easier to pour into the mixer bowl.

If you cannot find unsalted pistachios, rinse and thoroughly dry salted ones and proceed with the recipe.

If using 2 pans in 1 oven, place them so they do not block the circulation of air in the oven, and reverse the positions of the pans after 5 to 7 minutes.

FINGER MEALS

*E*ating with our fingers is a favorite American dining experience, whether eating in our cars or on our decks. Of course, we don't want to acknowledge too boldly that we are eating with our fingers—we use buns and tortillas and [cocktail napkins? The fancy French word *hors d'oeuvres*?] to cover up.

A finger meal is distinguished by one essential characteristic—the absence of utensils. A hamburger and hot dog cookout eaten off paper plates is the finger meal that comes most readily to mind, but an elegant wedding reception complete with rented china may be made up entirely of finger foods, too. In other words, the very simplest of parties may be a finger meal, and so can the most complex. That range—from a one-pot shrimp boil served straight off the stove to a full-scale hors d'oeuvres party suitable for a black-tie occasion—is covered here. (If you're wearing a tuxedo, no one would ever tell you not to eat with your fingers!)

Use these menus, mix their components with other recipes from the book or from your own repertoire: Just keep in mind that your guests need to be able to hold what you serve—and they need a free hand with which to eat it!

Seafood Party

Ripe Olive Bruschetta

Low Country Shrimp Boil

Cocktail Sauce (page 255)

Asian Dipping Sauce

P.D.C.'s Divine Saltines

Fresh Asparagus

Roasted Garlic Mayonnaise

Herb-Crusted Cherry Tomatoes

French Bread (page 44)

Drop Brownies

Strawberries with Balsamic Vinegar (page 141)

*L*iving in a central place, whether it is a college town—like Oxford, Mississippi, where there are regular games and fêtes, or a big city like New York or London—you are privy to impromptu, casual, last-minute affairs when friends wish to congregate. At times like these, a shrimp or lobster boil is ideal. If you know ahead of time you are expecting company and how many, so much the better, but even with no notice, it's all very easy—put on a large kettle of water and then embroider from there. I wouldn't trade a fancy evening anywhere— well, nearly anywhere—for a time like this with good friends and good seafood.

One of the virtues of shrimp is that they take a short time to cook and a long time to eat, and the conversation has time to gather steam and become animated and interesting, rather than the stop-and-start type that comes from jumping up and down for courses.

Initially, Low Country Shrimp Boil was probably designed to be served on a shrimp boat. Because it can be prepared easily and deliciously in the back yard, on the patio or deck, or even on the beach, it has become very popular.

This menu has wonderful versatility. The shrimp boil is a delicious meal in itself. If this is your first attempt at entertaining, add just a good bread and your easiest salad. (If need be, you don't even have to cook the seafood yourself—it can be purchased precooked in most grocery stores today.) The addition of fresh asparagus, the Herb-Crusted Cherry Tomatoes, bruschetta, or homemade or store-bought French bread make this a real feast. You can work your way toward the larger menu as you gain confidence, experimenting with lobster or bouillabaisse (page 268).

One note: A few unfortunate souls are allergic, often drastically so, to the fruit of the sea. One thing that helps your guests is to make the invitation very specific. Then they will know exactly what you're serving and can eat ahead of time if they need to! You can also make a small separate pot with only the sausage, potatoes, and corn and serve this for those allergic to seafood.

Store-bought alternatives: If you only have time to do the shrimp boil, asparagus, and tomatoes, store-bought olive paste, nice crackers, delicious bread, and cookies will be fine.

When I was living in New York as a young woman, I moved into a most peculiar apartment. It had curved walls, and the bedroom alcove contained a double-decker double bed. There were two exits from the "bedroom": either at ground level through a proper door or by catapulting through an opening in the wall at the height of the upper bed, onto the sofa in the living room area. In the living room, there were two day-bed-sized sofas. This meant my tiny apartment could accommodate six for sleeping, sort of, depending on size, sex, and marital configuration. It became a convenient way station for friends and acquaintances from Virginia, Washington, and Texas, and there was always someone camping out. It was here that I perfected shrimp boil and lobster boil. Friends would come dragging in from out of town, too tired and hungry (and often broke) to go out to eat, not to mention the arduous effort of finding a place to park their car. And so we would pitch in for shrimp or lobster, when not much more expensive than a pizza, and eat on the floor on spread-out newspapers, using paper towels for our napkins. What the apartment had in beds, it lacked in a table.

Cooking Time Line

Remember, each day, check your preparations list for things like cleaning, shopping, setting table, drop-dead time, and so on. If you elect to use a store-bought item (or more than one), make sure it's on your shopping list (and obviously, then, you don't need to make it).

UP TO 3 MONTHS BEFORE

1. Make the brownies, French Bread, and divine saltines. Wrap and freeze. If using store-bought, add to the grocery list.

UP TO 3 DAYS BEFORE

1. Make dipping sauces and mayonnaise and refrigerate.

The Day

1. In the morning, set out the bread, dessert, and saltines to thaw.
2. Prepare the cherry tomatoes.
3. Cook the asparagus.

UP TO 2 HOURS BEFORE

1. Set out the dessert.
2. Fix the bread for the bruschetta, slice it, put it on a platter, cover well.

1 HOUR TO 45 MINUTES BEFORE

1. Put on very large pot of water to boil. It will take at least 30 minutes to come to the boil, and you don't want to be held up waiting for the water. If the pot isn't really very large, you're better off using two or more pots. For each quart of water, figure about 5 minutes to come to the boil, depending on the fire and the pot.
2. Set out the cherry tomatoes, condiments, dip, and saltines. Recrisp the saltines if necessary.
3. Finish the bruschetta and pass.
4. When the water is boiling, check that everything—including guests—is ready. Add the sausage, potatoes, onion, seasonings; 5 minutes before, add the corn; 2 minutes before, add the shrimp. In 2 minutes, remove everything and toss into the middle of the newspaper-topped table, onto platters, or into a large bowl.

My TV crew once went to a crawfish boil in a beautifully groomed back yard in Louisiana. We were tired, hot, and dirty from filming rice planting as well as the crawfish that inhabit the rice stubble. The cameraman, who was ultra-professional, made the only mistake I ever saw him make—he sat a $50,000 camera down on the ground. A stray dog came through the yard, spotted the camera, and thinking that it was a competitor, lifted his leg and marked it. After much anguish, it turned out that the film was okay, but the lesson was, and is: A table is a protective device as well as a convenience.

Eating al Fresco

Eating outside, just standing around tables, works very well for ultra-casual affairs. Of course, pulling up benches or chairs is sometimes a plus, but I have been to many a seafood boil, oyster roast, and barbecue where standing up is the only alternative. In fair weather, you can just spread out a cloth instead of newspapers and "picnic" on the grass.

Disposable or plastic plates or bowls are the order of the day here—just double them if they're flimsy. Another small investment that will pay for itself many times is wicker plate holders, because even plastic plates can bend if loaded up with food. The plate holders will assure you of stability. Use heavy-duty coated paper plates. (Get bright colors so they don't look like the local white Styrofoam-type takeout plates.) Napkins can be big, heavy-duty colored paper, but your fingertip towels-turned-napkins are more chic.

Eating utensils in any size can certainly be plastic. Some remarkably sturdy versions are available. Be sure to have a few strategically placed *clean* trash cans—lined with plastic bag liners, of course.

When you are dining al fresco, nature doesn't usually need much help in the area of decorations. If you do need flowers, buy blooming seasonal plants. The benefits are twofold: The flowers don't die in a day or two, and they can be either brought in to be enjoyed in your house or planted in your garden. Having lanterns to light can add to the mood as evening falls.

When eating outdoors, plan to serve the food from a table or raised surface, even if you are using newspaper for a tablecloth. This inhibits animals, large and small, and usually discourages the intrusion of ants. And in case of a sudden shower, everything can be quickly scooted indoors.

Cold soft drinks, assorted beers, bottled water, and even bottled iced tea can be set out serve-yourself style in coolers or tin wash buckets filled with ice. If you are in the garden, a clean wheelbarrow can serve the same purpose as a washtub and look a little spiffier.

Ripe Olive Bruschetta

Bruschetta—from the Latin verb bruscare, *which means to toast—makes a wonderful appetizer or accompaniment to a meal. When I was in Florence, Italy, Faith Willinger, a famous cook, invited me to her home. We sat in the kitchen and she "toasted" the fresh bread on a special tin right over the gas flames. I occasionally do the same thing, but without the Italian tin, to get a lovely charred look to my bread, but broiling is much safer. Most toasters dry the bread too much, which is not as suitable, but my new Cuisinart bagel toaster does a great job!*

2 garlic cloves
½ cup pitted oil- or brine-cured black olives, preferably Kalamata, Italian, or French
¼ cup olive oil
1 teaspoon balsamic vinegar
1 loaf Italian bread, cut on the diagonal into ¾-inch slices
¼ teaspoon freshly ground black pepper
3 ounces imported Parmesan cheese, grated

Preheat the broiler.

Chop the garlic and olives finely and mix with the olive oil and vinegar. (This may all be done in the food processor if care is taken to avoid making it too pasty by overprocessing.) Set aside.

Place the slices of bread under the broiler or on the gas flame and toast lightly on both sides until flecked with gold and brown.

Spread the olive mixture on one side of the toast. Sprinkle the pepper and Parmesan on top. Broil until just heated, about 30 seconds. Serve warm.

If you prefer to serve the bruschetta at room temperature, the toasted bread may be placed in baskets, with the olive paste and Parmesan in separate bowls for the guests to make their own.

NOTE

This works fine with stale bread. Olive paste (sometimes called olivada) may be purchased in specialty shops and substituted for the garlic, olives, olive oil, and vinegar in this recipe. Or use tapenade (page 254).

Low Country Shrimp Boil

My brother, who is the chief cook and bottle washer of his family, routinely serves this to friends and neighbors. My daughter-in-law Bonnie discovered the ease of a seafood cookout before we met. Bonnie was a full-time pharmacist until her third child arrived, so she lacked time and energy for fancy, formal at-home dos. Her favorite entertaining meal came to be this South Carolina Low Country Shrimp Boil, which is sometimes called Beaufort or Frogmore Stew after Beaufort and Frogmore, South Carolina.

Why the sausage? Easy answer: Of ten women polled, all but three could have been happy without it; of ten men polled, nine loved it. No doubt those early shrimpers just wanted some meat! Authentic recipes call for kielbasa and Andouille, but to be honest I think them rubbery, with no affinity for the shellfish. This recipe may easily be multiplied by 2 or 4 or even more to serve more people. But be sure to compute the time it takes to boil water, or use more pots.

5   **quarts water**
16 **new potatoes (2 pounds) (1½ inches in diameter), still in their skins, scrubbed**
6   **medium onions, quartered, with roots**
2   **pounds hot country sausage links**
10 **garlic cloves**
    4 finger-sized hot red peppers, chopped
2   **to 4 tablespoons seasoning mix, such as Old Bay (optional)**
3   **tablespoons chopped fresh parsley**
    Salt
    Freshly ground black pepper
6   **ears fresh corn, husked and broken in half**
2   **tablespoons hot sauce (optional)**
3   **pounds shrimp, in the shell**

Condiments
    Quartered lemons
    Sour Cream
    Butter

Fill a 12-quart stockpot or water-bath canner with 5 quarts of water. Bring the water to the boil over high heat (takes approximately 30 minutes). Add the potatoes, onions, sausage links, garlic, hot peppers, and seasoning mix. Cover, bring to the boil, reduce to a simmer, and cook for 30 minutes. Add the parsley, salt and pepper to taste, and corn and bring quickly back to a rapid boil. Taste and add the hot sauce if desired. Add the shrimp, reduce the heat, and simmer until the shrimp are just done, no more than 5 minutes. Discard the onions and garlic. Heap the rest into a large bowl, or drain and dish out into individual plates, with the lemon for the shrimp, sour cream for the potatoes, and butter for the corn.

SHOPPING TIP

Corn

Corn is best in season and as fresh off the farm as possible, but in a shrimp boil there's no reason not to use frozen corn if there's a supermarket brand you like or if you've frozen it yourself. And it is certainly acceptable to buy already shucked corn at the grocery store, if it seems in decent condition.

MAKES 1 CUP

I've used a variation of this ever since I met my favorite former husband, who had lived in Asia and told me about the fish sauces known as nuoc nam in Vietnam, nam pla in Thailand, and shottsuru in Japan. The sauce is best when made several days in advance.

⅓ **cup nuoc nam, Thai, or other bottled fish sauce**
¼ **cup soy sauce**
¼ **cup lime juice**
1 **scallion or green onion, green part only, thinly sliced on the diagonal**
1 **tablespoon sugar**
1 **to 2 tablespoons chopped cilantro**
½ **to 1 tablespoon chopped fresh hot red pepper**
1 **teaspoon chopped fresh ginger**

Combine fish sauce, soy sauce, lime juice, scallion greens, sugar, cilantro, pepper, and ginger. Stir briefly to combine. Refrigerate for several days before serving for best taste.

VARIATION

Lobster boil

Omit the hot peppers, hot sauce, seasoning mix, parsley, and sausage. Add the lobsters (1 per person, with 2 or 3 extra if the lobsters weigh only 1 pound each) 25 minutes after starting to boil the first time. Add the corn, if desired, after 5 minutes more, cooking the lobster until they turn pink (a total of 10 minutes). You may, of course, add even more shellfish—oysters, clams, and so on—if you desire.

SHOPPING TIP

Shrimp

Unless you live within 50 miles of a seacoast, you probably won't find fresh shrimp. Along the coasts, most shrimp that looks fresh has actually been frozen and thawed. Don't worry, shrimp adapts very well to freezing, and much of the best shrimp is flash-frozen on the boat. Look for "F.A.S." (frozen at sea) on the package. My preference is to buy shrimp frozen in a block in the shell. It usually comes in 5-pound blocks and is quickly thawed by running tepid water over it. A good general size for a shrimp boil is 21 to 25 shrimp per pound. Most shrimp is sold thawed and has a sign on it that says "previously frozen." The good thing about this is you know you are dealing with an honest merchant. The bad thing is you can't tell how long it has been thawed. Even fresh shrimp sometimes has an ammonia smell. If you feel you can trust the word of your fish dealer, buy it anyway and rinse it in cold water when you get home. Store it surrounded by ice and try to cook it within 24 hours. Shrimp that has not been frozen, but might have been kept on ice on a large boat for up to a month, then shipped, can be sold as fresh.

P.D.C.'s Divine Saltines

MAKES ½ POUND SALTINES
(ABOUT 78 PIECES)

Generations have cocktailed and dined with these salty, buttery crackers on the table at the Piedmont Driving Club, Atlanta's oldest social club. You are in for a treat when you find out how good the lowly saltine can taste—and if you are desperate for a quick appetizer or snack, this one excels.

The saltines may be made up to a week in advance and stored at room temperature in an airtight container. If they get soggy, place them on a baking sheet and crisp them in a 300°F. oven for 5 to 8 minutes. They can be frozen for up to 3 months and recrisped if necessary.

½ pound (2 sticks) butter
½ pound saltine crackers
1 to 2 tablespoons
kosher salt (optional)

Preheat the oven to 300°F.

Melt the butter in a metal pie pan over low heat or in a shallow microwave-safe dish in the microwave.

Turn each cracker over in the warm butter briefly and place on a baking sheet. Sprinkle very lightly with kosher salt if desired and place in the oven until the saltines are very crisp and golden brown in color, about 8 minutes. Let cool thoroughly on a wire rack.

VARIATION

Sprinkle with herbs, cayenne pepper, curry powder, or grated Parmesan.

NOTE

You may brush the butter on, but you'll lose some of the rich, buttery taste. I say go ahead and dip.

Fresh Asparagus

SERVES 6 TO 8

While asparagus comes in many sizes, it's best to use the smallest ones, because you can allow more stalks per person, they cook more quickly, and they are more inviting to eat with your fingers.

1 pound pencil-sized asparagus (about 36 to the pound)
Roasted Garlic Mayonnaise (page 156)

Pick a skillet large enough to hold the asparagus lying down. Fill it halfway with water and bring to the boil. Meanwhile, cut the asparagus near the bottom where the stringiness begins. Add the asparagus to the skillet, making sure they are covered with water, and cook for 2 to 4 minutes. Cook in batches if the pan is too shallow to hold all the asparagus at one time. Remove the asparagus from the hot water and rinse with cold water to refresh (to stop cooking and to set the color).

Remove the asparagus from the cold water and drain the spears. You can hold them at room temperature if serving shortly or cover them with plastic wrap and refrigerate if cooking ahead.

Serve hot or cold with Roasted Garlic Mayonnaise.

Reheat them by tossing them in a skillet with 2 to 3 tablespoons melted butter or oil or running them under the broiler or putting them back in boiling water for a minute or two until hot.

TIPS

To stop a green vegetable from cooking any further, put it in a pan of cold or ice water or run it under the cold water tap. This is called "refreshing" and sets the color because it stops the cooking.

Never snap asparagus. It's an old wives' tale that it snaps where it changes texture. In fact, you lose a lot of expensive asparagus spear if you snap it. Cut it where the fibrous portion begins.

If you must purchase asparagus many days ahead of the time it will be used, it is important to keep the stem ends moist. You can store the asparagus standing upright in about ½ inch of water in the refrigerator or lying on the refrigerator shelf in a plastic bag with the ends wrapped in wet paper towels.

Roasted Garlic Mayonnaise

MAKES ABOUT 1 CUP

This mayonnaise is much like the classic Provençal sauce aïoli, but with a mellow, almost nutty flavor created by roasting the garlic. There are many ways to roast a garlic bulb, so choose oven-roasted or microwaved according to your needs.

If you are concerned about using and eating raw eggs, mix the roasted garlic with 1 cup good-quality store-bought mayonnaise. I don't recommend using the store-bought roasted garlic, however. Use a light-flavored olive oil.

1 large garlic head
1 large egg
¼ teaspoon salt
¼ teaspoon freshly
   ground black pepper
2 tablespoons fresh
   lemon juice
¾ to 1 cup light-flavored
   olive or vegetable oil

Preheat the oven to 375°F.

Remove the papery outer skin from the garlic head, leaving the unpeeled cloves intact as a bulb. Wrap the garlic in heavy-duty aluminum foil and roast it until soft, about 1 hour and 15 minutes. Remove the garlic from the oven and allow it to cool to the touch. If you prefer to use a microwave, cook, unwrapped, in the microwave until soft, 1 to 2 minutes at a time, testing it for soft doneness.

While the garlic is baking, whisk the egg with the salt, pepper, and lemon juice in a food processor or in a small bowl of an electric mixer. Process or whisk in 1 teaspoon of the olive oil and then add the rest in a slow, steady stream until the mixture becomes thick. Caution: Adding the oil too fast will cause the mixture to separate. You may refrigerate the mixture—now mayonnaise—until you are ready to blend it with the garlic. The mixture may separate when chilled, but if whisked again it will pull together.

When the garlic has cooled, separate the garlic head into cloves and, one at a time, squeeze each roasted clove into a sieve that has been placed over the mixing bowl holding the mayonnaise. Discard the skins. With the back of a spoon, press the roasted garlic through the sieve into the bowl. Whisk well to blend.

The mayonnaise may be stored in the refrigerator, tightly covered, for up to 2 weeks.

TIP

If the mayonnaise is too thick, add a little hot water to thin it. If it is too thin or has separated, place a tablespoon of store-bought mayonnaise or a fresh egg yolk in a clean bowl, whisk well, and add the curdled or thinned mixture to it.

Herb-Crusted Cherry Tomatoes

I'm hoping you will use this recipe over and over again whenever you want a finger-food tomato. Add it to your hors d'oeuvre table too. These tomatoes can be dressed down by serving them on platter-type oval or round baskets lined with herbs, kale, or other greens or dressed up by presenting them on a glass or silver plate. (Acidic foods, like tomatoes, can pit and tarnish silver, so don't use your good pieces.)

1 pint cherry tomatoes
½ cup finely chopped
   fresh parsley
1 tablespoon chopped
   fresh thyme leaves
Salt
Freshly ground black
   pepper
1 to 2 tablespoons
   balsamic vinegar

Cut the tomatoes in half horizontally and set aside. Mix the parsley and thyme together in a medium-sized bowl. Dip the cut side of each tomato into the herb mixture and place, cut side up, in a single layer on a serving platter. Sprinkle with salt and pepper. Just before serving, sprinkle the tomatoes with balsamic vinegar. Serve immediately, reserving the extra herbs for another use.

TIP

If you are multiplying this recipe to serve a larger crowd, you won't need to multiply the herbs. A half cup of parsley and a tablespoon of thyme is enough to coat as much as 3 pints of cherry tomatoes.

Drop Brownies

These are better than either brownies or cookies. I keep them in the freezer to serve with or without sorbets and ice cream.

12 ounces semisweet chocolate bits
3 tablespoons unsalted butter
¼ cup all-purpose flour
¼ teaspoon baking powder
⅛ teaspoon salt
2 large eggs
¾ cup sugar
½ teaspoon vanilla
2¼ cups pecans, coarsely chopped

Preheat the oven to 350°F. Grease or spray 2 cookie sheets with nonstick spray.

Remove one third (¾ cup) of the chocolate bits and set aside.

Place the rest of the semisweet chocolate bits and butter in a heavy 2-quart saucepan and melt over low heat (or melt in the microwave), stirring until smooth. Let cool slightly.

Meanwhile, on a piece of wax paper, sift together the flour, baking powder, and salt.

In a large bowl of an electric mixer, beat the eggs, sugar, and vanilla until well combined. With the mixer on slow speed, add the cooled chocolate mixture, then the dry ingredients. Blend well. Stir in the reserved chocolate bits and the nuts.

Drop by heaping teaspoons, 1 inch apart, onto the prepared cookie sheets. Bake 8 to 10 minutes. Or for 2-inch cookies, drop by heaping tablespoons 2 inches apart and bake 10 to 12 minutes. They puff but won't firm up until they are cool, so don't overbake. Place the pan on a rack to cool a few minutes, and then remove the cookies to the rack to cool completely. Serve at room temperature. The drop brownies can be stored, tightly covered, for up to 3 days or kept frozen for up to 3 months.

Tortilla Party

Fancy Cheese Quesadillas

Black Bean Swirl Dip with
Multicolored Tortillas★

Marinated Grilled Chicken

Lime Shrimp or Chicken, Beef,
and Roasted Pepper Fajitas

Green Bean, Zucchini,
and Orange Salad

Pico de Gallo Salsa

Guacamole (page 256)

Mango Sorbet

This party can put your guests in the kitchen (where people are the most comfortable anyway), in the back yard, or in the living room as well as in the dining room. A kitchen counter overflowing with tasty ingredients that can be combined in any number of ways with no hard-and-fast rules always conjures up fun in my mind! The whole entrée portion of this meal fits nicely on a small counter, using the stove burners for the quesadillas. Almost all the ingredients can be precooked and prepped ahead of time, with last-minute preparation easily executed by you and your guests. Many of the ingredients can be purchased ready to use if time is of the essence. If you must omit the chicken or shrimp, make sure that you have compensated with more cheese or other protein to guarantee a gracious plenty to eat. The last-minute work is just heating the tortillas, after all!

Buy one or two salsas that you have used before and liked. You can get various colors, depending on the ingredients, and various degrees of spiciness. People enjoy trying new flavors and combinations—just remember that not everyone likes extra hot.

Plain cheese quesadillas would be a fine starter for this menu, using the same size tortillas you do for the fajitas, or larger ones (they come in several sizes in the grocery store). To the cheese, you can add the lime chicken, hot peppers, and if possible, epazote. (Epazote is a strongly flavored herb that is reputed to lessen the aftereffects of beans.) Master the cheese quesadillas first, and then you are on your own. If you are uncomfortable cooking quesadillas at the last minute, you can substitute a cold soup such as gazpacho (page 56) or see the tips on page 163.

You may really do it up festively with a piñata (I purchased one in a toy store), a sombrero, a tortilla press (even if your tortillas aren't from scratch) and other Mexican cooking implements, and tapes of a mariachi band, or you can ignore all the trappings and just have a good time with a nonstick frying pan.

My father was stationed in El Paso, Texas, during my freshman year in college, so I quickly became a fan of Mexican-type fare, which ranges from the drive-in, fast-food Tex-Mex variety to very sophisticated cooking in metropolitan areas like Mexico City. I find that many of the names have changed in common usage—what I called a burrito is now called a fajita, for instance. This gives me a feeling of "anything goes." I've even had tortillas filled with canned tunafish mixed with cilantro, soy sauce, and wine vinegar.

My Favorite Parties

I often review the occasions I have hosted. In some cases, it's to analyze what I did versus what I should have, would have, or could have done, which can be very valuable in future planning. In other cases, I just find joy in reminiscing.

When I set myself to the task of selecting my favorite occasion, I find I must choose one from each category, my favorite one-to-one would mean choosing between a cozy tea, embellished with laughter and tears, with a dear friend, and a sensual repast with a sweetheart when excitement was more important than stability.

Of my favorite large gatherings, I would have to select one of two where my guests prepared the food. Both times I came up with this cook-your-own scheme as an icebreaker, since most of the people didn't know each other.

The first was years ago in London, when I was, if not a novice at entertaining, not more than an advanced beginner. My husband and I wanted to introduce his coworkers to my cooking crowd and to our friends from church. I explained what we were planning in the invitations. My cooking teacher, Eileen Smythe, agreed to help.

The necessary ingredients were arranged on trays with copies of recipes from class. I assigned boned and stuffed poussins (little birds) to some. The dessert crew filled the pecan cookies they made with peaches and cream. Perhaps the menu was a little ambitious.

I hadn't thought of having a munchie or starter while the food was being prepared, so by the time the entrée was ready, at 10:30 P.M., our guests were ravenous, but still laughing. On paper, it might look like a failure, but we had a wonderful time, and many years later, a friend spoke of that London party as being his favorite ever, too.

More recently, I hosted a dinner to introduce new neighbors—a television news anchor and her husband. Once again I divided the people into cooking teams. Learning from my past mistake, we started preparing the first course as soon as the guests came through the door. As the evening progressed, there was one group churning ice cream on the porch, another assembling canapés in the living room nearby, a third rolling fresh pasta in the dining room, and the fourth busily cutting apples and fennel for the salad.

Throwing people together and giving them a common goal is one way of building friendships. We all met many new people on those nights. This type of party can be more difficult for the host than preparing the food in advance, but the memories it brings are phenomenal.

Cooking Time Line

Remember, each day, check your preparations list for things like cleaning, cleaning grill, shopping, setting table, drop-dead time, and so on. If you elect to use a store-bought item (or more than one), make sure it's on your shopping list (and obviously, then, you don't need to make it).

UP TO 1 WEEK BEFORE

1. Make the sorbet.

UP TO 3 DAYS BEFORE

1. Soak the beans.

UP TO 2 DAYS BEFORE

1. Make the black bean dip, but do not include the cheese swirl; prepare the beans and zucchini; peel and slice the oranges and refrigerate.

UP TO 1 DAY BEFORE

1. Make the filling for the quesadillas, salsa, and guacamole; cover and refrigerate.
2. Put plastic wrap directly on the surface of the guacamole to keep it from discoloring.
3. Marinate and grill the chicken, if using.

The Day

1. If you're not using cones and if there's room in the freezer, scoop sorbet into bowls, cover, and freeze.

UP TO 1 HOUR BEFORE

1. Lay out the fillings for the quesadillas.
2. Set out the salsa and the guacamole, covered.
3. Heat the bean dip and add the cheese swirl; set out on a warmer with the tortilla chips.
4. Toss the salad; set out in a bowl.
5. Heat the fajita fillings.

When you are getting your things ready for the party, put all the necessary serving pieces for the quesadillas, fajitas, and salad in one place. You'll need a scissors or knife and board to cut the quesadillas. Put a piece of paper in each to indicate what goes where. If you put the dip and chips on a tray, you can whisk them away and whisk in the main course. If your kitchen is the size of a closet, look for a space like the top of the refrigerator to house your tray until you're ready for it. The salad can be in the bowl already, covered and waiting in the refrigerator. (Put a note with the other food so you will not forget to put it out.) Toss the salad with the dressing just before you bring it out. (It will need a fork.)

Fancy Cheese Quesadillas

SERVES 10 AS AN APPETIZER,
6 AS A MAIN COURSE

The host serves as a short-order cook by preparing quesadillas to order, filling the tortillas with cheese, chicken, peppers, and/or onions. Some people add refried beans, others tomatoes. Epazote, the pungent Mexican herb, can be added as you go along.

There are many forms of quesadillas, the most familiar being melted cheese tortilla sandwiches. Variations abound, such as Sonoran, which my friend Ric says are more like cheese pizzas, as they are open-faced. Karen likes a version where the tortilla is heated on a grill; you slit it in half when it puffs up, slide cheese into the slit between the layers, and eat it right off the grill.

When serving this as a main course, restaurants usually serve 3 per person. I also use filled and cooked quesadillas, in quarters or eighths, for a side bread for a soup.

6 cups (24 ounces) grated Monterey Jack or cheddar cheese

20 to 30 fresh tortillas or two 19-ounce packages flour tortillas (10 tortillas per package)

½ to 1 cup chopped jalapeños, fresh or canned (optional)

½ cup sliced scallions (optional)

3 pounds Marinated Grilled Chicken (page 166), slivered or torn

3 to 4 tablespoons butter, as necessary, or nonstick vegetable spray for cooking

2 cups Pico de Gallo Salsa (page 169)

2 cups guacamole

1 cup cilantro, finely chopped

1 (16-ounce) container sour cream

Sprinkle ⅓ to ½ cup of the cheese evenly over one tortilla. Top with some jalapeños, scallions, and grilled chicken slivers. Cover with another tortilla to make the quesadilla sandwich.

Meanwhile, melt about 1 tablespoon of the butter in a large nonstick skillet or spray the skillet with vegetable oil. Heat to medium-high. Place the quesadilla in the skillet and sauté until it is lightly brown and the cheese begins to melt, about 2 minutes. Turn and do the same on the other side, about 1 minute. Remove the quesadilla from the heat and cut into quarters. (I use a pizza wheel or scissors). You can, of course, use more than 1 skillet to speed the process.

Put the hot quesadillas on individual dishes or a serving platter and surround with bowls of Pico de Gallo Salsa, guacamole, cilantro, and sour cream.

Although quesadillas taste best when they are freshly baked or sautéed, they will hold for a few minutes while you are cooking them all. (Or they can be reheated. If made ahead, cut cooked quesadillas into wedges and lay them out on a baking sheet in a 200°F. oven to warm until ready.)

Black Bean Swirl Dip

MAKES 5 CUPS

This bean recipe was given to my friend Marion by Betsy Doughtie, a caterer in Hilton Head, South Carolina. Needing a hearty hot dip that was also pretty and enticing for a football party, Betsy took the beans, which are delicious by themselves, and developed the cheese swirl. Although the dip is best when kept warm, it does not separate and so can be served at room temperature. Like any bean mixture, it should not be held at room temperature for more than an hour for health reasons. If this is too cheesy a menu for you, omit the cheese in this recipe and do just the black bean dip, mashing the beans a bit. Note that the cheese swirl should be made ahead and refrigerated. This recipe halves easily.

Black Beans
- 1 **pound dried black beans, picked over and rinsed**
- ¼ **cup oil**
- 6 **garlic cloves, finely chopped**
- 2 **stalks celery, finely chopped**
- 4 **large carrots, finely chopped**
- 1 **medium red onion, finely chopped**
- 1 **small fresh jalapeño pepper, cored, seeded, and finely chopped**
- 1 **small fresh poblano pepper, cored, seeded, and finely chopped**
- 2 **bay leaves**
- 2 **tablespoons chili powder**
- 1 **tablespoon ground cumin**
- 1 **tablespoon freshly ground black pepper**
- 7 **cups fresh or canned chicken stock or broth**
- **Salt to taste**
- **Hot sauce to taste**

Soak the dried beans 24 hours in cold water to cover. If in a hurry, cover the beans with water, bring to the boil, cook 2 minutes, cover, and set aside for 30 minutes.

Heat a large heavy soup pot or stockpot and add the ¼ cup oil. Add the garlic, celery, carrots, medium chopped red onion, 1 small jalapeño, and poblano and cook over medium heat until soft, stirring occasionally, about 10 minutes.

Drain and rinse the beans. Add them to the pot along with the bay leaves, chili powder, cumin, black pepper, and chicken stock. Bring to the boil, then reduce the heat, cover tightly, and simmer until the beans are soft, about 1½ to 2 hours. Check occasionally to be sure there is enough liquid and add boiling water if the pot looks dry. Remove the bay leaves and discard. Remove a cup of the beans, mash them, and stir them back into the mixture. Taste and adjust the seasoning with salt and hot sauce to taste. The beans may be refrigerated at this point

VARIATIONS

The original recipe calls for ½ pound of fried bacon in addition to sautéing the vegetables in the resultant bacon fat, which I omitted. Feel free to add the bacon back, if you like, and purée it with the mixture.

❧

If using canned black beans, omit the soaking step. Use only 2 cups chicken stock at the start and simmer about 30 minutes.

Cheese Swirl

  4 **cups cubed pepper Jack cheese**

¼ **cup finely chopped red onion**

  4 **garlic cloves, finely chopped**

  2 **fresh jalapeño peppers, cored, seeded, and finely chopped**

  1 **medium red bell pepper, cored, seeded, and finely chopped**

  1 **medium green pepper, cored, seeded, and finely chopped**

¼ **cup olive oil**

      Tortilla chips, preferably blue, white, and yellow

SHOPPING TIP

Black beans

    Also sold as black turtle beans or frijoles negros.

---

for up to 3 days. The black bean dip may be served cold or at room temperature without the cheese swirl.

For the cheese swirl, mix the cheese, ¼ cup chopped red onion, 4 chopped garlic cloves, 2 jalapeños, red bell pepper, green bell pepper, and ¼ cup olive oil and marinate overnight or up to 2 days.

When ready to serve the black bean swirl, allow the cheese to come to room temperature. Bring the beans to the boil carefully to prevent burning in a heavy nonstick pot. Pour into a chafing dish. Drain the cheese and vegetables and swirl them in the hot black beans. Stir as little as possible so that you can see swirls of cheese and peppers in the black beans.

Serve hot in a chafing dish or over a warmer with tortilla chips or at room temperature.

TIP

Each 4 ounces dry black beans makes 1½ cups packed cooked beans, which equals 3 pounds (48 ounces) canned black beans.

Marinated Grilled Chicken

This is a very flavorful and versatile recipe. Left whole, the chicken breasts can be served on a bun for a casual meal or with rice and a nice sauce for a more formal dinner. If you slice the chicken into ½-inch strips before you marinate it, then it is perfect for fajitas (opposite), chicken salad, or pasta salad. Reduce the cooking time if necessary. Whether it is grilled or broiled, the possibilities are endless. The chicken can be made ahead in large batches for a crowd and frozen up to 3 months.

6 tablespoons lime juice
1 tablespoon olive oil
1 garlic clove, crushed
2 teaspoons chopped fresh oregano
3 pounds skinless, boneless chicken breasts, tenderloin removed and saved for another use
Salt
Freshly ground black pepper

Preheat the broiler or grill.

At least one hour before cooking, place the lime juice, olive oil, garlic, and oregano in a large plastic bag. Mix well.

If the chicken breasts are large, place 1 breast between 2 sheets of wax paper or plastic wrap and, with a meat mallet or rolling pin, lightly pound it on a flat surface until it is about 1 inch thick.

Add the chicken breasts to the lime marinade, close the bag tightly, and refrigerate for at least 1 hour. The longer the chicken is in the marinade—up to 2 days—the more flavor it will absorb.

Remove the chicken from the marinade, place on the grill or under the broiler, and cook 3 to 4 inches from the heat, depending on the size. Turn after 4 minutes and cook the other side until done, about 4 minutes. Remove from the oven and serve hot or cold. Season to taste with salt and pepper.

TIP

Try to buy smaller breasts, as they are more tender. If using larger ones, be sure to pound them according to instructions before grilling.

VARIATION

Various herbs and spices can be added or substituted in the basic marinade recipe. Be adventurous and experiment. Try ginger, soy sauce, lemon juice instead of lime, rosemary instead of oregano. Always start with less than you may need, tasting, then adding more.

Lime Shrimp, Chicken, or Beef, and Roasted Pepper Fajitas

SERVES 6 TO 8

Although fajitas are traditionally made from beef skirt steak (for which they are named), I find this seafood alternative makes me think more of hot Mexican summer days. The filling may be made ahead and reheated; it freezes up to 3 months.

3 pounds small shrimp, boned chicken, or beef
6 tablespoons lime juice
4 tablespoons olive oil
2 tablespoons whole cilantro leaves
1 tablespoon chopped cilantro
2 garlic cloves, finely chopped
¼ teaspoon freshly ground black pepper
¼ teaspoon ground cumin
⅛ teaspoon chili powder
2 roasted red bell peppers (below), coarsely chopped
20 flour tortillas

Shell, devein, and wash the shrimp. If using chicken or beef, cut into finger-sized pieces, about ½-inch thick.

In a medium-sized plastic bag, mix together the lime juice, 2 tablespoons of the olive oil, cilantro, garlic, black pepper, cumin, and chili powder. Add the shrimp and allow to marinate, refrigerated, up to 30 minutes before cooking. (Leaving them in the marinade any longer may "cook" them, resulting in tough shrimp.) Beef or chicken can marinate as long as 2 days.

Heat the 2 remaining tablespoons olive oil in a large skillet over medium heat. Remove the shrimp from the marinade, place in the skillet, and add the roasted pepper and cilantro leaves. Cook the shrimp until lightly done, about 2 to 3 minutes. Remove from the heat and place the shrimp and peppers on the flour tortillas and roll up. Serve hot.

Roasted or Charred Red Bell Peppers

To roast or char peppers, wash and cut them in half lengthwise. Remove the seeds and ribs. Place an oven rack on the top level and heat the broiler. Line a cookie sheet with aluminum foil and spray with nonstick spray. Place the peppers, skin side up, on the foil and place under the broiler until the peppers have blackened, 8 to 10 minutes. Remove the peppers from the oven, let cool slightly, and then place them in a plastic bag. Seal the bag and allow the peppers to cool completely. Peel away the charred skin from the peppers and discard. At this point, use the roasted peppers in a recipe or pack them in a small jar, cover with olive oil, and refrigerate.

Green Bean, Zucchini, and Orange Salad

SERVES 6

Finding something authentic and yet substantially green to go with this Mexican theme proved a bit of a challenge. I finally found a variation of this salad in Diana Kennedy's wonderful book The Art of Mexican Cooking. *I met Diana during my first trip to Mexico, and she was enormously helpful and kind. Like many cooks, I am indebted to her for her scholarly work and heartily recommend her books.*

¾ **pound zucchini**
¾ **pound green beans,
    tips and tails
    removed**
½ **medium red onion,
    thinly sliced**

Dressing
⅓ **cup red wine vinegar**
1 **cup vegetable oil**
1 **teaspoon Dijon
    mustard**
2 **teaspoons cumin seeds
    Sugar
    Salt
    Freshly ground black
    pepper**
2 **tablespoons fresh
    herbs, such as basil,
    rosemary, chives,
    and/or oregano**
2 **seedless oranges,
    peeled and sliced**

Cut the zucchini into halves crosswise and then into quarters lengthwise, then into sticks or batons about 3 inches long by ½ inch thick. Place in a microwave-safe dish and cook on high until crisp-tender, about 3 minutes. Alternatively, bring a pot of water to the boil, add the zucchini, and cook 5 minutes until crisp-tender. Remove with a slotted spoon and add the green beans to the water. Cook 3 to 5 minutes until crisp-tender. Remove the zucchini and beans from the hot water and rinse with cold water to stop the cooking and set the color. Cut the beans into thirds. Add the thinly sliced onion to the cooled zucchini and beans. The dish can be made to this point several days ahead.

Mix together the vinegar, oil, and mustard and season to taste with cumin, sugar, salt, and pepper. One hour before serving, toss the zucchini, beans, herbs, and onions in the dressing. Add the orange slices. Pile the salad on a platter or in a bowl.

Pico de Gallo Salsa

Pico de gallo, which means "rooster's tooth," perhaps because of its spicy bite, is a loose, runny salsa. It can be used any time a tomato salsa is required, because the word salsa *just means sauce, and this one is full of tomatoes.*

2 whole tomatoes,
   peeled, cored, seeds
   removed, and hand
   chopped (about 2
   cups)
½ cup chopped onion
2 scallions, chopped,
   including green parts
4 garlic cloves, finely
   chopped
¼ green bell pepper,
   finely chopped
2 tablespoons chopped
   cilantro
2 to 4 small fresh
   jalapeño peppers,
   seeded and chopped
   (optional)
Salt
Freshly ground black
   pepper

In a medium-sized bowl, mix the tomatoes, onion, scallions, garlic, green pepper, cilantro, and jalapeño. Stir in salt and pepper to taste. Cover and let sit for an hour to allow the flavors to blend, or refrigerate for up to 3 days. (Drain if watery.)

Note on hot peppers: Put a plastic bag over your hands when seeding and chopping the pepper to prevent pepper juice from burning tiny cuts or scrapes on your fingers.

SHOPPING TIPS

Hot peppers vary—they can be canned, jarred, or fresh. I prefer fresh because they are crunchier, greener, and hotter. As a rule of thumb, the smaller a pepper the hotter, but 2 peppers on the same bush can vary greatly in heat. When in doubt, always add less. I buy jalapeño and cayenne peppers unless otherwise noted.

Cilantro

This is the leaf counterpart to coriander seed. They are both from the same plant but totally different in taste. Cilantro has a very definite flavor, for which there is no substitute. It is not available year-round in my grocery store, so I sometimes have to leave it out.

TIP

Adding chopped cilantro to a commercial salsa frequently results in a dip that can pass for homemade.

Mango Sorbet

I use mangoes so much these days I buy them sliced and packed in refrigerator jars ready to use. The size of these jars is odd—1 pound 10 ounces, which makes about 1⅔ cups purée.

There are many sorbet makers available for the freezer or to be turned electrically or by hand. Follow their directions, making careful note of the quantity they hold.

4 large ripe mangoes (4 pounds), or 3¼ pounds slices
¾ cup sugar
½ cup light corn syrup
1 cup vanilla yogurt (optional)

Using a small, sharp knife, make 4 lengthwise slits through the skin of the mango, cutting the skin into quarters. Peel off the skin and discard. Slice the flesh from both sides of the large, flat pit, as well as from around its edges.

Place the mango flesh in a food processor or blender and purée until smooth (you should have 3⅓ cups). Add the sugar and corn syrup and blend well. Add the yogurt if you wish.

Pour the mixture into a bowl and refrigerate until cold, about 1 hour.

Transfer the sorbet to an ice cream maker and follow the manufacturer's instructions.

After making the sorbet, put it in a container, cover tightly, and freeze until firm, from 20 minutes up to 4 hours, depending on the manufacturer's instructions.

VARIATIONS

Fresh or frozen peaches are a wonderful alternative to mango.

Add 1 tablespoon chopped mint.

Buffet for Twelve to Fifty, in Four Hours or Less

Toasted Cheese Cutouts (page 215)

Toast Points

Basil Oil

Grilled Sides of Salmon

Hot or Cool Mango Salsa

Rosemary Buffet Sandwich Rolls★

Buffet Tenderloin Mini-Rounds

Lemon-Orange Asparagus Spears

Herb-Crusted Cherry Tomatoes (page 157)

Apricot and Almond Tartlets★

The menu for fifty is designed to be prepared in less than four hours by one person, or in two hours by two people working together. (It will take much less than that for twelve people.) For this time frame, some of the items—such as the cheese appetizers, bread, toast points, and desserts—are best made ahead and frozen, or purchased. This timing also assumes that all dishes, glasses, and napkins are clean and ready for placement and that the flower and table arrangements are simple. All the food preparation is designed to allow the host to have everything ready for the party in time to relax and dress before the guests arrive.

This menu has many uses. It can be dressed up to be appropriate for a wedding reception, an engagement party, an elegant cocktail party, or a Christmas party. It even may become your "standby" for sit-down dinner parties, and it will be a good one. (For a sit-down dinner you will have to up the quantities—we eat more when we sit down (see page 18). The recipes can be easily doubled for a larger party or divided in half to accommodate fewer guests.

If you are entertaining a large number of people, a spectacular buffet party is the ideal choice. It can be set to enhance any tone you choose—casual to dressy. A buffet provides a full meal while being much simpler to prepare than a cocktail party, which requires lots of smaller, individual pieces. (Also, when people eat well they consume less alcohol, so in many ways a buffet is less expensive, yet it appears grander and more gracious than a cocktail party that costs much more.) At such an occasion, your best choice is a safe menu with which you feel thoroughly at ease.

My core buffet main-course recipes are salmon and tenderloin of beef. I dress them up—mango salsa is the current accessory to my old salmon standbys poached and grilled salmon. So, too, grilled or roasted tenderloin is the meat answer, equally dressed up with red peppers in balsamic vinegar or in a delicious marinade of mustard and ginger.

I have learned that large meats are easier to cook than smaller, that they can be sliced thinly or cut into chunks or wedges to go further, and that they can be served on small plates or tiny rolls to stretch them to serve a crowd, or cut thickly and sauced and put on a large plate and served to a few.

With that secret, you can feed any number of people, anytime. In this case, twelve to fifty, multiplying the recipes as you need to, to accommodate the number you wish.

None of the recipes require any great skill in the kitchen, but it's a good idea to practice grilling salmon for four or six people as a main course before you tackle it for fifty as an appetizer. This exercise can form the basis of an excellent sit-down dinner party, along with the tenderloin and asparagus.

Make this menu for family or close friends until you feel comfortable with it. (Expensive as it might be, it is still less expensive than eating out!) It will make an elegant dinner party that will give you great confidence for entertaining anyone in the world. From feeding family and friends comes the savvy and grace to fix for fifty. After that, the sky's the limit.

To test the durability of this menu, I toted it several places—one was to a friend's home in Washington for a party during the second Clinton inaugural weekend. I did substitute Greens with Grits for the salmon because I wanted a Southern feel, and besides I didn't want to smell up the airplane with the salmon. You can substitute your time-honored hors d'oeuvres too!

I don't like my buffet tables to look all one level—it's boring! Place something sturdy, like an upended box, on the table and drape a pretty cloth—from a remnant to a sari—over the box. Gather the cloth attractively at the back and set a bowl or platter on it. The cloth and the height add a splash of color and interest and draw your eye to the food. This technique is particularly helpful if the food is not elaborately garnished. Rolls, breads, and toast points can all be put in baskets with handles, which lift the eye.

Look for inexpensive glass compotes to put your condiments or sauces in. They don't all have to be the same height—or even match, for that matter. You can find old ones in antique shops, flea markets, and consignment shops. Modern ones are available but usually cost more. While you're out searching the junk shops, look for glass platters, too. They fit in with a lot of looks.

Setting the Scene

This Stand-up-Plates-Only Buffet was designed with food that can be eaten easily without forks while standing. (Some seating should always be provided for those who are unable to stand for long periods of time.)

Where to place the food and drink:

To begin, take a good look at the space available in your home or apartment. Consider the space and the traffic pattern when deciding where to position the food and drink as well as the used glasses and plates. The guests should have ready access to the food and drink as they move about visiting with one another. Furniture should be arranged so the guests can move freely about while holding plates and glasses.

I know I'm repeating myself, but it is important to make a very good list of the food, the platter on which it is to be served, and the time and way you are heating and putting it out. Be sure to mark all empty platters and bowls ahead of time with a piece of paper to indicate what is to go in them. When you put each food out, check it off on your list so you know it is not hidden in the refrigerator or an ice chest.

When you have fifty people to feed, unless you have hired help for refilling platters, you may have to make a decision about whether to set up two complete buffet tables, or whether to have duplicates of each food item on one larger buffet. Either way will mean that you have to have more trays, platters, and so forth to serve on. Two separate tables allow more freedom: The serving pieces on one can be very different from those on the other, which may be preferable, visually, to a hodgepodge on one large table. It is usually quicker to serve from two tables, but the amount of total space for the party may determine this for you. That said, perhaps you would rather cluster food and bread-and-butter plates on a number of small tables or "stations."

Find a separate space—such as a bedroom, a porch, or the laundry room—for a staging area to hold the extra plates, glasses, and napkins, as well as the storage boxes and any used dishes that would crowd the kitchen area. Having a definite place where the extra items are kept and where the used dishes can be taken will allow you to avoid the rush, confusion, and overcrowding of cabinets and tables. Your guests will enjoy the uncluttered appearance of your party rooms and your dishes will not be in danger of being bumped and broken.

Beverages should have their own table (or bar). You should have this very organized for fifty—maybe even get some extra help if you don't have a reliable, dedicated family member and if you are offering choices more extensive than wine, beer, bottled water, and sodas. At least determine how you will replenish the bar and clean up the used glasses and napkins. You'll need ice and tongs as well as bar napkins.

My accountant, who also serves as a recipe-development assistant and entertains frequently herself, bought 250 ten-ounce wineglasses at a cost of about one dollar each in 1981. She stores them in a closet in cardboard liquor boxes, the glasses turned upside down on clean paper towels. She lends them often to friends and to her church and has lost only a few in the many years of use. If, in the after-party cleanup rush, there is no time to wash all the glasses, she puts the glasses back in the boxes right side up. This alerts her to the need to wash them. If you have a closet or attic that would hold them, you might consider buying enough glasses for fifty people. A 10-ounce glass can also be used as an iced-beverage glass for luncheon buffets or other events. My friends Marion and Elise prefer all-purpose, 12-ounce, large bowl, red-wine glasses for all beverages.

The Right Equipment

Having the right equipment is an important consideration. Glasses, plates, and linen napkins can be rented; good-quality paper napkins and plastic plates and glasses are available today; and you might find that you can borrow from friends. If you are going to entertain this way, keep an eye out for garage and estate sales where you can purchase attractive, inexpensive plates, glasses, and linens, which you keep stored in boxes until needed.

For a plates-only standing buffet such as this one, I use small bread-and-butter plates and napkins, such as those used for dessert and cocktails or salad plates, because the guests can manage them more easily as they move around. Dinner plates encourage people to take more than they can easily handle standing up. You will need to allow more than one per person, since people may put one down and pick up another. Glass or salad plates are a good compromise size.

Figure one clean glass per person per hour, as people also set glasses down.

Cooking Time Line

Remember, each day, check your preparations list for things like cleaning, cleaning grill, shopping, setting the table, drop-dead time, and so on. If you elect to use a store-bought item (or more than one), make sure it's on your shopping list (and obviously, then, you don't need to make it).

UP TO 3 MONTHS BEFORE

1. Make the rolls and tartlets and freeze them.

UP TO 6 WEEKS BEFORE

1. Make the Toasted Cheese Cutouts and Toast Points and freeze.

UP TO 3 DAYS BEFORE

1. Marinate tenderloin in the refrigerator; bring to room temperature before baking.

UP TO 2 DAYS BEFORE

1. Make the two mango salsas.
2. Marinate the salmon in the refrigerator.

UP TO 1 DAY BEFORE

1. Grill or broil the salmon, cover, and chill.
2. Bake the tenderloin, let cool, slice, and arrange on platter. Cover and refrigerate.
3. Prepare the asparagus, cover, and chill.
4. Take the rolls, tartlets, and Toast Points from the freezer to thaw.

The Day

In the morning, prepare the tomatoes, arrange on a platter, cover, and refrigerate or set aside at room temperature.

UP TO 3 HOURS BEFORE

1. Slice the rolls if they haven't been sliced already and arrange on platters or baskets. Put on the buffet.
2. Put the tartlets on the buffet, still covered.
3. Put the Toast Points on the buffet next to the spot for the salmon.

UP TO 2 HOURS BEFORE

1. Assemble the ice, coolers, and so on.
2. Put the asparagus and tomatoes on the buffet.
3. Garnish the tenderloin and salmon platters and put on the buffet.

1 HOUR BEFORE

1. Remove the salsas from the refrigerator and place on the buffet.

30 MINUTES BEFORE

1. Preheat the broiler.

15 MINUTES BEFORE

1. Broil the Toasted Cheese Cutouts directly from the freezer. They can be kept warm in a 200°F. oven.

Weddings

Anyone who decides to do a major wedding dinner for someone they love very much is slightly crazy, because a wedding, like a family holiday, is full of other things that take time and emotion, and being responsible for something so important is very stressful. That said, if you are asked, of course you will do it, and of course I have. It is necessary because we've been asked, and not always because it is "simpler" or less expensive than a professionally catered affair.

I have done several such weddings. One was for LuLen, who came to live with me when she was sixteen, when her parents, my dear friends, were going to Upper Volta, Africa, where her dad was sent as United States ambassador. LuLen had just finished the New York City Ballet School and came to Atlanta to apprentice with the Atlanta Ballet. She came to stay with me for a few weeks while she was waiting for student housing. And ended up staying several years—through her second year at Emory University, when her parents returned. We are close friends, and so of course I wanted to do the main part of her wedding reception.

I could not have made it without Virginia Willis, who apprenticed with me, then worked for me, then went to study at the Académie de Cuisine, in Washington, so was available here and in Washington. There was a serving staff for the wedding at the rental site. (They were married outside under a bower, and the meal was served inside.) The wedding feast was highly successful, and everyone was happy, including me. We followed a number of the suggestions here. Since the in-house staff caterer didn't want us in her kitchen, we had to turn a small library into our staging area, and I'll never forget Virginia on her hands and knees, plating the trays as they came in for refills.

I also did the food for Gail's wedding. When Gail was less than sixteen, she and her sister Audry moved in with me. Their mother had died when they were very young. We never have found a good name for the relationship, and so I refer to her and Audrey in various ways—daughter, foster daughter, and nearly daughter being the most usual ones. None of the names ever quite fit the feelings we have for each other. Gail wanted her wedding in the club room near her apartment, and so we did it there.

I would dearly have loved to have had Audrey's wedding here at home. As it was, it was held in France, and Pierre Henri's mother, Jozette, graciously did all the organizational work, while I champed at the bit, frustrated at being so ineffectual, here in the States. I don't think it much mattered, however, since Jozette is so skilled at entertaining. Not only did we have a seated meal after the wedding, we had a little cocktail party at their home in Rousillon first, serving many of the types of things in this book's hors d'oeurves menu, including Madame Titine's pâté. The grand finale of Audrey's wedding was a croquembouche, a traditional French wedding "cake" made from piled cream puffs.

It is crucial at these emotional times to be organized way in advance, to have even your purchasing finalized and the food in hand ahead of time, so that there can be no last-minute glitches that appear overwhelming when stress is high.

Toast Points

I keep some of these toast points in my pantry at all times. My family and guests enjoy them with cheese spreads, pâtés, and soups and salads. I sometimes cut the bread into fancy shapes for special occasions, but that creates some scraps of bread and takes longer to prepare. The toasts will keep for several months if they are tightly sealed and kept free of moisture. They are cheaper than crackers and infinitely better.

2 loaves thin-sliced sandwich bread

Preheat the oven to 250°F.

Using a sharp knife, remove the crusts from the bread and cut each slice diagonally into four triangles. Place the triangles on an ungreased baking sheet and bake until lightly browned, about 15 to 20 minutes. Let cool on a wire rack and store in plastic bags or a tightly covered tin.

VARIATION

Brush with melted butter or oil and sprinkle with kosher salt, garlic, or grated Parmesan before baking.

TIP

I simplify the process of removing the crusts and cutting the bread into triangles by working with 3 slices of bread at a time. The 12 triangles left in squares fit nicely on my baking sheet. The pieces do not need to be spaced apart, because they will separate slightly as they brown. If you are baking more than one sheet at a time, check the toasts after 10 minutes and swap the positions of the pans so that all will brown evenly.

Basil Oil

MAKES 2 CUPS

Infused oils can be a real flavor boost to perk up marinades, as well as to brush on food before grilling, and this variety is one of my favorites.

⅓ cup roughly chopped basil leaves
2 cups olive oil

Put the basil and olive oil in a sterilized glass jar and tightly cover or seal. Keep, refrigerated, up to two weeks.

Grilled Sides of Salmon

A boned side of salmon—filet, as it is called in French—is a very versatile item to use for entertaining. Grilled it can be dressed up for a fancy cocktail buffet by serving it on a beautiful silver tray, topped with mango salsa or garnished with cucumber, fresh dill, or an edible flower, like a rose, or it can be served in an outside casual buffet on anything from a pottery platter to a wooden plank cut to size. If you are truly afraid, and can only afford to do one side, so must make no mistakes, broil the salmon on an oiled broiler pan or cookie sheet. The broiled salmon colors and cooks quite nicely and is very easy.

This recipe may easily be multiplied for a crowd. A rule of thumb is 1½ ounces per person for an appetizer. When the crowd grows, people eat less per person—maybe because it's harder to get to the food. To convert this dish into a main course, figure 3 ounces per person for a buffet, 4 to 6 ounces for sit-down dinner.

Note: The generally accepted rule for the length of time a fish should be cooked is 10 minutes per inch of thickness (5 minutes per side), measured at its thickest point, at 400°F. or more, or 4 to 5 inches from the heat if broiled or grilled. If the salmon is more than 2 inches thick, add 1 more minute per side per inch.

2 (2½- to 3-pound) sides of salmon, bone removed, skin on
¼ cup extra-virgin olive oil or Basil Oil (page 177)
¼ cup lemon juice
2 tablespoons chopped fresh basil leaves
Salt
Freshly ground black pepper

Garnish
Mango salsa (page 180)
Curly lettuce
Sprigs of herbs, such as basil, dill, or fennel
Tomato rose or edible flowers
Lemon slices or wedges
Cucumber slices

Prepare the grill.

Place the salmon sides in a glass or plastic container that is long enough to accommodate them unfolded and with high enough sides to keep the marinade from spilling when you move the salmon to the grill. In a small bowl, mix the olive oil, lemon juice, basil, salt, and pepper. Pour the marinade over the salmon, cover with plastic wrap, and leave at room temperature while the grill is heating, about 30 minutes.

Place the salmon sides on the grill so that the nonskin side is down so that the hot grill will mark the presentation side. If the salmon sides are 1 inch thick, cook for 5 minutes then turn, using a wide spatula to loosen the fish underneath carefully be-

VARIATIONS

Omit the marinade. Before grilling, coat each salmon side with a dry-rub mixture of ⅓ cup each paprika, toasted and crushed coriander seed, toasted and crushed cumin seed, and light brown sugar.

Serve with the Pico de Gallo Salsa (page 169), or mix yellow tomatoes with red in the Pico de Gallo Salsa.

Salmon is available in numerous sizes—it ranges from 2 to 38 pounds—and several types of cuts. Sides, or fillets, are the meat along the spine, with the bone removed, and occasionally the skin left on. If the skin has been removed, it is fine to purchase the salmon fillets, but they will be a little harder to handle. Since salmon freezes well, tightly wrapped, I purchase it on sale and keep it until I need it.

TIP

If using briquettes, oil the rack to avoid sticking in case the coals are not hot enough. Light the charcoal and wait until the coals become very hot: 15 minutes after the coals turn gray-white (about 30 minutes in all) and hot enough to hold your hand 4 or 5 inches over the fire for 4 to 5 seconds only. Spread the coals out so that you have a surface of coals as large as your salmon sides.

fore turning. Cook 5 minutes on the second side. (It is better to undercook the salmon slightly, since it will continue to cook on the platter, just from the residual heat.)

Using 2 wide spatulas, remove the salmon sides from the grill to serving platters. Don't panic if the salmon splits into pieces when you lift it from the grill. If you are careful, you can rearrange it on the serving platter so that the break will not be evident to your guests. The salmon can be served hot or it can be refrigerated, covered with plastic wrap, and served cold. Garnish with the mango salsa, curly lettuce, herb sprigs, tomato rose, lemon slices, or cucumber slices.

Hot Mango Salsa

I use this salsa for tortillas, grilled chicken, or fish as well as to add interest to soups. I vary the ingredients according to the colors and flavors I want, and I frequently use mangoes from a jar for salsa.

1 (14-ounce) mango, peeled, seeded, and chopped (about 2 cups)
¼ cup chopped scallion
¼ cup chopped yellow or red bell pepper
1 teaspoon chopped cilantro or basil
1 to 2 teaspoons chopped jalapeño peppers, preferably fresh
2 tablespoons fresh lime or lemon juice

Mix together the mango, scallion, bell pepper, cilantro, jalapeño, and lime juice. The salsa can be kept, refrigerated, for up to a week.

Cool Mango Salsa

MAKES 2 CUPS

This mild, friendly, fresh-tasting salsa is not only special any time you'd use a hot salsa—for example chicken, fish, pork, or beef—but it can double as a dessert salsa.

1 (14-ounce) mango, peeled, seeded, and chopped (about 2 cups)
1 tablespoon chopped fresh ginger
1 tablespoon fresh lime juice
1 tablespoon packed light brown sugar or honey or to taste

Toss the mango with the ginger and add the lime juice. Taste and add sugar or honey as needed.

VARIATION

To either of these salsas, add 1 to 2 chopped avocados and serve on lettuce as a salad.

Rosemary Buffet Sandwich Rolls

MAKES FIFTY 1½-INCH ROLLS

These rolls are an adaptation of a family recipe—updated with the addition of rosemary and made small enough to serve as a buffet sandwich roll. For a buffet for fifty people, make the recipe twice and place the dough in separate bowls or bags to rise. Do not try to double the recipe, because the dough will be difficult to manage when doubled. The rolls freeze well for two to three months.

1 package active dry
  yeast
4 tablespoons sugar
½ cup warm water
  (105°F. to 115°F.)
¾ cup milk
3 tablespoons butter
2 teaspoons salt
3½ to 4½ cups bread flour
1 large egg, lightly
  beaten
2 tablespoons finely
  chopped fresh
  rosemary leaves

Glaze
1 egg, lightly beaten
  with 1 tablespoon
  water

Preheat the oven to 350°F. Lightly grease two 10x13-inch baking sheets.

Dissolve the yeast and 1 tablespoon of the sugar in the warm water. Scald the milk by heating it almost to the boil; small, simmering bubbles will appear around the edge of the pan. Add the remaining 3 tablespoons sugar, the butter, and the salt to the milk and let the mixture cool to 105° to 115°F.

Put 3 cups of the flour in the bowl of a food processor or a large mixing bowl. Pour in the yeast mixture and the cooled milk mixture. Add the lightly beaten egg. Process or beat until smooth.

Adding flour as needed, process about 1 minute in the food processor or 10 minutes in the electric mixer to knead, or turn out onto a floured board and knead by hand. Knead in the rosemary. The dough should be smooth and elastic and soft like a baby's bottom. Place in an oiled bowl or in an oiled plastic bag and turn to coat. Cover with plastic wrap or seal the bag and set aside in a warm place to rise until doubled, about 1 hour. (Note: The dough may be refrigerated before or after doubling and finished the next day.)

Punch the dough down and knead it lightly. Pinch off small pieces about 1 inch in diameter and roll the pieces into balls. Place them 2 inches apart on the baking sheets. Set aside and let rise until doubled, about 45 minutes. Brush the tops of the rolls with the egg glaze and bake until golden brown, and the dough is cooked, about 15 to 20 minutes.

Buffet Tenderloin Mini-Rounds

Tenderloin is the most loved of all beef party dishes and simple to cook. What's scary is the major investment. You may feel you have just one shot at doing it right. So get a good timer and a meat thermometer and don't do anything else while it's cooking. That said, tenderloin is the most forgiving piece of meat—even if overcooked it's tender and tasty.

Cut to fit the rolls, this self-sauced, all-inclusive approach is easy on you and your guests, and it's delicious. If you'd rather not cut and tie, fold under the thinner end of each tenderloin, spread with the mustard, and roast approximately 30 minutes. When it's cooked it will need to be sliced in half horizontally as well as sliced vertically.

For a buffet main course where the meat is served sliced, plan on 3 ounces trimmed tenderloin per person; for a sit-down dinner party, 7 ounces per person. A whole trimmed tenderloin serves 8 people generously at a formal seated dinner, where the meal is plated.

This recipe halves easily for cooking just 1 tenderloin.

2 cups Dijon mustard
¼ cup crumbled fresh rosemary
¼ cup finely chopped fresh ginger
4 garlic cloves, finely chopped
¼ cup Worcestershire sauce
2 tablespoons peanut oil
Salt
Freshly ground black pepper
2 (approximately 5-pound) trimmed beef tenderloins
100 (2- to 3-inch) Rosemary Buffet Sandwich Rolls (page 181), halved

Preheat the oven to 425°F.

Mix the mustard, rosemary, ginger, garlic, Worcestershire, and oil and salt and pepper to taste.

Trim off any excess fat and membrane from the meat. To make the cylinders, slice each tenderloin lengthwise from end to end to form 2 pieces of meat from each tenderloin. Turn about 2 inches of the thinner end under to make a uniform cylinder. Tie each cylinder at about 2-inch intervals with kitchen twine, forming a cylindrical shape of the same diameter as the bread rolls. Repeat with the remaining 3 pieces of beef. Spread the mustard mixture all over the 4 pieces of meat and set aside. (At this point, you can wrap the meat and refrigerate it for up to 2 days.)

> ### NOTE
>
> *The purpose of tying the meat is to form cylinders about the diameter of the rolls, so the filled rolls may be eaten easily at a stand-up meal without the need for forks. The mustard-covered surface means forgoing extra mustard and sauces, which speeds up the ease of service for the guests.*

Reserving the mustard mixture, put the tenderloins in a heavy baking pan, leaving space between them. There must be plenty of room to let the heat circulate and the meat brown rather than steam. Roast them in batches if necessary. Put the pan in the hot oven on the top shelf and roast until an instant-read thermometer inserted in the middle of the tenderloin registers 135°F., about 15 to 20 minutes, longer if straight from the refrigerator. Remove the roasts from the oven and let them rest at least 15 minutes. Remove the strings and carve the meat into thin slices. (They can be made ahead up to 2 days and refrigerated and carved a day or two later. It's easier to carve a cold roast.)

While the meat is resting, add any leftover mustard mixture to the roasting pan and bring to the boil, scraping up the browned bits on the bottom and sides of the pan. Boil until the juices have reduced by about half. Let cool.

Put the cold or room-temperature meat on a serving tray and pour any reduced mustard mixture over the meat. Put the tray on the buffet and place the rolls nearby. If you are making up the sandwiches, put 2 or 3 of the thin slices of the meat on the roll. (It is easier to eat 2 thin pieces than 1 thick one.) Otherwise, let everyone help themselves. The sliced tenderloin may be kept, frozen, for up to 3 months, for family use.

Lemon-Orange Asparagus Spears

SERVES 50

Asparagus goes so well with citrus, my first thought is frequently lemon or orange. Alas, like any other green vegetable, asparagus will fade when it comes into contact with citric acid. And this won't do. My friend Shirley Corriher taught me to use just the peel of citrus fruit to give food its citrus flavor boost. The peel can be added ahead of time and doesn't bleach the color of the green vegetable as vinegar, lemon juice, or orange juice does.

5 to 6 pounds asparagus spears, about 100 spears
2 lemons
2 oranges

Wash the asparagus, and then cut off the bottom where the stringiness begins. Peel the stalks if they are thick.

Choose a skillet large enough to hold the length of the asparagus and half fill it with water. Bring the water to the boil. Add the asparagus in batches and cook 2 to 4 minutes, or until nearly tender. Do not crowd the pan. Remove the asparagus from the hot water and rinse with cold water to refresh (to stop the cooking process and to set the color).

Repeat the cooking process until all the asparagus has been cooked and refreshed. Arrange the asparagus on serving platters, or place in plastic bags.

Remove the peel from the lemons and oranges using a zester. If a zester is not available, grate the peel, making sure no white is attached, or peel and slice very thin. Sprinkle the peels on top of the asparagus in a decorative manner. Cover the asparagus platter with plastic wrap and refrigerate, or if they will be served within 3 hours, place directly on the serving table.

TIP

Leftover asparagus can be refrigerated and served cold at a later time, or quickly heated in a microwave or under a broiler and served as a hot vegetable to accompany a meal. If you will not use the asparagus in a few days, freeze in plastic bags and then thaw and reheat when needed. Tightly wrapped asparagus can be kept, frozen, for up to 3 months. It will lose its crunch but will be especially nice for soup or cooking in a casserole.

Apricot and Almond Tartlets

MAKES FORTY-EIGHT 1-INCH TARTLETS

Tartlets are ideal pick-up desserts. I suspect this is because people tell themselves they are too little to have calories. Made ahead and frozen, they can almost be eaten out of the freezer. I urge you to make them ahead so you are sure you are happy with them and are not making fiddly things under stress.

Frangipane is a traditional almond filling. Other fruit can be substituted for the apricots, or the tarts can be baked and have fresh fruit such as strawberries put on the baked crust and frangipane. There are four steps in this—the crust, the filling (frangipane), the apricots, and the glaze.

These pretty tarts are a classic and never fail to please. I've seen them made at the best cooking schools, at The Ritz in Paris, and by Nick Malgieri, New York's famous pastry chef, for a party for Ivana Trump. This is an adaption of Nick Malgieri's recipe.

I make these delicious tartlets in various molds and tartlet pans, rather than in one shape. The variety of sizes makes an interesting serving platter and also allows my guests to choose a tartlet that suits their tastes. Some people like a one-bite tartlet, while some prefer a two-bite one. If you do not have 48 tartlet tins, you must bake in batches, cleaning the tins as necessary, and reuse those you have. Allow at least two 1-inch tartlets per person for a buffet party. A store-bought pie pastry can be used if necessary as a substitute for the pâte sucrée, but be sure to roll it thinly (⅛ inch).

Frangipane filling
- ⅓ cup (4 ounces) canned almond paste
- ¼ cup sugar
- 1 large egg yolk
- 1 teaspoon grated lemon peel (no white attached)
- 4 tablespoons (½ stick) unsalted butter, at room temperature
- 1 large egg
- 3 tablespoons all-purpose flour

- 2 recipes Pâte Sucrée (Sweet Pastry Dough) (page 280), chilled
- 2 (17-ounce) cans apricot halves in heavy syrup, drained, syrup reserved

Preheat the oven to 350°F. Spray the molds with nonstick cooking spray or oil.

Combine the almond paste, sugar, egg yolk, and peel. Beat with a mixer or food processor until smooth. Beat in the butter, then the egg. Continue beating until light. Stir in the flour until well combined. Set aside.

Remove the chilled dough from the refrigerator and pound briefly to soften it enough to shape. Divide into 48 pieces.

To line 1½- to 2-inch molds, tartlets, or boats with the dough, put a piece into a tin and gently press with your fingers or a floured tart tamper (a wooden implement that is shaped on both ends to fit into tart shells) until ⅛ inch thick. Press down on the edges of the tins to cut the dough. Line more molds in the same way until all the dough, including the trimmings, is used. Chill in the freezer for 15 minutes or up to 3 months, covered.

Place on a baking sheet and bake the chilled shells until lightly brown at the edges, 8 to 10 minutes. Remove from the oven to a rack until completely cooled. The thinner they are, the more quickly they brown. They may puff up, in which case remove the puffed up portion with a sharp spoon.

Glaze
½ **cup apricot preserves**
½ **cup canned apricot**
   syrup or nectar

Garnish
¼ **cup finely chopped**
   almonds

TIP

Tartlet molds are a good investment. They do, however, need care, because without it they will rust. Wipe them after use. Scrub and dry only the ones that have residue sticking to them. Place the cleaned tins on a cookie sheet and bake at 350°F. until dry, about 5 minutes. Remove from the oven and turn upside down overnight to be sure they are dry. Pack in an airtight container or plastic bag.

Spread the bottom of each tartlet crust with the frangipane filling. Top with an apricot half or a small piece, skin side up, that has been cut to fit. Place back in the oven and bake until the crust and filling are baked through and the apricots color at the tips, about 20 minutes.

While the tartlets are still warm, carefully remove them from the tins and cool on a wire rack. Caution: If the tartlets are not removed from the tins while they are warm, they may be difficult to remove. If they are, place them back in the warm oven for just a few minutes before trying again.

Make the glaze: Combine the preserves and syrup in a small heavy saucepan. Carefully bring the mixture to the boil and simmer briefly to thicken slightly.

Brush the hot glaze over the cooled tartlets. To garnish, sprinkle each tartlet with chopped almonds. Allow the glaze to drip, then place the tartlets on serving platters or in storage containers. The tartlets may be made several days in advance and refrigerated or frozen up to 3 months.

Two Hors d'Oeuvres Parties

An "Hors d'Oeuvres Only" menu with the food set out on tables or a sideboard is perfect for black-tie cocktail parties, wedding receptions, holidays, and other special occasions. Here are two such menus for you, depending on your time and budget. Neither requires a fork. The items in each can be mixed and matched like a well-planned wardrobe. Hors d'oeuvres parties probably are appropriate for more occasions and offer the host more items to choose from than any other type of entertaining. They are also the most labor-intensive and can be very costly. When you want things to be the simplest, and least time-consuming, start with one or two of the large meat or fish items that are cooked and then cut into small portions, or with the Elegant Cheese Platter Garnished with Sugared Grapes, a lovely hors d'oeuvre that doesn't require any cooking at all. Add to these as you feel you need to, to set the tone you want and to meet your time and space requirements. (Obviously, your budget will be the other deciding factor in your menu.) Feel free to mix in your own favorites.

I usually change the focus of "cocktail" parties to the food rather than the drinks. If you are serving alcohol, I suggest a menu formula of about 60 percent protein divided between meat, seafood, and dairy, so that all kinds of eaters have something to enjoy. Then add about another 30 percent in vegetables and fruit—items such as the Stuffed Cherry Tomatoes, Tomato Bruschetta, and Basket of Crudités with Yogurt-Coriander Sauce. Your last 10 percent can come from the Small Hors d'Oeuvres category or, if you wish, the smaller sweets from the dessert menu.

How Many Hors d'Oeuvres? How Much Help?

For an hour-and-a-half- to two-hour party, estimate about ten "bites" per person, but you don't have to make ten different hors d'oeuvres. There can be five bites of two different items or two bites of five items. If you know that you are serving something that will be very popular, like the Scallop and Shrimp Seviche, plan on at least two bites per person of those.

Unless you are having a really big party, you can probably make the food yourself by selecting a menu that allows you to do a good bit of freezing ahead and very little last-minute preparation for the "fresh" items like the meats and vegetables.

When you are doing an elaborate party, however, such as a black-tie cocktail party—possibly your fanciest—and if it is large, it really is almost essential to have someone who will come in and help you when it's time to put the food on the trays, garnish them, and get them out to the table. This person can also make the evening a lot easier for the host if he or she can be relied on to replenish trays, pick up the empty glasses, and keep things neat and tidy. If you don't have a friend who will help, you may be able to hire a helper from a catering company or find someone in town who knows how to "work" a party. Figure this cost into your budget. Your guests will all have a better time if you aren't all worn out before they even arrive.

Of course, there is no sense in getting anyone's help if you don't leave time to direct the person. This will be simpler if you make sure that you have written down everything that your helper will need. You can do the list early on when you do your own time line—including your drop-dead time—particularly important at party time, when you always want to do "just one more thing."

OTHER HORS D'OEUVRES

SMALL, PICK-UP HORS D'OEUVRES
Ripe Olive Bruschetta (page 151)
Parmesan Coins (page 89)
P.D.C.'s Divine Saltines (page 154)

MEATS
Buffet Tenderloin Mini-Rounds (page 182)

SEAFOOD
Grilled Sides of Salmon (page 178)

CHEESE
Toasted Cheese Cutouts (page 215)

FRUITS, VEGETABLES
Black Bean Swirl Dip (page 164)

Herb-Crusted Cherry Tomatoes (page 157)
Lemon-Orange Asparagus Spears (page 184)
Oven-Roasted New Potatoes Stuffed with
    Potato Salad (page 266)
Strawberries with Balsamic Vinegar (page
    141)
Melon Basket (page 95)

BREADS
French Bread (page 44)
Toast Points (page 177)

COCKTAIL SWEETS
Almond Crescents (page 277)
Apricot and Almond Tartlets (page 185)
Anise Cookies (page 142)

Setting the Scene

Hors d'Oeuvres Party Presentation

*P*resentation is what really sets an hors d'oeuvres party apart from the mundane. For big parties especially, to avoid congestion, put items like the Elegant Cheese Platter Garnished with Sugared Grapes or a tray of sweets on separate tables, or even in another room if there is a logical place. Or cluster several smaller tables in one place and divide the menu between them and the sideboard. Whenever you do this, keep an eye on the tables and move items when an empty space is left.

You can certainly use an assortment of serving pieces. Silver, glass, pottery, wood, brass, bamboo, copper—almost anything can be appropriate if garnished prettily. Beware of containers that were not made to hold food. If in doubt, line the container with a glass bowl, plastic wrap, aluminum foil, or some other safe material. Keep biscuits or rolls warm by serving them in a basket lined with a hot roll cover or spiffy cloth napkin.

Even if you are serving from a buffet, you may want to consider having one passed item. There's just something a little sophisticated about passing an hors d'oeuvre on a pretty tray. (If you can't find a willing helper—be it spouse, child, friend, or hired helper—don't try to do it yourself.) If the food is likely to slide on a tray, like the cherry tomatoes, or to leave oil or grease, like the Scallop and Shrimp Seviche, line your trays with herbs, parsley, or edible greens. I avoid using doilies for any hors d'oeuvres that will extrude juices or leave a messy blot. Wheat grass, lemon leaves, kudzu, and trimmed palm fronds from the florist will also work well, especially if you are putting something hot on them, because they don't wilt. Be sure that you only use greens that are not poisonous and have not been sprayed with pesticide. Edible garnishes such as pansies can be purchased, often from wholesalers. Garnishes could be a single striking flower, a tiny bouquet of flowers, or a pretty shell for seafood items.

To Pass or Not to Pass

For maximum elegance, you can do a completely "passed" hors d'oeuvres party, which I rarely do, because this is something for which you really *do* need a *trained* staff. It's also about impossible to feed people a meal—and meet my protein requirements (Nathalie Dupree's Rule)—from passed hors d'oeuvres. (This has nothing to do with a shortage of appropriate food and everything to do with the difficulty of getting food to guests who don't want their conversation constantly interrupted by a tray of hors d'oeuvres.) If you're a little adventuresome and want to pass, however, here's how:

The logistics are extremely important, because someone has to do the traying up and passing. It could be you, your charming children, or a friend. If you have twenty or more guests, the best choice is to hire someone. From twenty to thirty guests, one server can handle things. From thirty to fifty, you'll need two.

Give your guests a few minutes to settle in and get a drink before you start passing.

If the first item you pass is a cold or room-temperature one, the next one can be warming in the oven.

Have the passer prepped to begin with at least half as many hors d'oeuvres on the tray as there are guests. When the server goes back in to refill the tray with the other half, he or she should try to have a sense of where to start back so that he doesn't serve only the same people he served the first time. If you have two servers, assign each an area.

Have refilled trays come out at once if everyone hasn't been offered an item. Otherwise, wait about ten minutes between items, if that timing works with the time allowed for the party, depending on how thoroughly fed you want your guests. People like to sip their drinks and chat a little between hors d'oeuvres.

The trays should be wiped up and spruced up *each* time they are refilled. A server should carry cocktail napkins in one hand and offer them with the hors d'oeuvres. If the item is on a pick or skewer, a small plate, tray, or bowl should be carried in the hand with the napkins so that guests will have something to do with the used ones.

If you are planning to have a sweet, offer it last.

What About the Bar?

Cocktails are becoming fashionable again after a hiatus, but they take a lot more work than wine. Specific cocktails, such as martinis, require special glasses. If you are planning to have a variety of cocktails, you may need to hire one more person: a bartender with experience. People are particular about cocktails and want them made exactly right. Consider limiting what you are offering if you are not having a bartender.

Cocktails also require garnishes—lemons, limes, cherries, olives—and toothpicks for them. Make a list of what you plan to serve and get good help from your local liquor store or bartender about how much you'll need for how many. The fruit can be cut, put in its serving dishes, wrapped with plastic wrap, and put in the refrigerator the day before the party. Plan on three napkins, three glasses, and three drinks per person for a three-hour party. Plan on a pound of ice per person for a summer cocktail party. That may be a bit much, but better to have too much than too little.

ENDING THE EVENING

Cocktail parties are frequently so much fun that no one wants to leave. If that is fine with you, then let the party go on. But if you want a limited time for your party, or want the party to end while your guests can still drive, here are a few tricks to end it:

At the scheduled time for the party to end (as on the invitation), or fifteen minutes or so before, put the food and drink away. This is easier if there are caterers, but if not, keep a carton for the bottles, and fill and close the carton while continuing to smile and chat. Leave a bottle or so of wine out if you don't want to seem inhospitable, and a few glasses. Offer coffee, decaf, and tea, which extends your hospitality but is a signal that the evening is coming to a close. If people still won't leave and you have other plans, such as a follow-up dinner to a celebratory occasion, politely but firmly mention them, or include the guests if you prefer. Check to be sure your guests are capable of driving, and offer them a ride or to call a cab if necessary.

Winter Hors d'Œuvres Menu

Caponata with Cucumber Rounds

Phyllo Crab–Goat Cheese Kisses

Stuffed Cherry Tomatoes

Chili Jicama Sticks with Lime

Elegant Cheese Platter Garnished
with Sugared Grapes

Frosted Salmon Platter with
Toast Points

Mère Titine's Chicken Liver and
Pork Terrine

Marinated Roasted Pork with
Chutney Butter

Angel Biscuits

Rosemary Roll "Grape Cluster"

Italian Meringue Kisses

Pecan Crescents (page 278)

Cooking Time Line

Winter Hors d'Oeuvres: Remember, each day, check your preparations list for things like cleaning, shopping, setting the table, drop-dead time, and so on. If you elect to use a store-bought item (or more than one), make sure it's on your shopping list (and obviously, then, you don't need to make it).

UP TO 3 MONTHS BEFORE

1. Make the caponata, phyllo kisses, terrine, Toast Points, biscuits, roll cluster, meringue kisses, and Pecan Crescents; freeze.

UP TO 2 DAYS BEFORE

1. Cut the jicama sticks, wrap, and refrigerate.
2. Prepare the Chutney Butter.
3. Cook the salmon; refrigerate.
4. Marinate the pork.
5. Remove the Pecan Crescents from freezer; thaw in tin.

AT LEAST 1 DAY BEFORE

1. Remove the caponata, Toast Points, biscuits, rolls, and meringue kisses from the freezer and thaw.
2. Ice and decorate the salmon; refrigerate.

UP TO 1 DAY BEFORE

1. Slice the cucumber rounds for the caponata and stuff the cherry tomatoes; refrigerate.

2. Cook the pork, let cool, slice, and refrigerate.
3. Defrost the terrine in the refrigerator; slice and refrigerate.

The Day

UP TO 8 HOURS BEFORE

1. Finish and set out the cheese platter.

UP TO 2 HOURS BEFORE

1. Set out the jicama sticks, caponata and cucumber rounds, cherry tomatoes, Toast Points, biscuits, and crescents, covered.

UP TO 30 MINUTES BEFORE

1. Bake the phyllo kisses and heat the roll cluster. Set them out as they are ready.
2. Set out the salmon, pork, and meringue kisses.

Caponata
with Cucumber Rounds

MAKES 10 CUPS

This tasty dish makes a handy appetizer dip. I keep it in the freezer in small containers. It goes well with bagel chips, toasted pita triangles, Melba toast, or on cucumber or zucchini rounds. It can also serve as sauce for hot cooked pasta and can be spread on bread for a sandwich with cheese or turkey slices.

½ cup olive oil
1 large red onion, chopped
3 stalks celery, chopped
3 garlic cloves, peeled and chopped
2 medium regular or 3 long Italian eggplant, peeled and chopped
1 (28½-ounce) can Italian plum tomatoes, drained
1 cup chopped green olives
⅓ cup roasted red bell peppers, chopped
½ cup capers, drained
½ cup chopped fresh parsley
¼ cup chopped fresh oregano or marjoram
½ cup red wine vinegar
¼ cup tomato paste
2 tablespoons sugar
Salt
Freshly ground black pepper
Thin cucumber rounds

Heat the oil in a large skillet over medium heat. Add the onion and celery and cook until soft, 5 to 7 minutes. Add the garlic and eggplant and cook until soft, about 5 minutes more. Add the tomatoes, olives, red peppers, capers, parsley, oregano, vinegar, tomato paste, sugar, and salt and pepper to taste. Simmer about 5 minutes, stirring occasionally to break up the tomatoes. The caponata may be kept refrigerated 5 days or frozen. Turn the caponata into a serving bowl, place it on a tray, and surround with cucumber rounds.

Phyllo Crab–Goat Cheese Kisses

MAKES 40

These delectable kisses are best when assembled and baked just before serving, but they can be made a few hours in advance: Underbake them slightly and reheat briefly before serving. The major mistake novices make is using too much butter when assembling the phyllo sheets. After baking one tray, check to see if the kisses are greasy or if there is residual butter on the sheet. If so, cut back on the butter.

½ **pound flaked crab meat**
½ **pound soft, mild goat cheese**
1 **shallot, very finely chopped**
2 **tablespoons finely chopped fresh parsley**
Freshly ground black pepper
18 to 28 **sheets (one 16-ounce package) phyllo dough**
¼ **pound (1 stick) butter, at room temperature**

Preheat the oven to 350°F. Line two jelly roll pans with foil and lightly grease.

Place the crab meat, goat cheese, shallot, parsley, and pepper in a small mixing bowl. Blend well with a fork or mixer on low setting and set aside. Unwrap the phyllo dough and cover with a damp (not wet) cloth. As you work, keep this stack of phyllo covered with the damp cloth. Carefully transfer one sheet of phyllo dough onto a work surface and brush lightly with the very soft butter. Spread a second sheet of phyllo over the first. Brush lightly with butter. Repeat with a third sheet.

Cut the layered phyllo with a pizza cutter or sharp knife into 20 rectangles—4 columns by 5 rows—and place a teaspoonful of the crab meat mixture in the center of each. Bring the four corners of the phyllo up over the filling and "kiss" them together, twisting a bit like a candy kiss. Brush them lightly with additional butter. Place the kisses on a baking sheet about 1 inch apart.

Repeat with the remaining phyllo and filling to make 20 more "kisses," and continue until the filling is gone. You will have phyllo left over.

Place the baking sheets in the oven and bake about 10 minutes or until the phyllo is nicely browned. Transfer the kisses to a platter and serve.

To freeze, place in a sturdy airtight container up to 3 months. Reheat directly from the freezer in a 350°F. oven for 5 to 8 minutes.

TIP

Phyllo dough, also called filo, is easily obtained. If it tears, just fold in any torn dough. If, however, you have messed up a piece of phyllo, brush it with butter and bake it anyway—even in pieces. It will make a welcome addition to a fruit or ice cream dessert. Or dust it with salt and pepper, curry powder, or grated Parmesan and serve it as a savory munchie. I prefer to use up extra dough rather than trying to refreeze it.

Stuffed Cherry Tomatoes

There are so many uses for these bite-sized, tasty morsels. I can hardly name them all. Just keep the recipe in mind—you'll find dozens of ways to use it!

2 pints small, firm, ripe cherry tomatoes (one-bite size)
2 bunches parsley
6 ounces Monterey Jack cheese, grated or finely chopped
½ cup finely chopped cooked ham or chicken
1 tablespoon finely chopped pimiento
2 tablespoons finely chopped onion
⅔ cup mayonnaise
Fresh thyme
Freshly ground black pepper

With a very sharp knife, slice off the top quarter of each tomato and set aside. Remove the insides and seeds with a small spoon, grapefruit spoon, or melon baller and discard. Invert the shells on a wire mesh rack or paper towels to drain.

Up to a day ahead, finely chop 1½ bunches of the parsley, reserving the rest. Mix together the chopped parsley, Monterey Jack cheese, ham, pimiento, onion, mayonnaise, thyme, and pepper. Spoon this mixture into the tomato shells or use a piping bag with a large tip. The top can be set back on, a little askew, if not broken. Keep refrigerated until needed, preferably stored in a sturdy airtight container.

Garnish with the remaining parsley sprigs.

NOTE

You may have extra, unfilled tomatoes—it's hard to predict nature's gifts.

Chili Jicama Sticks with Lime

SERVES 12 TO 14 AS AN APPETIZER

Jicama is a fresh-tasting, crunchy vegetable that looks like a giant potato. Peeled, it is marvelously refreshing and munchy. The jicama sticks can be refrigerated without the lime juice up to two days in advance.

I've known people to use straight cayenne pepper for this recipe instead of the chili powder, but that's too hot for me!

1 **large jicama (about 2 pounds)**
½ **cup lime juice**
  Grated peel (no white attached) from 2 limes
  Salt
1 to 2 **tablespoons chili powder**
1 to 2 **tablespoons finely chopped cilantro**

Peel the jicama and cut into 3x½-inch-long sticks. Place in a plastic bag, add the lime juice, and briefly soak the pieces (5 minutes to several hours) to moisten. Put the jicama on a tray and sprinkle with the grated peel, salt, chili powder, and cilantro. You may use any remaining lime juice as a dip for these refreshing sticks.

Elegant Cheese Platter Garnished with Sugared Grapes

SERVES 8 TO 10 AS AN APPETIZER

Brie makes a particularly elegant presentation, but certainly other kinds of cheese could be used—or several different types—but keep in mind that their flavors must be compatible, and that working with one cheese is easier than working with several. You may buy rounds of Brie up to a kilo, in which case you would need to double or triple the grapes and sugar. If serving Brie on silver, take care as the cheese knife may scar the silver. Marble, wood, and other natural materials enhance the appearance of cheese.

Gingersnaps vary widely in quality. I use Moravian cookies when I'm feeling flush, or the best kind of gingersnaps I can find.

1 (8-ounce) wheel of
   Brie
1 large bunch seedless
   green grapes
Nonstick spray or
   vegetable oil
¼ cup confectioners'
   sugar
Thin gingersnaps or
   crackers

Place the cheese on a large round serving platter. Cut a small wedge out of the cheese and turn it on its side on top of the round.

Leave the washed grapes attached to the stems. Put them on a rack in a jelly roll pan. Spray the grapes lightly with nonstick spray or vegetable oil. Put the sugar in a fine sieve and shake it over the grapes until they are lightly covered. Drape the grapes on top of the cheese allowing them to cascade off the edge. Surround the cheese with gingersnaps. The dish can sit at room temperature up to, but not more than, 8 hours, depending on the ripeness of the cheese.

SHOPPING TIP

Brie should be fully ripe but should not have the ammonialike smell that indicates overripeness. At room temperature, it should feel soft to the touch, especially in the middle. To speed up the ripening process, leave it at room temperature overnight or until it feels very soft in the middle.

Frosted Salmon Platter

SERVES 20 TO 30 AS AN APPETIZER,
4 TO 6 AS A MAIN COURSE

Here is a real showstopper for looks and, more important, for taste. The salmon is perfect as the focal point of a cocktail buffet table or as the main course for an important summer dinner party. You will need to have space cleared in your refrigerator for the fish pan as it cools and for the decorated fish the day of its decoration and use. Some people poach the salmon in a combination of white wine and water, but I prefer using court bouillon.

It is unfortunate that a long recipe looks intimidating. This takes very little "people time" and is remarkably easy. The finished dish just looks as though it took a lot of time. Only you will know. Peggy's Secret Sauce may be made in advance or while the fish is cooking.

3 pounds boneless, skinless salmon fillet
3 cups Court Bouillon (page 260)
1 tablespoon gelatin
¼ cup cold water
1½ to 2 cups Peggy's Secret Sauce (page 255)
Several sprigs of chives
1 ripe tomato
2 tablespoons butter, at room temperature
1 large hard-cooked egg yolk
Dill sprigs
Toast Points (page 177) or crackers

Preheat the oven to 300°F.

Up to 2 days before you plan to serve it, place the fish in an ovenproof glass or enamel lined pan large enough to hold it with an inch or so surrounding it, and deeper than the fish. If the fish is too long for the pan, fold the tail under. Pour in enough court bouillon to cover the fish. (You can add water or bouillon if you need more liquid.) Cover the pan tightly with aluminum foil, place in the preheated oven, and poach until the fish is barely cooked, about 20 minutes or until an instant-read thermometer inserted at the top of the fish next to the bone reads 140°F.

Remove the pan from the oven and allow to cool 30 minutes in the pan and its liquid. Refrigerate until completely cold, 4 to 5 hours. This will make the fish easier to move as well as giving it a chance to take on the flavor of the poaching liquid.

At least 6 hours before serving, make the "icing," using Peggy's Secret Sauce. Start by placing the gelatin in a small pan or metal measuring cup, add the cold water, and wait a few minutes until it is absorbed and spongy. Place over low heat and melt the gelatin. Let cool slightly and whisk into Peggy's Secret Sauce. Allow to sit in the refrigerator for up to several hours, until it is cold and spreadable but not set. (If it sets, gently stir it over very low heat until spreadable.) If you are in a hurry, set the bowl over a lot of ice and water and keep stirring until cold, up to 30 minutes.

Drain the fish and move it onto a strip of foil if you do not have a large enough spatula to move the fish later. Cover it completely with the "frosting" mixture. Reserve some of the mixture for touching up later.

Meanwhile, drop the chives into boiling water for just 3 seconds and then dip in ice water to bring out the color. Make a design on the top of the fish using the chives to represent flower-stems. Take a sharp paring knife and cut two tulip-shaped flowers from the tomato. Place them on the top of two of the chive stems. Mash the softened butter and the egg yolk together and place them in a small pastry bag with a #4 open star pastry tube. Make a flower on one of the chive stems. Using the foil or a large spatula, move the entire fish to the serving platter and surround it with dill or another garnish of your choosing. If it comes apart, push it together and touch up with the reserved icing mixture. Refrigerate until serving. Serve with the Toast Points.

Mère Titine's Chicken Liver and Pork Terrine

This requires the simplest of ingredients, all of which could come from the pantry, refrigerator, or freezer. It is one of the most delicious pâtés I've tasted. My son-in-law's adored great-grandmother was called Titine. She was born in 1866 in Poitou, in the west center of France and married a schoolteacher when she was sixteen years old. She was fond of cooking and made her famous terrine often. Her secret recipe, passed to the family as an inheritance, will keep up to a week in the refrigerator and can be frozen for several months. Caul fat is very hard to find, so bacon is given as a first choice, although caul fat is preferred. It is important to have equal amounts of chicken livers and pork.

1 **pound chicken livers**
1 **teaspoon salt**
1 **teaspoon freshly ground black pepper**
1 **teaspoon dry or fresh thyme**
   Pinch of mace or nutmeg
½ **cup Cognac or Armagnac**
1 **pound pork loin or back scraps, in pieces**
2 **shallots (or 3 if small)**
2 **large eggs**
8 **ounces bacon, thinly sliced, or 10 ounces caul fat**
1 **bay leaf**

French Bread (page 44)
Toast Points (page 177)

Preheat the oven to 350°F.

Wash the chicken livers in cold water, pat them dry, and refrigerate in a plastic bag or large bowl with the salt, pepper, thyme, mace, and cognac for 3 to 4 hours.

In a food processor, process the livers, soaking liquid, pork, shallots, and eggs. Form 1 tablespoon of the mixture into a small patty, cook it in the microwave or a small skillet, and taste for seasoning. It needs to be highly seasoned since it will be served cold, so add more seasoning to the mixture if necessary.

Wash the bacon or caul fat in cold water and dry it. Line a 3x11-inch terrine (see Note) with foil and then with the fat, allowing the ends to hang over the sides of the terrine. Caul is very thin and fragile. If it breaks, patch with another piece. Pack the pâté mixture into the prepared terrine, top with the bay leaf, and fold the fat over the top. Cover tightly with a lid or foil. Place the terrine in a larger pan and pour hot water to reach halfway up the sides. Place in the oven and cook 2½ hours.

Pour off the excess fat. Cover the pâté with a double layer of foil and a board. Top with 1 or 2 cans to weigh it down. Let the terrine cool, then chill 3 to 4 hours or overnight. Remove the weights, board, and foil. Serve from the terrine or remove and serve sliced on bread or Toast Points. Keep in the refrigerator up to a week or freeze.

NOTE

If you do not have a terrine, you can use a 3½x8½-inch loaf pan.

Marinated Roasted Pork with Chutney Butter

MAKES 40 THIN SLICES
FOR ROLLS OR BISCUITS

Pork is a marvelously adaptive meat. I've done this recipe with pork tenderloin as well as pork loin roasts. Tenderloin is prettier and easier to slice, but the loin variation is more economical, feeds more people, and is better for a family-style dinner. When I multiply this recipe for a crowd, I multiply the marinade accordingly. The chutney butter is also terrific with lamb.

¼ pound (1 stick) butter, at room temperature

1 (8-ounce) jar mango chutney, roughly chopped if the pieces are very large

2 pork tenderloins (about 1 pound each), silver skin trimmed off

⅓ cup sherry

⅓ cup vegetable oil

2 tablespoons soy sauce

20 Angel Biscuits (page 202), sliced almost through

Preheat the oven to 500°F.

Beat the butter until creamy. Fold in the chutney and set aside, refrigerated if necessary.

Put the pork in a large plastic bag or shallow dish. Whisk together the sherry, vegetable oil, and soy sauce. Pour over the meat, seal or cover, and marinate 45 minutes to 8 hours, refrigerated.

Remove the meat from the marinade and put on a rack in a pan large enough to allow the heat to circulate. Discard the marinade. Roast the meat 11 to 15 minutes, until a meat thermometer registers 160°F. Allow to cool for 10 minutes and then slice thinly. Spread a little room-temperature chutney butter on each roll and add 2 slices of pork. Pile the rolls on a serving platter. The pork may be roasted several days ahead and reheated.

VARIATIONS

Substitute a 3-pound boneless trimmed pork loin for the tenderloins and roast it for 45 to 60 minutes.

❧

The marinade may be enhanced by the addition of a small amount of toasted sesame oil, chopped ginger, chopped garlic, ground coriander, or five-spice powder to your taste. You can, of course, omit the sherry if you wish.

Angel Biscuits

Traditional biscuits are so intimidating to novices in part because most recipes require you to make them at the last minute. I wanted to come up with something anyone can do, and this is it. The yeast makes the day! The dough is easy to work with, and both dough and baked biscuit can be made ahead.

1 package active dry yeast
¼ cup sugar
3 tablespoons warm water (105°F. to 115°F.)
1 teaspoon baking soda
1 tablespoon baking powder
1 teaspoon salt
7 cups all-purpose or cake flour
1 cup vegetable shortening
2 cups buttermilk

Dissolve the yeast and a pinch of the sugar in the warm water. Into a large bowl, sift the baking soda, baking powder, salt, and the remainder of the sugar, with 6 cups of the flour. Cut the shortening into the dry ingredients with two forks, a pastry cutter, or your fingers until the size of garden peas. Add the yeast mixture to the buttermilk and stir into the flour mixture until all the flour is barely moistened to make a sticky dough. Cover with plastic wrap and refrigerate overnight or up to a week before using.

When ready to cook, preheat the oven to 425°F.

Place about 1 cup additional flour on the work surface. Place the sticky dough on top of the flour and sprinkle with more flour. Pat out into a round ⅓ inch thick and then fold over to a height of ⅔ inch. Using a 2½-inch biscuit cutter, cut out the biscuits. If you desire a 1½-inch round, make the dough thinner—a total of ½ inch. Place the biscuits, their sides touching, on the baking sheet. Bake 10 to 12 minutes, until lightly tinged with brown.

The biscuits can be kept frozen for up to 3 months.

SHOPPING TIP

All-purpose flour

Even all-purpose flours vary considerably, according to the brands and the geographic location. Soft wheat flour, sold primarily in the South, and cake flour are much better for biscuits and pie crusts. Hard wheat flours, sold primarily in the North and Midwest, are better for breads. There can be a variation of a half cup per pound of flour according to the type of flour.

Rosemary Roll "Grape Cluster"

SERVES 28

Not only are the rolls delicious, the grape cluster shape is a great conversation piece as well. Taking a roll is like plucking a grape from the vine.

Do not be intimidated by this recipe. It is easy to make and can be done ahead and frozen. If it breaks apart from handling, push it together on the serving dish and it will look fine. It's nice to garnish it with a large sprig of rosemary.

1 recipe Rosemary Buffet Sandwich Rolls (page 181) dough and glaze ingredients

Glaze
⅓ cup milk
1 tablespoon sugar

Preheat the oven to 350°F. Lightly grease a large baking sheet.

When the dough has finished its second rise, punch it down and knead briefly. Pinch off a piece of dough and roll it into a ball about 1½ inches in diameter. Repeat this process until you have 6 balls prepared. Place them in a straight line across the middle third of the baking sheet (you are leaving room at the top of the pan for the stem and leaves). Make 5 more balls and place them below the 6 balls on the baking sheet. They should be touching. Repeat the process, making 4 more balls, then 3 and then 2, then 1. Make one more and place at slight angle to the last one. Then make a stem by forming a small piece of dough into a thin cylinder. Attach it to the top of the grape bunch by tucking one end under the top row of 6 balls. Press gently to attach. Pinch off 3 more pieces of dough, flatten them, and cut into 3 leaves. Attach these to the stem, again by pushing gently.

Form the remaining dough into balls and place them randomly on the first layer, filling in where there are gaps and where the rows come together. Place balls of dough randomly on top of second layer to make a third layer.

When you have used all the dough, cover loosely with plastic wrap and let rise until doubled, about 45 minutes.

Mix the milk and sugar together, and brush the milk glaze over the doubled dough. Bake until an instant-read thermometer reads 200°F., about 30 to 40 minutes.

Let cool completely on a wire rack.

If you are going to freeze the cluster, place it on a cookie sheet or on a large piece of cardboard in the freezer until frozen. Once frozen, place the bread in a large freezer bag, squeeze out all the air, and seal. If using cardboard, you may place the bread on the cardboard in a freezer bag and leave until time to defrost.

To reheat, remove from the cardboard and place on a cookie sheet. Cover with foil and heat at 300°F. until warm.

Italian Meringue Kisses

Meringues are enormously adaptable, whether served alone or with berries and cream or chestnut purée. They are well worth mastering. Choose a dry day to work on them, because humidity fights against you. These can be made into kisses of all sizes, into rounds, or into baskets and cooked according to size. They are supposed to be white, but pale brown is acceptable.

1 **cup sugar**
½ **cup water**
4 **large egg whites**
½ **teaspoon vanilla**
    extract

TIPS

In working with sugar syrup, to stir or not to stir is not as important as making sure no granules of sugar enter the boiling mixture. To prevent this, use a clean wooden spoon each time you stir. The sides of the pan are brushed down with water to dissolve sugar granules so that when the syrup boils, it will not grab up any crystals from the side and crystallize. Stirring after boiling should not be necessary, as the sugar should already be dissolved.

Preheat the oven to 200°F. Line a 10x15-inch cookie sheet with baking parchment paper or use a nonstick baking sheet.

Put the sugar and water in a heavy 2-quart saucepan and cook over low heat, washing down the sides of the pan with a pastry brush dipped in additional water, until the sugar is dissolved. Bring to the boil and cook until the liquid reaches the hard-ball stage (248°F. on a candy thermometer), approximately 25 minutes.

When the syrup is a few minutes away from completion, put the egg whites in the bowl of an electric mixer. Beat slowly at first and increase the speed as the whites start to thicken. When the whites are in soft peaks—that is, stiff enough to cling to the bowl when tipped—and the syrup is at the hard-ball stage, turn the mixer to low and slowly beat in the hot syrup. Continue to beat until completely cool. Add the vanilla and beat well.

Fit a #16 piping bag with a large star or plain tip. (You can also use a sealable plastic bag for the piping bag: Cut out one corner, insert the tip, and continue as if it were a regular piping bag.) Fill the bag only half full with the egg white mixture or it will spill out. Twist the top to "close" the bag. Push from the top only or the whipped egg will dissolve.

Pipe shapes onto the prepared pan ¼ inch apart. For kisses, put the tip nearly on the pan, squeeze out the desired-size mound, lift the bag straight up, and squeeze again, then pull up quickly. For a basket, pipe a large round and then coils around the sides two or three times. For a filigree, put a paper doily under a piece of parchment and follow the filigree design of the doily.

Bake 15 minutes in the middle of the oven and then reduce the temperature to 200°F. and bake until dry but not brown—about 50 minutes, depending on thickness. For thick shapes, turn one over and check to see if it is dry on the bottom, or break it open to check. Store in a tightly sealed container for up to a week or in a sturdy freezer container for up to 3 months.

Summer Hors d'Oeuvres Menu

Chicken Saté
with Spicy Peanut Sauce

or

Lemony Cilantro Chicken
Drumettes

Cheddar-Date Black-eyed Susans

Tomato Bruschetta

Scallop and Shrimp Seviche

Spicy Phyllo Envelopes

Broccoli or Spinach Tart

Toasted Cheese Cutouts

Basket of Crudités

Yogurt-Coriander Sauce

Florentine Fruit Triangle Cookies

Cooking Time Line

Summer Hors d'Oeuvres: Remember, each day, check your preparations list for things like cleaning, cleaning grill, shopping, setting the table, drop-dead time, and so on. If you elect to use a store-bought item (or more than one), make sure it's on your shopping list (and obviously, then, you don't need to make it).

UP TO 3 MONTHS BEFORE

1. Make the chicken drumettes, phyllo envelopes, black-eyed Susans, tart, and fruit triangles; freeze.

UP TO 3 DAYS BEFORE

1. Prepare the vegetables for the crudités; refrigerate.

UP TO 2 DAYS BEFORE

1. Make the Spicy Peanut Sauce.

36 HOURS BEFORE

1. Move the chicken drumettes from the freezer to the refrigerator to thaw.

UP TO 1 DAY BEFORE

1. Remove the black-eyed Susans, tart, and fruit triangles from the freezer.
2. Chop the tomato and slice the bread for the bruschetta; wrap well.
3. Make the Scallop and Shrimp Seviche and the sauce for crudités; refrigerate.
4. Marinate the chicken and grill; refrigerate.

The Day

UP TO 3 HOURS BEFORE

1. Set out the crudités and sauce.

UP TO 2 HOURS BEFORE

1. Toast the bread for the bruschetta and spread with the garlic; set out with the tomato.

UP TO 1 HOUR BEFORE

1. Set out the seviche.

30 MINUTES BEFORE

1. Heat the chicken drumettes, black-eyed Susans, and saté.
2. Bake the phyllo envelopes; set out when done.

Chicken Saté

Virginia Willis developed this recipe for saté, which is pronounced "satay." With her penchant for green vegetables, she added the scallions as a bonus to the dish. They, too, can be dipped in the sauce.

Skewered chicken tenders make great finger food. Consider combining the saté with another appetizer or two for a tapas-style dinner.

6-inch bamboo skewers

2 pounds chicken tenders or 4 boneless, skinless breasts

1 garlic clove, finely chopped

1 tablespoon toasted sesame oil

1 tablespoon rice wine vinegar

1 teaspoon salt
Freshly ground black pepper

8 to 10 scallions, white and pale-green parts only
Spicy Peanut Sauce (below)

Soak the skewers in water while you work.

Preheat the broiler or heat a grill. If broiling, grease a large cookie sheet with nonstick spray or cover it with foil.

If tenders are not available, slice the chicken breasts across the grain into ½-inch-wide strips.

In a large bowl, mix the garlic, sesame oil, vinegar, salt, and pepper. Add the chicken and scallions and toss to cover. Let marinate 30 minutes to 1 hour.

Thread the meat onto the bamboo skewers. Place on the prepared cookie sheet. Remove the scallions from the marinade and place on the cookie sheet with the skewers. Broil or grill 4 to 5 inches away from the heat source for 5 to 8 minutes, turning once. Serve with the Spicy Peanut Sauce.

SPICY PEANUT SAUCE

SERVES 6 TO 8

2 tablespoons finely chopped fresh ginger
2 garlic cloves, peeled and chopped
⅓ cup red wine vinegar
⅓ cup creamy peanut butter
2 teaspoons hot red pepper flakes
⅓ cup soy sauce

In a blender or food processor, combine the ginger, garlic, vinegar, peanut butter, red pepper flakes, and soy sauce. Process until well blended and chill. The sauce can be made and refrigerated up to 2 days in advance.

VARIATION

Substitute 4 boneless pork loin or lamb chops for the chicken. Slice the meat in strips, as with the chicken breasts.

Lemony Cilantro Chicken Drumettes

SERVES 20

Drumettes, the top joint of the wing, are like miniature drumsticks. They may be purchased pre-cut, or the whole wing may be separated at the joints. Pre-cut ones may be smaller than the ones you would cut yourself. I use the wing tips for family snacks or in stock. The second (middle) portion has 2 bones. It is tasty, but I don't use it if people are eating off napkins, because it is more difficult to handle. I do use it for family.

Drumettes require an abundance of paper napkins next to the place they are set out, as they are the ultimate finger-licking food. Saffron adds wonderful flavor, but if you are watching pennies or using saffron in another item in the menu, use turmeric instead, because this recipe can be expensive. Cilantro is also called Chinese parsley or fresh coriander and is very strong in flavor. For subtlety, use the lesser amount. If you love it, as I do, go the whole route!

8 **pounds chicken drumettes**
1 **teaspoon saffron threads or turmeric**
¼ **cup lemon juice**
¼ **cup boiling water**
¼ **cup grated fresh ginger**
1 **cup water**
3 **tablespoons vegetable oil**
10 **garlic cloves, finely chopped**
2 **to 6 cups (2 to 6 bunches) very finely chopped cilantro**

Preheat the oven to 500°F. Line two 9x13-inch baking and freezing pans with aluminum foil.

Cut wings into drumettes if necessary (see box) and arrange on the foil, trying not to overlap. Lay the wing on a clean surface, skin side down, and sever at each of the joints with a knife. In addition to the drumettes, you may use the portion with two bones as well, although its meat is not as accessible, or you may save them for another time. Save the tips for stock.

Place baking pans on the top rack of the oven until brown, about 5 minutes. Turn the drumettes over and return to the oven to brown, another 3 minutes. When both sides have browned, transfer the drumettes to paper towels and set aside, saving the pans.

Stir the saffron and lemon juice into the boiling water. Combine this mixture with the ginger and 1 cup water in a blender or food processor and purée to a smooth consistency.

In a heavy 10-inch skillet, heat the oil over medium-high heat. Add the garlic and cook until softened, about 2 minutes. Turn down the heat and stir in the cilantro, green chile, cumin, coriander, and salt. Add the saffron mixture to the pan and stir to mix. Turn up the heat, bring to the boil, and reduce the liquid until the sauce is thick, like salsa.

To serve now, arrange the drumettes on a serving platter and top with the warm sauce.

1 or 2 fresh, hot green chile peppers, very finely chopped
4 teaspoons ground cumin
2 teaspoons ground coriander seeds
1 to 2 teaspoons salt, or to taste

Garnish (optional)
Cilantro sprigs
Lemon wedges

To make ahead, reline the two 9x13-inch baking/freezing pans with clean heavy-duty freezer aluminum foil. Arrange the drumettes in the pans and pour the sauce over the wings. Let cool. Wrap with heavy foil and label. Freeze flat in the pan rather than bunched in a plastic container. Remove the pan when frozen. If you are short of freezer space, use plastic freezer bags for storage.

Defrost the drumettes 36 hours in the refrigerator or remove from the foil and defrost in the microwave.

Thirty minutes before serving, preheat the broiler to 500°F. Drain the sauce into a microwave-safe container or saucepan. Bring to the boil, reduce the heat, and keep warm.

Run the drumettes on the foil under the broiler, being careful not to burn them, until crisped, about 5 minutes. Turn them over and crisp them on the other side. Arrange the drumettes on a serving platter, top with the reheated sauce, and garnish with sprigs of cilantro or lemon wedges, if desired.

TIPS

Do not peel ginger unless the skin is very thick and tough if you chop it in the food processor.

One bunch cilantro from my grocery store, removed from stems, is about 1 cup chopped.

To chop large quantities of herbs, wash them, dry thoroughly on paper towels, spread out to air dry half an hour, and chop, being careful not to over chop, by hand or in the food processor. The rule is if you can tell what it is, it's not chopped finely enough!

Cheddar-Date Black-eyed Susans

MAKES 120 TO 125

The dough for these savory treats is a traditional cheese straw dough. The dates and almonds update it with a great new look. This recipe came from a friend whom I met in my restaurant in Social Circle many years ago.

2 cups grated sharp
  cheddar cheese
½ pound (2 sticks)
  unsalted butter
2 cups all-purpose flour
¼ cup grated imported
  Parmesan cheese
½ teaspoon salt
¼ teaspoon cayenne
  pepper
2 boxes pitted dates
  (120 to 125)
1 cup slivered blanched
  almonds
  Freshly ground black
  pepper (optional)

Preheat the oven to 350°F.

In a food processor or mixer, blend the cheddar cheese and butter until combined. Blend in the flour, 1 cup at a time. Add the Parmesan, salt, and cayenne and blend well. Form the mixture into 2 oval logs, 1 inch in diameter, and refrigerate for at least 1 hour, until firm.

Meanwhile, halve each date and stuff with slivered almonds; set aside. Cut the logs into ¼-inch slices. Shape each slice of dough into a boat shape. Wrap around the bottom and up to the cut edges of each almond-stuffed date.

Place on a baking sheet and sprinkle with black pepper, if desired. Bake until golden, about 15 to 20 minutes. Remove and let cool slightly on a wire rack. Serve warm.

You can bake these ahead and store them for up to 3 months in the freezer. Reheat in a 350°F. oven until heated through, approximately 5 minutes.

Tomato Bruschetta

SERVES 4 TO 6

Author Faith Willinger, who lives in Italy, taught me to rub unpeeled garlic on rough toasted bread. The rough bread peels and grates what it needs. Get the best olive oil you can afford, and only use fresh ripe tomatoes, using 2 plum tomatoes or 1 large ripe tomato. If you have neither, make something else.

4 to 6 thick (¾-inch) slices long Italian bread
1 garlic clove
1 ripe tomato or 2 plum tomatoes, peeled and chopped
⅓ cup extra-virgin olive oil
6 leaves fresh basil, chopped (optional)
Salt
Freshly ground black pepper

Place the bread under the broiler, on the gas flame, or in a very good toaster oven with a bagel setting until it has flecks of gold and brown on both sides. Rub the unpeeled garlic clove on the toast. Top the bread with the chopped tomato and place on a serving plate. Sprinkle with the olive oil and season to taste with basil, if desired, salt, and pepper.

Scallop and Shrimp Seviche

SERVES 8 AS AN APPETIZER

Seviche has many names, including escaveche *and* caveach. *It's very popular in the South, especially in Florida, and in Mexico and South America. Traditionally it is made with raw fish, with the acid from the lime juice seemingly cooking it and the peppers preserving it. Because of modern parasites, I am reluctant to use finfish and shrimp uncooked. If desired, the scallops may be poached quickly after being sliced, about 30 seconds. I also do not leave seviche sitting for weeks on my counter in a jar, as I first saw it, but keep it refrigerated. Though traditional, cilantro and epazote are so strong that I prefer the basil.*

1 **pound sea scallops, rinsed**
1 **pound medium shrimp, cooked, peeled and deveined**
½ **cup fresh lime juice (4 to 5 limes)**
3 **tablespoons chopped fresh basil, cilantro, or epazote**
2 to 3 **garlic cloves, finely chopped**
1 **medium red onion, finely chopped**
⅓ **cup finely chopped red bell pepper**
½ **cup olive oil**
   Salt
   Freshly ground black pepper
1 to 2 **small hot chile peppers**

Slice the scallops horizontally into ¼-inch-thick discs. Combine the scallops, shrimp, lime juice, basil, garlic, onion, and bell pepper and half the olive oil. Season to taste with salt and pepper and add more olive oil if desired. Add some or all of the hot peppers. Cover and marinate in the refrigerator at least 6 hours or overnight. Serve in a pretty glass bowl with toothpicks or spoon onto individual chilled plates.

VARIATIONS

Add 2 avocados, peeled and sliced.

❧

For a Thai-inspired seviche, slice limes and lemons and stagger in the glass bowl to make prettier. Add a few kafir lime leaves, if desired. Add a little very fresh chopped lemongrass.

SHOPPING TIP

I'd buy already cooked and peeled shrimp from the supermarket for this recipe. There is no need to make extra work when you're hosting a party of this size.

Spicy Phyllo Envelopes

MAKES 60

Whether you prefer ground lamb or ground beef chuck, this is a very tasty bite. These hors d'oeuvres make a very nice pre-theater snack, as well as a good accompaniment for soup or salads. Because the task can be tedious, try making envelopes with a friend and splitting the results for your freezers. Frequently two people make this better than one. First time around, it may take you well over an hour to make the triangles, but the second time will be considerably faster.

1 tablespoon olive oil
1 large onion, chopped
2 large garlic cloves, finely chopped
1 pound boneless lamb shoulder or beef chuck, coarsely ground
½ teaspoon cayenne pepper
1½ teaspoons dried ground coriander
1 teaspoon curry powder
Finely grated peel (no white attached) of 2 lemons
Juice of 1 lemon
1 tablespoon sesame seeds
Salt
Freshly ground black pepper
18 to 28 sheets (one 16-ounce package) phyllo
½ pound (2 sticks) butter, at room temperature

Preheat the oven to 350°F.

In a large, heavy saucepan, heat the oil, add the onions, and cook until soft, about 6 minutes. Add the garlic and cook another 2 minutes. Add the ground meat and sauté until light brown, stirring occasionally to break up the clumps, about 5 minutes. Add the cayenne, coriander, curry powder, lemon peel, lemon juice, and sesame seeds. Taste and add salt, pepper, and other seasonings as needed.

Defrost the phyllo sheets if frozen and unroll. Cover the stack with a slightly damp (not wet) tea towel and keep it covered while you work. The sheets dry out very easily. Move the top sheet of phyllo to a work surface. Brush the sheet very lightly with the very soft butter. (The most common mistake when assembling phyllo pastries is using too much butter.) Place a second sheet of phyllo on top of the first and brush it with butter. Cut each double sheet lengthwise into 6 strips. Put 1 teaspoon of filling at the top (or bottom) of each strip. Fold each dough strip down (or up) like a flag, making triangles. Brush again with butter. Transfer to a baking sheet with sides to prevent the butter from dripping.

These may be kept, frozen, for up to 3 months in a sturdy freezer container. Place frozen on a baking sheet and bake until golden brown, 20 to 25 minutes, or bake them before freezing and reheat directly from the freezer for 5 to 8 minutes until hot.

VARIATION

Cooked and chopped spinach may be used in place of a portion of the meat.

Broccoli or Spinach Tart

SERVES 6 TO 8

With the cream cheese and blue cheese as deliciously rich thickeners, this cheese tart is particularly suited for an hors d'oeuvre or appetizer. If you are in the mood to experiment, use other green vegetables—such as broccoli rabe or cooked turnip greens. A tart pan with a removable bottom is a good addition to the kitchen because it makes for a much prettier presentation than a pie pan or plate. If you are using a pan without a removable bottom, slice and serve the tart in thin wedges. I frequently double the recipe, make two tarts, and freeze one for later.

4 ounces blue cheese
8 ounces cream cheese, at room temperature
3 tablespoons butter, at room temperature
2 tablespoons heavy cream
2 large eggs
Salt
Cayenne pepper
2 teaspoons snipped fresh chives
½ cup broccoli florets, lightly steamed and well drained, or 5 ounces frozen chopped spinach, thawed and drained
1 (9-inch) prebaked pastry shell (page 279) in a round tart pan with a removable bottom

Preheat the oven to 375°F.

In the bowl of a food processor or electric mixer, blend the blue cheese, cream cheese, butter, and cream. Add the eggs, salt, and cayenne to taste and process or mix. Sprinkle the chives over the mixture and pulse the machine twice or stir in well. Scrape the custard into the prebaked pastry shell and sprinkle the broccoli or spinach evenly over the pie.

Bake until the tart is puffed and the pastry golden brown, about 25 minutes. Cover the edge of the pie with foil if it gets too dark. Let cool on a wire rack.

For hors d'oeuvres, remove from the pan and cut a circle 3 inches in diameter in the center using a biscuit cutter. Cut the outer "doughnut" and the inner circle into bite-sized pieces.

The tart can be kept, refrigerated, for several days, or frozen for up to 3 months, tightly wrapped and in a sturdy container.

Toasted Cheese Cutouts

MAKES 100 APPETIZERS

I use my favorite flower-shaped cookie cutter, which is quite festive and just the right size to cut 4 cutouts from 1 slice of bread. Choose any other simple shape that appeals. If you do not have a cutter, trim the crusts from the bread slices and cut each slice into 4 squares or 4 triangles of the same size.

Uncooked, but ready to broil, these cutouts are a wonderful item to keep in your freezer for when unexpected guests come for afternoon tea or for drinks.

4 slices bacon
2 cups shredded Gruyère or other Swiss cheese
2 whole scallions, chopped
½ cup mayonnaise
25 slices thin-sliced sandwich bread
3 tablespoons butter, at room temperature

Preheat the broiler.

In a heavy skillet or the microwave, cook the bacon until brown and crisp. Drain, cool, then crumble into small pieces. Place the bacon, cheese, scallions, and mayonnaise into a blender or food processor and process until mixed but not puréed. Set aside.

Cut the bread into shapes using a 1½- to 2-inch cookie cutter. Place the bread cutouts on baking sheets under the broiler. Toast each of the bread cutouts on 1 side until lightly browned.

Turn the cutouts over and thinly spread butter on the untoasted side. Top with 1 teaspoon of the cheese mixture, and return to the baking sheets.

To complete, place about 4 inches from the heat and broil until golden, approximately 2 to 4 minutes. Watch carefully so they don't burn. Serve warm.

To make ahead, place the baking sheets with the cutouts into the freezer. When the cutouts are frozen, remove them from the baking sheets and place them in plastic freezer bags or containers. Carefully sealed, the cutouts may be kept in the freezer for up to 6 weeks.

When ready to serve, remove the cutouts from the freezer, place on baking sheets, and broil while frozen. Serve as directed above.

Basket of Crudités

SERVES 25 TO 30

"Crudités" is the French word used to describe raw vegetables. They've become ubiquitous, but I remember the first time I saw crudités: It was at the restaurant La Colombe d'Or in the South of France. Our table was outside, overlooking a stunning valley. Famous actresses and actors like Anouk Aimée and Jean-Paul Belmondo were milling around, and incredible art hung on the walls. As soon as we were seated, out came a basket of crudités. I was hooked forever.

The vegetables have been marinated in a sauce that has no oil, resulting in a subtle flavor that makes them particularly tasty accompaniments for stronger foods, but you could certainly add a dipping sauce if you want to. These may be made a day or two ahead and kept refrigerated.

3 pounds asparagus
1 head cauliflower
2 red bell peppers, about ¾ pound
2 yellow bell peppers, about ¾ pound
8 cups fresh or canned vegetable broth
Juice of 2 lemons
1 pound baby carrots, trimmed
1 Savoy cabbage
2 teaspoons salt
Freshly ground white pepper
Hot sauce to taste (optional)

Cut the woody stems off the asparagus and place the asparagus in a pan of rapidly boiling vegetable broth or salted water for 2 minutes. Remove from the hot water and rinse with cold water to refresh (to stop the cooking and set the color). Remove and dry on paper towels.

Cut the cauliflower into bite-sized florets. If tender, leave as is. If not, place them in a large pot of rapidly boiling vegetable broth or salted water until tender, about 4 minutes. Remove from the pot and put in iced water to stop the cooking. Remove and dry.

Cut the peppers in half, remove the seeds and ribs, and cut into wedges. In a large bowl, mix the vegetable broth and lemon juice. Add all of the vegetables, except for the cabbage to the broth mixture. Cover and refrigerate 2 hours or up to 3 days.

Up to 3 hours before serving, line a basket with savory cabbage leaves. Drain the vegetables and place on the cabbage leaves. Sprinkle with salt, white pepper, and hot sauce if desired.

TIP

Scrape any brown spots on cauliflower with a fork instead of cutting them out to preserve more of the cauliflower. Use a paring knife to separate the florets from core, breaking apart along natural divisions. Trim any stems that are too large.

Yogurt-Coriander Sauce

MAKES 1½ CUPS

This cool yogurt sauce goes well with grilled salmon, chicken, lamb, and grilled or raw vegetables.

1 cup plain yogurt
3 tablespoons sour cream
3 tablespoons lemon juice
2 to 3 tablespoons chopped green onion tops or chives
2 garlic cloves, chopped
1½ tablespoons ground coriander seeds
Pinch of sugar
Salt
Freshly ground black pepper
¼ cup chopped cilantro

In a small bowl, whisk together the yogurt, sour cream, lemon juice, green onion tops, garlic, and coriander until well blended. Season to taste with the sugar, salt, and pepper. Pour into a serving bowl and garnish with the chopped cilantro.

Florentine Fruit Triangle Cookies

These butter-laden fruit cookies are pretty to look at and delicious to eat. They freeze well, so I would advise making extra and keeping them on hand for that unexpected guest. There are some who prefer them without the chocolate, so sometimes I omit the chocolate or drizzle it over half the pan.

Crust
1½ cups all-purpose flour
 ½ cup confectioners' sugar
 ¼ pound (1 stick) unsalted butter, cut into pieces
 2 teaspoons vanilla extract
 2 tablespoons heavy cream

Topping
1½ sticks butter
 ½ cup sugar
 ¼ cup heavy cream
 ½ cup chopped red candied cherries
 ½ cup chopped candied pineapple
 ½ cup sliced blanched almonds
 2 tablespoons grated orange peel (no white attached)
 ½ cup semisweet chocolate pieces, melted

Preheat the oven to 375°F. Line a 15x10-inch jelly roll pan with foil.

In the bowl of a food processor fitted with a steel blade or in an electric mixer, combine the flour and confectioners' sugar and the ¼ pound butter. Process or beat until well blended. Through the feed tube, with the motor running, add the vanilla and cream and process until the dough begins to form a ball. Press the dough evenly into the foil lined pan and refrigerate for at least 30 minutes.

In a medium saucepan, combine the 1½ sticks butter, the sugar, and the cream. Bring the mixture to a boil over medium heat, stirring often. Boil 1 to 2 minutes and then add the cherries, pineapple, almonds, and orange peel. Spread the mixture evenly over the chilled crust. Bake until golden, 15 to 20 minutes. Allow to cool in the pan. While still slightly warm, drizzle with the melted chocolate. When cool, cut into 5 lengthwise strips, and then cut each strip into about 13 triangles. These cookies should be stored in the refrigerator or frozen in a sturdy container with the layers separated with wax paper.

TIP

Use a fork to drizzle the chocolate over the cookies.

Thanksgiving

Much as I now love Thanksgiving, it was not always my favorite holiday. In fact, I still remember my mother serving a turkey that was not completely cooked one Thanksgiving when I was in high school. I had invited a boy home for the holiday, and I was mortified. The first time I cooked a Thanksgiving meal was not much better. I was cramming food into the refrigerator, trying to find space for the turkey, frustrated and harried. Since then, blessedly, I've come up with a number of tricks that make the day a joyous pleasure. I share them with you, in hopes you will use some of them.

Planning starts sometime in the summer, when I buy some turkey wings and make the stock for the turkey, simmering it down so I have room for it in the freezer. I dedicate a shelf and a large storage container to hold the freezer bags of stock and other things I make ahead for Thanksgiving, so nothing gets lost or used. Those things might be cheese straws for nibbles, the zucchini casserole made when the zucchini are overrunning the garden, or something else I plan to serve over the Thanksgiving weekend—tarts or meringues—that I don't want to be tempted to use earlier. I label them in such a way that they won't entice freezer marauders. I have even been known to write "poison" on them in large and forbidding letters, although frankly that really doesn't deter the people who raid *my* freezer. I did some of this preparation, particularly the stock part, before I got a free-standing freezer, using the top freezer of my refrigerator. A large freezer is an enormous boon!

By August I have made a list of everything I want to serve and adjusted the recipes for the number of servings needed.

I have freely mixed Christmas and Thanksgiving items in the photographs, since I cook ahead in the early fall and use what I need, depending on how many show up for Thanksgiving and what they bring, and save the rest for Christmas.

Southern Oyster Casserole (page 269)

Two-Hour Turkey and Gravy

Grandma Stoll's Moist Dressing

Basil-Garlic Green Beans with Pine Nuts

Butter Beans and Carrots

White Acre Peas with Caramelized Onions
and Garlic (page 268)

Sweet Potato and Turnip Gratin

Brussels Sprouts with Poppy Seeds and Lemon

Creamed Spinach

Zucchini and Sausage Casserole

Ginger-Spiced Sweet Potatoes

Bob Lynn's Wild Rice Salad

Cranberry-Orange Relish (page 257)

Bonnie's Challah

Pumpkin Pie with Ginger and Almonds

Ginger-Pumpkin Cheesecake

Pumpkin Spice Roulade (page 283)

Chocolate-Walnut Pie

Ray's Sweet Potato Pie (page 281)

Star-Spangled Cranberry-Apple Pie (page 140)

Ambrosia (page 284)

As I complete the cooking for each dish, I indicate on the list where it is stored in the refrigerator or freezer, what dish it will be served in, whether it is heated on top of the stove (so I don't try to heat six things on four burners) or in the oven, and how long I think it will take to cook in an oven crammed beyond its capacity. (When the oven is jammed wall to wall, the things on the bottom will cook, and burn, from the bottom and the things on the top will cook, and burn, from the top, since the air doesn't circulate.) Many of us overtax the oven on Thanksgiving. To ease this problem, we can stagger the final cooking of some things. Some dishes have to be very hot to be good, but many can be served room temperature plus a little, so they can be heated first, then held on a warming tray while others are being heated. And a microwave is great for reheating. I note which dishes will need space when they come out of the oven—where will I put the turkey to carve? The list is also helpful in reminding me that something is still in the refrigerator—like the salad I might otherwise forget. I use ice chests to store additional things that need to be kept cold and to defrost things in overnight if the refrigerator is full, taking care to keep things cold that should stay cold. As I empty the ice chest of things defrosted overnight, I fill it with drinks to chill.

When I invite guests for Thanksgiving (usually about thirty people—longtime friends, relatives, and sometimes a stranger who had no other place to go), I ask them if there is anything special they crave or that they will miss if they don't have it. People are funny about Thanksgiving. Most of us have some special food we are used to, that we attach to the holiday. It can range from lumpy mashed potatoes to mincemeat pie. If I can make it, I promise to do so. If I can't, I ask the guest if they would like to bring it, since I won't be able to. (I especially try to accommodate those emotionally dependent on their favorites but truly unable to cook.)

I set the time for Thanksgiving at a normal midday meal time, although I have done some Thanksgiving evening dinners. There was once a reason for serving Thanksgiving dinner late in the afternoon—cooking turkeys took a long time (hence my mother's raw one). Eating at that peculiar time became tradition, as did family fusses because many people become touchy when they are hungry and can't eat at a regular time. Now that smaller turkeys are widely available, we may eat at a regular hour.

I attend church on Thanksgiving close to my home and am home by noon. We eat dinner at 1:00 P.M. or shortly thereafter. (If I think people are going to be cranky, I make an oyster casserole—peanut butter sandwiches for the kids—to nibble on.) When I issue invitations, I tell everyone we are sitting down at a specific time and that if they are late we will have started, since I do not think it is right to keep the children and the elderly waiting. (Also, I, too, get mean when I get hungry.)

The night before, or early Thanksgiving morning I cook

Try to include in your menu items that can be made ahead and frozen. Line oven-to-table serving dishes with aluminum foil. After you cook the item, chill it and freeze it in its serving dish. When frozen, lift out of the dish, wrap up in the foil, and slide the whole thing into a labeled plastic zippered freezer bag. To thaw, unwrap the foil and defrost. Place the item back into its dish. You've saved space in the freezer, freed up the dish, and made it easy to put back together. (Be sure to make a note of the dish you used so you don't count on it for another item in the menu.)

The week before the week before Thanksgiving, the refrigerator becomes critical. I buy only products that can be used up before my major shop for Thanksgiving—pastas and rice dishes, for instance—and make an effort to use up everything in the refrigerator. Before shopping day, I clean out the refrigerator—a chore I hate. Anything I am not going to use Thanksgiving weekend is evaluated. Am I ever going to use the rest of that jar of okra pickles someone gave me that I really didn't like? What about that bottle of ketchup? Any unopened good food I've had for a while goes to the Mission. Any stray vegetables, bacon, or sausage, gets a good sniff. If it smells good, it goes in a big pot of soup.

my turkey and carve it. We set up the extra tables, clean and polish the dining room table. The tablecloths, napkins, glasses, and silver are laid out on the tables and the serving platters marked with yellow stickums according to the list. (If someone wants to help me, I suggest looking at the list and matching it up with the dish. That way I don't have the turkey platter used for the green beans by someone who was trying to be helpful.)

I put everything I can into bake-and-serve dishes. (There are some lovely ones out there, from posh china manufacturers, so don't turn your nose up.) I put some things, like the mashed potatoes, into containers that can go in the microwave. I put out a warming tray, which I only use once a year, and an electric skillet, which I've borrowed, for stovetop-type heating. I may cook something like the butter beans that I will later re-rewarm.

On Thanksgiving, my friend Beverly usually brings a second turkey. Otherwise, I cook a second turkey, putting it in before church and turning it down as I'm ready to walk out the door. We serve the first turkey, which reheats easily. The whole turkey looks pretty, on the buffet, and we carve it later for second helpings and leftovers.

Set up a dessert "buffet" if there is room. Have all the components—dishes, silverware, desserts, and so on—ready on a tray. People can then help themselves. Look at the coffee tip (page 24).

Here's a cleanup tip that will keep you from facing the kitchen alone after a holiday dinner: my friend Cynthia puts a little message on the inside of place cards: "Please bring the dishes to the kitchen and scrape them," or "Please rinse the dishes and put them in the dishwasher" or "Please wash the dishes that can't go in the dishwasher."

Lay in a good supply of foil and zip-type bags for leftovers.

Plan ahead for where dirty pots will go. One solution is to clear out the space under the sink and place a cooler filled with soapy water there.

Thanksgiving Cooking Time Line

Remember, each day, check your preparations list for things like cleaning, cleaning the oven, shopping, setting the table, drop-dead time, and so on. If you elect to use a store-bought item (or more than one), make sure it's on your shopping list, and obviously you don't need to make it. This list includes all the recipes I might use for Thanksgiving in addition to the ones on the menu.

UP TO 3 MONTHS BEFORE

1. Make the turkey stock, gravy, dressing, green beans, Sweet Potato and Turnip Gratin, Zucchini and Sausage Casserole, bread, Ginger-Spiced Sweet Potatoes, and desserts; freeze.

UP TO 1 MONTH BEFORE

1. Make the Cranberry-Orange Relish; refrigerate.

UP TO 2 DAYS BEFORE

1. Make the Creamed Spinach, wild rice salad, and Ambrosia (without the bananas); refrigerate.

UP TO 1 DAY BEFORE

1. Remove the frozen dishes from the freezer.
2. Make the Southern Oyster Casserole.
3. Cook the turkey; carve; make the gravy if not already done.
4. Make the white acre peas, butter beans and carrots, and Brussels sprouts; refrigerate.
5. Defrost desserts overnight in refrigerator.

The Day

UP TO 3 HOURS BEFORE

1. Cook the turkey, if not done, or if doing a second one.

UP TO 1 HOUR BEFORE

1. Carve the turkey if not already done, make the gravy (if not already done).
2. Reheat the Sweet Potato and Turnip Gratin, Zucchini and Sausage Casserole, and Ginger-Spiced Sweet Potatoes.

UP TO 30 MINUTES BEFORE

1. Reheat the dressing, peas, butter beans, spinach, and Brussels sprouts.
2. Add the bananas to the Ambrosia.
3. Reheat the oyster casserole, the turkey if necessary, the gravy, and the challah (if desired).
4. At serving time, heat desserts if desired.

Two-Hour Turkey and Gravy

SERVES 10 TO 12

The trick to having a turkey ready in two hours is to use a hot oven and a small turkey. I learned this recipe originally from Julia Child, but I've changed it along the way. The turkey should be no more than 14 pounds. If the roasting pan is more than 2 inches larger than the turkey, the juices may burn. (If you use a larger pan, add a little broth to the pan as needed.) Always remove any bags or parts from the large and small cavities before cooking, and start with a clean oven to avoid excess smoking.

Because I make my turkey broth months ahead of time and freeze it, I can use that for the bird and the gracious amount of gravy. After Thanksgiving, I make another broth or stock from the turkey bones, leftover skin, and parts. I even add any leftover gravy, and freeze that whole stock for yet again another turkey.

1 onion, halved or
    quartered
2 to 3 garlic cloves
3 to 4 rosemary sprigs
    (optional)
1 (12- to 14-pound)
    turkey
¼ pound (1 stick)
    butter, melted, or
    vegetable oil
    (optional)
1 quart turkey broth
    (page 263) or canned
    chicken broth
½ cup flour
1 cup cream (optional)
    Salt
    Freshly ground black
    pepper

TIPS

If the pan juices burn, make the gravy in a separate pan. Use ¼ pound (1 stick) butter instead of the fat in the pan. Cook the ½ cup flour in the butter and whisk in the broth and any of the pan juices that may still be good.

If you have one of those sturdy V-shaped roasting racks, you can try starting the turkey breast down, then turning it over halfway through its cooking time. This does seem to produce moister breast meat as well as a breast that's nicely browned, but it is almost impossible to turn a large turkey without one of those racks.

Preheat the oven to 450°F.

Put the onion, garlic, and rosemary, if using, into the empty turkey cavity. Place the turkey in a large roasting pan, breast side up, and brush with the butter or oil. Place in the oven, uncovered, and roast, unattended, for 1 hour. Carefully remove the turkey from the oven (close the door of the oven), watching out for the steam. Brush the turkey with butter or its juices. Return to the oven quickly and reduce the heat to 400°F. Roast another 30 minutes, checking the pan juices occasionally. Cover with foil if the breast is too brown. Cook another 30 minutes, adding stock if the pan juices evaporate.

The turkey is done when a meat thermometer inserted in its thigh registers 170°F. and the juices run clear. Let rest 10 minutes (the temperature should rise 10 degrees in 10 minutes). Remove the turkey to a board or platter for carving. Carve. Discard the onions and garlic from inside the turkey. The turkey can be made a day ahead and refrigerated before reheating, carved, or it can be carved 10 minutes after resting.

If you decide to roast and carve the turkey ahead of time or if you want to freeze a portion of the turkey for another occasion, place the carved turkey in a shallow baking dish, cover it with broth, then wrap with foil or place the dish in a plastic bag; refrigerate for up to 2 days or freeze for up to 1 month. When you are ready to serve, defrost, if necessary, in the refrigerator, then bake in a 350°F. oven for 30 to 45 minutes or until heated completely through (or heat in the microwave).

While the turkey is resting, place the pan over medium-high heat. The skin, fat, and juices should be a beautiful dark bronze, not black. Remove all but ½ cup of the fat. Keep as much of the juices as possible. Whisk the flour into the fat and cook, stirring, until the flour turns light brown. Whisk in the rest of the broth, and boil until thick and flavorful, stirring occasionally. Strain if lumpy or any part is burned. Add water or canned broth or stock if a thinner gravy is desired. Add as much cream as desired. Season to taste with salt and pepper.

Grandma Stoll's Moist Dressing

SERVES 6 TO 8

Beverly's Grandma Stoll lived in Deep River, Connecticut, and her whole family converged on her house during the holidays. They all have taken the recipe with them to wherever they moved. My Southern friends love this variation to their traditional turkey dinner because of the natural, down-home, unexotic flavors of the dressing. Beverly uses the liver, but I don't.

Turkey giblets
3 to 4 cups turkey broth (page 263) or chicken stock
1 large (1½-pound) loaf white bread, stale or day-old, torn into 1-inch pieces
¼ pound (1 stick) butter
2 onions, chopped
1 cup chopped celery
1 to 2 tablespoons poultry seasoning
¼ cup chopped fresh parsley
2 teaspoons salt
½ teaspoon freshly ground black pepper

Preheat the oven to 350°F. Grease a 9x13x2-inch oven-proof serving dish or spray with nonstick spray.

Put the turkey giblets in a medium pot, add 1½ cups broth, place over high heat, and bring to the boil. Reduce the heat and simmer, uncovered, for 1 to 1½ hours, adding water if the liquid boils out. Strain and reserve the broth. Coarsely chop the giblets, removing any bones or extra fat. You should have about 1 cup giblets.

In a large bowl, mix together the turkey giblets and the bread. In a large skillet on medium-high heat, heat the butter until it sings (is foamy). Add the onions and celery and cook until soft, about 5 minutes. Pour into the bread mixture. Stir in the poultry seasoning, parsley, salt, and pepper, and enough reserved giblet broth to moisten the mixture, adding plain broth, if necessary, so that you are using about 1½ to 2½ cups all together. Toss thoroughly and pour the dressing into the prepared dish. Bake 30 minutes, adding more stock as needed to keep the dressing moist.

The dressing can be refrigerated up to 3 days or frozen for up to 3 months. Let it defrost in the refrigerator overnight, cover with foil, and reheat at 350°F. for 30 minutes.

Basil-Garlic Green Beans with Pine Nuts

SERVES 4 TO 6

These beans are very refreshing and add a lot of verve to even a simple dinner. The beans may be made ahead and frozen and used for several meals; just toss over heat until hot through.

1 to 1½ pounds green beans, tipped and tailed (ends broken off)
1 tablespoon olive oil or butter
2 tablespoons pine nuts
1 garlic clove, peeled and finely chopped
¼ cup chopped fresh basil
 Salt
 Freshly ground black pepper

Bring a pot of water to the boil. Add the beans and cook 5 to 7 minutes, depending on their size. (Test one to see if they are done.) Remove the beans from the hot water and rinse with cold water to refresh (to stop the cooking and to set the color). Drain again. The beans may be refrigerated at this point up to several days or frozen up to 3 months.

In a large skillet, heat the olive oil over medium heat. Add the pine nuts and carefully toast 2 to 3 minutes. (They burn easily.) Remove them and set aside. Add the garlic to the skillet and cook until soft, 1 to 2 minutes. (If desired, the garlic, pine nuts, and oil may be kept refrigerated several days.) When ready to serve, add the drained beans to the hot skillet and stir in the pine nuts and basil. Toss over the heat until heated through. Season to taste with salt and pepper. Pour into a serving bowl and serve hot.

Butter Beans and Carrots

SERVES 6

If you've never had our Southern butter beans, you are missing a real treat. Baby limas will do, but they aren't quite as flavorful or such a pretty color.

1 **(10- to 12-ounce) package frozen butter beans, butter peas, or baby limas**
1 **dozen small baby carrots, scraped if necessary**
2 **tablespoons unsalted butter**
Salt
Freshly ground black pepper
Chopped fresh parsley, chives, thyme, or oregano (optional)

Bring 3 cups of water to a boil. Add the beans, carrots, butter, and salt and pepper to taste and bring to a boil. Reduce the heat, cover, and cook until the beans are tender but not mushy, 20 to 25 minutes. Remove the lid and boil down slightly. Add chopped herb of your choice if desired. The dish can be made ahead a day or two and reheated.

SHOPPING TIP

Where I come from, butter beans are small and a beautiful pale green, but in some parts of the country, the frozen vegetable sold as a butter bean is large and brownish-tan—more like what I think of as a broad bean. If you can't find small green butter beans, make something else.

Sweet Potato and Turnip Gratin

SERVES 10 TO 12

This gratin is particularly welcomed on the holiday table by those who love sweet potatoes and hate marshmallows. The cream and butter make this so delicious your guests will lie in bed and remember it happily all year long. You only serve this kind of dish once in a very long while, so the caloric intake is moderated. If your meal has too many sweet potatoes, see the variation for turnip gratin.

2 to 3 pounds white turnips, peeled and sliced ¼ inch thick
2 to 3 pounds sweet potatoes, peeled and sliced ¼ inch thick
¼ pound (1 stick) unsalted butter
1 to 2 tablespoons finely chopped fresh tarragon leaves
Salt
Freshly ground black pepper
1 cup grated imported Parmesan cheese
1 cup bread crumbs
2 cups heavy cream

Preheat the oven to 350°F. Butter a 3-quart casserole.

To blanch the turnips, bring a large pot of water to the boil. Add the sliced turnips and cook 5 minutes. Remove them and drain thoroughly in a strainer.

Gently combine the turnips and sweet potatoes. Place a layer of the vegetables in the casserole and dot with half the butter. Sprinkle generously with tarragon, salt, and pepper, and cover with half the Parmesan. Make another layer. Top with the bread crumbs and pour the cream around the sides. Dot with the remaining butter and Parmesan. Bake until the vegetables are soft but not mushy, 1 to 1½ hours.

The gratin can be made ahead several days, or frozen for up to 3 months. Let defrost in the refrigerator and reheat for 30 to 45 minutes in the oven, or reheat in the microwave.

VARIATION

Turnip gratin
Omit the sweet potatoes and double the amount of turnips.

Brussels Sprouts with Poppy Seeds and Lemon

SERVES 8 TO 10

Brussels sprouts are much maligned because they are so frequently poorly cooked. This recipe will convert even the most adamant sprout hater to a sprout lover, knowledgeable enough to know a properly cooked sprout from a badly cooked one. And oh yes, sprout lovers will love it, too!

2 **pounds large Brussels sprouts**
2 **cups chicken stock or water**
2 **tablespoons olive oil**
2 **garlic cloves, finely chopped**
  Grated peel (no white attached) of 1 lemon
1 **tablespoon poppy seeds**
  Salt
  Freshly ground black pepper
  Sugar

Cut the stems from the Brussels sprouts and halve each one lengthwise.

Heat the stock, add the sprouts, and cook until the sprouts are bright green and barely crunchy, 5 to 7 minutes. Drain well.

When ready to serve, heat the olive oil, add the garlic, and cook until soft, 1 to 2 minutes. Add the Brussels sprouts, lemon peel, and poppy seeds. Season to taste with salt, pepper, and sugar and toss for 1 minute more. Transfer to a warm serving bowl and serve.

The Brussels sprouts can be made ahead several days and reheated, but be careful not to overcook them.

VARIATION

Baby carrots and Brussels sprouts

Cook 1 to 2 pounds scraped baby carrots in boiling water to cover, covered with a lid. When the carrots are just tender enough for a fork to pierce, add 1 tablespoon butter and 1 teaspoon sugar, and quickly boil down until the carrots are tender and glazed. Add them to the drained Brussels sprouts and season with salt and pepper if desired.

Creamed Spinach

SERVES 6 TO 8

This dish, an old-fashioned French classic, is elegant on its own or as a base for cooked chicken, meat, fish, or poached eggs and English muffins. It can easily be made ahead and reheated, and it freezes and reheats well. Using frozen chopped spinach saves the time needed to wash and stem all that spinach, but fresh, uncooked spinach may be used—cover the saucepan as it is cooking in the milk mixture. Creamed spinach is a nice side dish for Italian-flavored main dishes.

2 **cups milk**
3 **tablespoons unsalted butter**
 Sugar
3 **tablespoons all-purpose flour**
 About ⅛ teaspoon freshly grated nutmeg
2 **garlic cloves, finely chopped**
2 **(10- to 12-ounce) boxes frozen chopped spinach, thawed and drained well**
 Salt
 Freshly ground black pepper

Heat the milk to simmering in a small pot over low heat. In a medium saucepan over low heat, melt the butter. Stir in the sugar to taste and the flour and cook until pale blond, about 3 to 5 minutes, stirring often. Add the hot milk all at once and stir until smooth and thick and the mixture comes to the boil. Continue to cook about 3 minutes. Stir in the nutmeg, garlic, and spinach and cook 3 to 5 minutes over low heat until the spinach is hot. Season with salt and pepper to taste.

The creamed spinach can be made ahead several days and reheated.

VARIATION

Fresh Creamed Spinach

Stem and clean 2 pounds fresh spinach. Chop roughly. Add the chopped spinach to the boiling sauce with the nutmeg and garlic.

Zucchini and Sausage Casserole

My friend and colleague Ric Lands learned a similar recipe, using squash, from my book New Southern Cooking. *He and his family so enjoy this zucchini version that they make it every Thanksgiving, as do I. It can also serve as a rich main course for a light supper.*

2 pounds zucchini or yellow squash, coarsely grated
¾ pound sage sausage
¾ pound hot sausage
2 onions, chopped
3 garlic cloves, chopped
1 cup heavy cream
1 cup fresh bread crumbs
5 large eggs, lightly beaten
2 to 3 cups grated sharp cheddar cheese
2 cups chopped pecans
  Salt
  Freshly ground black pepper
  Hot sauce

Topping
6 tablespoons butter, melted
¾ cup fresh bread crumbs
¾ cup chopped pecans
½ cup grated cheddar cheese

Preheat the oven to 350°F. Grease a wide, 2-quart baking dish or spray it with nonstick spray.

Put the zucchini in a colander to drain for about 30 minutes or wrap it in a clean tea towel and gently squeeze it to remove the excess liquid. Put the zucchini in a large mixing bowl.

Heat a large skillet and add the sage sausage and hot sausage. Cook until the sausage starts to brown, stirring to break it up. Pour off all but about 3 tablespoons grease. Add the onions and cook until soft, about 5 minutes. Stir in the garlic and cook 1 more minute. Combine the sausage and onions with the zucchini.

Stir in the cream, the 1 cup bread crumbs, the eggs, the 2 to 3 cups cheese, and the 2 cups pecans. Add salt, pepper, and hot sauce to taste. Pour this mixture into the baking dish. The casserole may be refrigerated at this point for up to 2 days or frozen for up to 3 months.

For the topping, combine the butter, the ¾ cup bread crumbs, and the ¾ cup pecans. Sprinkle evenly over the casserole. Bake, uncovered, until hot through, about 30 minutes. Sprinkle the top with the ½ cup cheese and return to the oven just until the cheese is melted and lightly browned.

Ginger-Spiced Sweet Potatoes

SERVES 4

Sweet potatoes should be big for baking, because they yield more meat in the ratio of cooked meat to skin, but I wish I knew the trick to choosing good sweet potatoes. One Thanksgiving, I selected three from the same bin at the grocery store. They all looked alike and they all were of approximately the same size. Two were sweet and bright orange inside. The other one was low in flavor and color. It also was stringy. Trust me, the string doesn't bake or beat out. I ended up having to sieve my potatoes. If I went to buy them again, I still wouldn't have any idea of what to look for, so I'd buy twice as many as I needed, cook them, and use the best!

This casserole freezes beautifully.

3 pounds sweet potatoes
6 tablespoons (¾ stick) unsalted butter, at room temperature
6 tablespoons packed dark brown sugar
½ teaspoon salt
½ teaspoon ground coriander seeds
½ teaspoon ground cinnamon
1 teaspoon finely chopped fresh ginger
1 teaspoon finely chopped lemon peel (no white attached)
¼ cup fresh orange juice

Preheat the oven to 350°F. Grease a 1- to 1½-quart oven-proof serving dish or spray with nonstick spray. Line a baking sheet with foil.

Wash and dry the sweet potatoes. Stick them with a knife several times each to allow the steam to escape. Put them on the baking sheet and bake them until soft—1½ to 2 hours, depending on size.

Peel the potatoes as soon as they are cool enough to handle. Beat them with the flat beater in an electric mixer, put them through a ricer, or mash them. Beat in 4 tablespoons of the butter. Add 4 tablespoons of the brown sugar and the salt, coriander, cinnamon, ginger, and lemon peel. Mix well. Beat in the orange juice.

Place the potatoes in the prepared baking dish. Sprinkle the top lightly with the remaining 2 tablespoons brown sugar and dot it with the remaining 2 tablespoons butter. Bake for 30 minutes until heated through.

After you put it together, and before baking, cover it tightly with foil and freeze. When ready to use, defrost the casserole and bake in a 350°F. oven for 30 minutes.

Bob Lynn's Wild Rice Salad

I so love wild rice that I try to use it whenever I can. Since so many people have never had wild rice that makes their heart pound, this is my wooing recipe. It converts the hard-of-heart. Bob Lynn develops recipes for the restaurant chain Houston's and was kind enough to share this recipe with me. I find using all olive oil overpowers the taste of the wild rice, so I dilute it with a milder vegetable oil. Sometimes I add ¼ cup of dried figs or cherries, other times the arugula, sometimes both.

4 cups water or chicken stock
1 cup wild rice, rinsed thoroughly under running water
¼ cup chopped dried figs or cherries

Dressing
2 tablespoons red wine vinegar
1 tablespoon lemon juice
2 garlic cloves, finely chopped
1 teaspoon Dijon mustard
1 teaspoon sugar
Salt
Freshly ground black pepper
½ cup vegetable oil
¼ cup olive oil

½ cup toasted pecans or walnuts, chopped into ¼-inch pieces
½ cup toasted unsalted cashews, macadamias, and/or almonds, chopped into ¼-inch pieces

2 tablespoons finely chopped celery
2 tablespoons finely chopped red onion
¼ cup finely chopped scallions or green onions, green part only
1 bunch arugula or watercress (optional)

In a large, heavy saucepan, bring the water or stock to the boil. Add the rice, cover, and cook until the rice grains split, approximately 50 to 60 minutes.

Place the dried figs or cherries in ½ cup hot water to plump. After 30 minutes, drain.

In a blender or food processor, combine the vinegar, lemon juice, garlic, mustard, sugar, salt, and pepper. Process until smooth, and then slowly add the vegetable and olive oils to emulsify. The dressing can be made 3 or 4 days in advance and refrigerated.

In a large mixing bowl, toss together the rice, pecans, cashews, celery, red onion, green onions, and dried figs or cherries. Pour enough of the dressing over the rice to coat lightly. Toss well with the optional arugula or watercress. Serve warm or at room temperature.

> ## VARIATION
>
> *For a more festive appearance, add 1 or 2 cups of orange sections or peeled orange slices.*

Bonnie's Challah

My daughter-in-law Bonnie makes challah every Friday for her family of five. This recipe doubles and can be frozen.

1 package active dry
   yeast
2 tablespoons sugar
½ cup warm water
   (105°F. to 115°F.)
2½ to 3 cups bread flour
1 teaspoon salt
2 large eggs, lightly
   beaten
½ cup margarine,
   melted, or ½ cup
   vegetable oil

Glaze
1 large egg beaten with
   1 tablespoon water
Poppy seeds, sesame
   seeds, or kosher salt

Preheat the oven to 375°F.

In a small bowl or measuring cup, dissolve the yeast and 1 teaspoon of the sugar in the warm water. In a large bowl or food processor, mix together 2½ cups of the flour, the remaining sugar, and the salt. Stir in the yeast mixture, then the eggs, margarine, and enough additional flour to make a thick dough. Continue adding flour as necessary as you knead the dough on a floured board or in an electric mixer until the dough is elastic and smooth as a baby's bottom, 5 to 10 minutes (or about 1 minute in the processor). Place the dough in an oiled bag or bowl, seal or cover with plastic wrap, and let rise 1 hour until doubled.

Remove the dough, punch it down, and divide it into thirds. Roll the pieces into ropes about 14 to 16 inches long. Braid the 3 dough ropes, pinch the ends together, and place the braid on a lightly greased baking sheet. Pinch all the ends to keep the braid joined. Let rise until doubled, about 45 minutes.

Brush the braided dough with the egg glaze. Sprinkle with seeds, or salt if desired. Bake 15 minutes, then reduce the heat to 350°F. and bake until the loaf is golden and sounds hollow when tapped and registers 200°F. on an instant-read thermometer, 15 to 20 minutes longer. Cover the bread with foil if it begins to brown too quickly. Remove the pan from the oven and place on a wire rack about 5 minutes, then remove the bread from the pan and let it continue cooling on the rack.

Pumpkin Pie with Ginger and Almonds

MAKES 1 PIE

Although classic pumpkin pie is a favorite of mine, so too is this zippy combination, layered with candied ginger and almonds.

1 cup firmly packed light brown sugar

½ cup finely chopped almonds

½ cup chopped candied ginger

3 tablespoons unsalted butter, at room temperature

2 teaspoons all-purpose flour

¼ teaspoon almond extract

1 (9-inch) unbaked deep-dish pie shell (page 279)

4 ounces cream cheese

2 large eggs, lightly beaten

2 cups solid-pack pumpkin

½ cup heavy cream

⅓ cup sour cream

1 tablespoon maple syrup

1 teaspoon ground cinnamon

½ teaspoon freshly grated nutmeg

½ teaspoon salt

½ teaspoon vanilla extract

Preheat the oven to 425°F.

Combine ½ cup of the brown sugar and the almonds, ginger, butter, flour, and almond extract until well blended. Spoon into the unbaked pie shell and press firmly onto the bottom and partway up the sides of the shell. Chill for 30 minutes.

Beat the remaining ½ cup brown sugar and the cream cheese until light, 3 to 4 minutes. Beat in the eggs, pumpkin, cream, sour cream, and maple syrup. Add the cinnamon, nutmeg, salt, and vanilla. Beat well to combine. Spoon over the chilled almond-ginger layer.

Bake for 15 minutes. Reduce the temperature to 350°F. and bake for 50 to 60 minutes more. Cover the edge of the crust with foil, if necessary, to prevent overbrowning.

The pie may be made ahead several days and refrigerated, or frozen for up to 3 months. Let come to room temperature before serving.

Ginger-Pumpkin Cheesecake

SERVES 16

I remember my friends as I fix recipes they gave me. Lillian Marshall was the food editor of the Louisville Courier Journal. *At a late stage in life, after a devastating bout with cancer, she decided to attend the Cordon Bleu in London. After she emerged triumphant, she gave me this recipe with its snap of ginger.*

1 (6-ounce) package graham crackers, crushed into 1 cup fine crumbs

⅜ pound (1½ sticks) unsalted butter, melted

2⅓ cups plus 2 table-spoons sugar

3 ounces candied ginger, very finely chopped

4 (8-ounce) packages cream cheese

¼ cup flour

Grated peel (no white attached) of 1 lemon

2 cups solid-pack pumpkin (not pumpkin pie filling)

6 large eggs, beaten to mix

2 cups sour cream

⅓ cup honey

Preheat the oven to 400°F.

Mix the graham cracker crumbs with the melted butter, ⅓ cup of the sugar, and the ginger. Reserve ⅓ cup of this mixture and press the remainder firmly on the bottom and about a third of the way up the sides of a 9-inch springform pan.

In a food processor or by hand, blend the cream cheese, 2 cups of the sugar, and the flour, lemon peel, pumpkin, and eggs. Add ¼ cup of the sour cream and blend together well. Pour gently into the pan and place on a baking sheet. Bake for 15 minutes. Reduce the heat to 225°F. and bake 1½ hours or until set.

While the cake is baking, mix the remaining sour cream and the remaining 2 tablespoons sugar. Remove the pan from the oven and spread the sour cream mixture on top. Top with crumbs. Return the pan to the oven, and bake 10 minutes more. Let cool completely in the pan on a rack. Refrigerate overnight and remove the cake from the pan the next day. Drizzle the honey over the top before taking the cake to the table.

The cheesecake may be made ahead several days, or frozen for up to 3 months.

Chocolate-Walnut Pie

SERVES 8

This is a variation of a classic pecan pie recipe with the addition of chocolate. It's a bit hedonistic. It is very easy to assemble, but it takes 45 to 50 minutes to bake.

**4 ounces semisweet
    chocolate**
**1 unbaked 9-inch pie
    crust (page 279)**
**3 large eggs, lightly
    beaten**
1 cup light corn syrup
1 cup sugar
**2 tablespoons (¼ stick)
    butter, melted and
    allowed to cool**
**1 teaspoon vanilla
    extract**
2 cups broken walnuts

Garnish (optional)
Whipped cream

Preheat the oven to 350°F.

Melt the chocolate in the microwave or in a heavy pot on low heat. Pour it evenly into the unbaked pie shell.

In a large bowl, mix the eggs, corn syrup, sugar, butter, and vanilla well. Stir in the walnuts. Pour the mixture into the chocolate-lined pie shell and bake until the filling is set, 45 to 50 minutes. Remove to a rack and let cool.

The pie may be made ahead several days, or frozen for up to 3 months. Serve with whipped cream if desired.

Christmas

*N*ow that I have a larger family, with my husband's added to mine, I need to plan large holiday meals. I used to ignore the winter holidays, feeling sorry for myself because my birthday was so close to Christmas it would get ignored. We get all the children together between Christmas and New Year's, when they join us on vacation on Hilton Head Island. It's so much fun I can't feel sorry for myself and that's when I serve my big holiday dinner.

I do my primary grocery shopping and my cutting and chopping ahead of time, carting many of my meals with us from Atlanta in coolers, so I do not have to be Pitiful Pearl, chopping and slicing and washing pots and pans while they are with us. (Huge stacks of dirty pots and pans are the worst thing to be faced with in a small condo kitchen.) With so much of this meal prepared in advance, I can cook the rib roast—which looks so impressive and important and calls out "I love you and think you are very special" to the family—in the tiny oven and reheat other things in their serving containers on the stove or in the microwave, reducing the clutter visible from the table.

Of course, you may (and should) select from the recipes listed, depending on your own preferences and how many will be at your table. This meal is a lovely one for any winter's occasion.

If I am going out to a party or early children's service, I serve the soup to keep us from starvation. Otherwise, I may omit it. There is very little wild rice in the soup, so I don't mind some duplication between the soup and the salad.

Christmas Cooking Time Line

Remember, each day, check your preparations list for things like cleaning, cleaning oven, shopping, setting table, drop-dead time, and so on. If you elect to use a store-bought item (or more than one), make sure it's on your shopping list (and obviously, then, you don't need to make it).

UP TO 3 MONTHS BEFORE

1. Make the soup (omit the wild rice), Layered Vegetable Purée, mincemeat and pumpkin pies, and cheesecake; freeze.

UP TO 2 DAYS BEFORE

1. Cook the wild rice, beans, leeks, and mashed potatoes; refrigerate.
2. Assemble the wild rice salad except for the green beans; reserve some of the cooked rice for the soup.
3. Make Chocolate Roulade (do not roll or fill) and refrigerate.

UP TO 1 DAY BEFORE

1. Remove the frozen foods from freezer.
2. Fill and decorate Chocolate Roulade.

The Day

2 HOURS BEFORE

1. Put the roast in the oven.
2. Make the popover batter.

UP TO 45 MINUTES BEFORE

1. Add the wild rice to the soup and reheat.

30 MINUTES BEFORE

1. Remove roast from oven; tent with foil; let stand at least 20 minutes.
2. Put the popover pan in oven to heat.
3. Assemble the wild rice salad.

20 MINUTES BEFORE

1. Add the batter to the popover pan; bake.
2. Reheat the potatoes, vegetable purée, beans, and leeks.

If you believe that it isn't dessert if it isn't chocolate, serve a Bûche de Noël (yule log), a typical French cake served for Christmas Eve or Christmas dinner. Make the Chocolate Roulade (page 45), decorate it with meringue mushrooms, chocolate or almond paste leaves, and dust it all over with cocoa powder to look like the woods in winter.

Wild Mushroom and Wild Rice Soup

Standing Rib Roast

Yorkshire Pudding Popovers

Roasted Garlic Mashed Potatoes

Layered Vegetable Purée

Braised Leeks

Buttered Green Beans with Hazelnuts

or

Wild Rice with Oranges, Green Beans,
and Spinach

Mincemeat Pie (page 281)

Ginger-Pumpkin Cheesecake (page 238)

or

Pumpkin Pie with Ginger
and Almonds (page 237)

Chocolate Roulade (page 45)

Wild Mushroom and Wild Rice Soup

SERVES 4 TO 6

This recipe has changed with the times. Originally, I made it with button (now called white) mushrooms. Now I find the many varieties of mushrooms available punch it up and give it a startlingly rich and earthy flavor brightened up with the mint, lemongrass, or basil. Use whatever variety (or varieties—it's even more fun to mix them up) of mushrooms you can find. You can even include dried mushrooms reconstituted according to their package directions.

2 tablespoons butter
2 medium onions, chopped
½ pound mushrooms, such as portobello, shiitake, cèpes, and/or morels, chopped
2 tablespoons all-purpose flour
5 cups fresh or canned chicken stock or broth
3 to 6 tablespoons cooked wild rice
1 bay leaf
Salt
Freshly ground black pepper
½ teaspoon chopped fresh lemongrass, mint, or basil

Heat the butter in a heavy pan until it sings (becomes foamy). Add the onions and mushrooms and cook until soft, 5 to 6 minutes. Stir in the flour until smooth. Pour in the stock, stirring, and bring to the boil. Add the wild rice and bay leaf, turn down the heat, cover, and simmer for 15 to 20 minutes. Remove the bay leaf. Taste and add salt and pepper as necessary. Serve hot or cold.

The soup may be refrigerated for several days, or frozen for up to 3 months.

To serve, sprinkle lemongrass, mint, or basil over each serving.

VARIATION

Substitute cooked white or brown rice for the wild rice.

TIP

To freeze

Cool soup, then pour into zipper-type freezer bags. Lay the bags flat on a cookie sheet for easy stacking when frozen. Label and freeze up to 3 months. Thaw in original container and then reheat, bringing to the boil in the microwave or stovetop in a suitable container.

Standing Rib Roast

Rib roast has to be one of the easiest, most forgiving dishes you can make. I've seen all kinds of instructions—from slow roasting at a low temperature to almost broiling—and all from well-respected cooks. Each one is perfectly satisfied with the results. Apparently, a rib roast can stand up to almost any method—as long as it isn't overcooked! The technique in this recipe is my favorite, since it is so easy on your time.

If the pan is too snug, it will steam the roast. If you want to add potatoes, carrots, and/or onion wedges to the roast to caramelize around it, the pan should be even larger.

The "cap" on a roast is perfectly good, but it's not as good as the rest of the roast. At the end of the roast is a well defined "eye" or round piece of meat (not to be confused with the eye of round, which is much tougher). Above it may be a line of fat or membrane and then another layer of meat. These make up the cap. Remove them and save for a cook's treat, stroganoff, or even hamburger. Cut and scrape the meat and fat from the lower 1 or 2 inches of the ribs using a sharp, stout knife. Add these cuttings to the "hamburger-to-be" pile.

1 (5- to 5½-pound) 3-rib roast, trimmed
Oil
1 garlic clove per rib, finely chopped
1 teaspoon fresh rosemary leaves per rib
Freshly ground black pepper

Preheat the oven to 350°F.

Rub the ends of the meat with the oil and sprinkle all over with the garlic, rosemary, and pepper. Place the roast, bone side down, directly into a low-sided roasting pan large enough to hold the roast and have an inch or so room around it. The bones form their own rack. Put the pan in the oven and roast for about 90 minutes (30 minutes per rib for rare at the large end). Check the internal temperature with an instant-read thermometer. It should register 140°F. at the large end for rare. Remove the roast, tent it with foil, and let it stand at least 20 minutes before carving.

SHOPPING TIP

There are 13 ribs in a beef, but only 7 of them—6 through 12—go into a "whole" rib roast. The other 6 go with other cuts. The meat with the ribs from the small, or loin, end are a better value than the meat from the large, or shoulder, end. The small end is tenderer and has a smaller cap. The rib numbering system is the reverse: Large numbers are from the small end and small numbers from the large end. So, ribs 10 through 12 are better than 6 through 8. Make sure the butcher has removed the chine, or backbone—this will make carving infinitely easier.

To give very generous portions, figure on two people per rib. With several courses and lots of side dishes and thinly sliced meat, you might be able to serve three or even four people per rib. The roast should have at least three ribs.

Yorkshire Pudding Popovers

MAKES 8

These are so impressive, I love serving them for special occasions. A popover pan is one of the few specialty pans I own. A muffin tin can be used, but the popovers will not be as tall and may fall. I usually make two batches when I am serving these for a family meal, since everyone wants two. Any leftovers can be served at lunch the next day, maybe even filled with a salad from the leftover roast beef. Bread flour is a must! I confess I do not know the source of this recipe, which is an old standby. You will get a soggy popover if the batter is not at room temperature before using.

1⅓ cups bread flour
⅔ teaspoon salt
3 large eggs
⅔ cup milk
1⅓ cups water
8 teaspoons beef
    drippings or oil

Preheat the oven to 450°F.

Sift the flour with the salt into a bowl. Whisk together the eggs, ⅓ cup of the milk, and ⅔ cup of the water. Mix the egg mixture into the flour carefully until you have a smooth batter. Mix the remaining ⅓ cup milk and ⅔ cup water, add half, and beat again for several minutes. Stir in the rest of the liquid, cover, and let rest in the refrigerator for at least 1 hour and up to overnight. Bring it to room temperature before using if refrigerated.

Pour 1 teaspoon of the fat into each of the cups of an 8-cup popover pan. Place the pan in the oven to heat.

When the pan is very hot, remove it from the oven and half fill each popover cup with batter. Bake until very firm to the touch and puffed and brown, on top and bottom, about 20 minutes. Turn out onto a serving platter and serve hot.

Roasted Garlic Mashed Potatoes

SERVES 4 TO 6

This is true comfort food but without much fat. It is a very flavorful accompaniment to chicken or beef. Roasting the garlic requires a little forethought, but the results are well worth the effort. Just put the garlic in the oven first and then do the other prep for the meal. (Avoid the commercially prepared roasted garlic.) The trick in a good mashed potato is to be sure the potatoes are very soft before mashing and to add hot liquid to the potatoes over heat when mashing. I always make my mashed potatoes in advance. Peeling or not peeling the potatoes is up to you!

1 **head garlic (about 15 cloves)**
2 **tablespoons olive oil**
Salt
Freshly ground black pepper
6 **large potatoes, scrubbed and cut into ½-inch pieces**
1 **to 2 cups fresh or canned chicken stock or broth, boiling**
1 **tablespoon chopped fresh rosemary**

Preheat the oven to 400°F.

Toss the garlic cloves in olive oil and place in a small baking dish or pie plate. Season with salt and pepper. Place in the oven until lightly brown and soft, about 45 minutes, or cook in the microwave for 1 to 2 minutes.

Place the potatoes in a medium-sized pot with the garlic cloves. Add water to cover. Bring the water to a boil, reduce the heat to a simmer, and cook the potatoes until very soft, about 20 minutes.

Remove from the heat and drain. Return the potatoes and garlic to the pot over low heat and add ½ cup of the hot chicken stock. Mash the potatoes with a mixer or a potato masher, adding just enough more stock to get the desired consistency. Season to taste with chopped rosemary, salt, and pepper.

If not serving immediately, cover the surface of the potatoes in the pot with a layer of hot broth to keep a skin from forming. When ready to serve, turn up the heat, stir in the broth, and heat through. Alternatively, put the cooled mashed potatoes in a plastic bag, seal tightly, and refrigerate for up to 3 days. Reheat in the microwave or with additional hot broth in a pot.

VARIATION

Creamy Garlic Mashed Potatoes

Use 1 to 2 cups heavy cream instead of the chicken broth and butter rather than oil. Omit the rosemary.

Layered Vegetable Purée

This medley of vegetables is beautiful as well as delicious, filling, and satisfying. It is ideal for taking to some-one else's holiday meal, or when a glamorous all-in-one side dish is required, as it reheats so easily.

1 pound white turnips, peeled and sliced ¼ inch thick

½ pound potatoes, peeled and sliced ¼ inch thick

1 large head cauliflower

1 pound carrots, peeled and sliced ¼ inch thick

4 to 5 cups White Sauce (page 255)

2 (10- to 12-ounce) packages frozen chopped spinach, thawed and drained

Salt

Freshly ground black pepper

Freshly grated nutmeg

¾ pound Gruyère cheese, coarsely grated (about 1½ cups)

1½ cups grated imported Parmesan cheese

¼ pound (1 stick) butter

¾ cup bread crumbs

Preheat the oven to 350°F. Butter a 3- to 4-quart gratin or soufflé dish.

Put the turnips and potatoes in a large pot of cold water and bring to the boil. Simmer until tender, about 15 minutes. Break off the cauliflower florets and add to a pot of boiling water. Cook until tender, about 7 minutes. Add the carrots to another pot of boiling water. Cook until tender, about 7 minutes. Drain each vegetable thoroughly.

Purée the turnips and potatoes together in a food processor or in batches in a blender with 1 cup of the white sauce. Purée the cauliflower, carrots, and spinach separately, each with 1 cup of the white sauce. Season the mixtures with salt, pepper, and nutmeg to taste.

Mix the Gruyère and Parmesan cheeses. Spread the turnip-potato mixture on the bottom of the baking dish and sprinkle with one-fourth of the cheese mixture. Reserve 2 tablespoons of the butter. Dot the cheese layer with small pieces of 1 to 2 tablespoons of the butter. Add the spinach layer, sprinkle with one-third of the remaining cheese mixture, and dot with butter. Repeat with a cauliflower layer and then a carrot layer. Sprinkle the top with the bread crumbs and dot with the 2 tablespoons reserved butter. Bake until browned and heated through, 35 to 40 minutes. Serve right away, or keep frozen for up to 3 months.

Braised Leeks

The pale green of the leeks adds beautiful color to the holiday table, and the mild onion-like flavor enhances the meal as well.

6 slices bacon
4 leeks, white and pale green parts only, cut into thin strips lengthwise
1 bay leaf
1 sprig fresh parsley
1 sprig fresh thyme
½ cup fresh or canned chicken stock or broth
Salt
Freshly ground black pepper

Cut the bacon into small bits and place in a hot medium-sized stockpot. Add the leeks, bay leaf, parsley, and thyme. Add the chicken stock and bring to the boil. Reduce the heat to a simmer and cook until soft and tender, about 20 minutes. Season to taste with salt and pepper. Remove the parsley, thyme, and bay leaf before serving.

Buttered Green Beans with Hazelnuts

SERVES 8

Hazelnuts (also called filberts) or pecans add a touch of glamour to the simple bean—perhaps after you have pulled the dish from the refrigerator or freezer at the last minute!

2 pounds green beans, trimmed
2 to 3 tablespoons unsalted butter
½ cup roasted hazelnuts or pecans, coarsely chopped
Peel (no white attached) of 2 oranges, finely chopped
Salt
Freshly ground black pepper

Bring a large amount of salted water to the boil in a large saucepan. Place the beans in the boiling water for 3 to 5 minutes, until crisp-tender. Remove from the hot water and rinse with cold water to refresh (to stop the cooking and to set the color). The beans can be prepared up to 2 days ahead and refrigerated or frozen for up to 3 months. Return them to room temperature (or hot) before proceeding.

In a large, heavy skillet, melt the butter. Add the hazelnuts and orange peel and cook 1 minute. Add the room-temperature green beans and toss to coat evenly with the mixture. Season to taste with salt and pepper. Heat through and serve.

Wild Rice with Oranges, Green Beans, and Spinach

SERVES 8 TO 10

This glamorous but nutritional dish can be served warm, cold, or at room temperature and can be made several days in advance. One cup uncooked wild rice makes 3½ to 4 cups cooked wild rice. There are mixes made with wild rice and rice that can be substituted for wild rice. In that case, follow the package directions to cook.

1½ cups wild rice
1 tablespoon olive oil
2 pounds fresh, tender green beans, washed and tops and tails removed
4 seedless oranges, peeled, sectioned, and all pith and membranes removed, with their juice
3 scallions, sliced, including green tops
Salt
Freshly ground black pepper

Vinaigrette
⅓ cup red wine vinegar
2 teaspoons Dijon mustard
⅔ cup olive oil
¼ teaspoon salt
⅛ teaspoon freshly ground black pepper

Garnish
1 pound fresh spinach, washed, drained, and stems removed

In a large, heavy saucepan, bring 4 cups water to a boil. Add the rice and the olive oil. Cover and simmer over low heat until the rice is cracked and puffy, approximately 50 to 55 minutes. Drain.

In a large, heavy saucepan, over high heat, bring a large amount of salted water to the boil. Add the green beans and boil until they are just crisp-tender, about 3 to 5 minutes. Drain and rinse with cold water to refresh (to stop the cooking and to set the color). Drain and set aside. Both the green beans and the rice may be made to this point ahead several days and refrigerated or frozen up to 3 months.

In a large bowl or container, combine the room-temperature cooked rice, the orange sections, and the scallions.

Make the vinaigrette: Mix the vinegar and mustard. Slowly whisk in the olive oil and season with salt and pepper.

Toss the vinaigrette with the salad. Add the green beans shortly before serving (the acid in the vinaigrette will discolor the beans). Taste and add salt and pepper to taste.

To serve, line a platter or bowl with clean, dry spinach leaves and arrange the salad on top. Serve warm or at room temperature, or chill and serve cold.

NOTE

The spinach may be torn into pieces and tossed with the rice mixture if desired. It may also be used in place of the green beans with a lettuce garnish.

CORE RECIPES

This section includes recipes that are the core of my entertaining but have not been used elsewhere in this book. If I don't know what I'm in the mood to cook for company, I start with foods I am in the mood to cook for myself. Cooking those meals frequently makes me want company to share them.

I'm often asked what my favorite meal is. When pushed, I think a roast chicken, Mock Potatoes Anna, a green salad, and a chocolate roulade would very quickly rise to the top. I think that until I start thinking about other favorites—Shrimp and Fennel Risotto, for instance. And what could top a bouillabaisse?

So this is a broad collection of my favorites for entertaining. Some are more ambitious than others, and some are here because they are so easy they can be assembled quickly and still make me look as though I had put forth a bit of effort. Others—like the osso bucco—are here not just because they are delicious but because they offer a bit of excitement while working well when made in advance.

Emergency Meals

No one I know has a perfect life. We all have unexpected emergency situations where we have to appear gracious and feed others. To ease those times, I have a list of simple-to-make dishes posted inside my kitchen cabinet. It lists ten emergency hors d'oeuvres, ranging from goat cheese and sun-dried tomatoes on crackers to cheese toast fingers. Others listed in this book are P.D.C.'s Divine Saltines and Oven-Toasted Pecans.

I have ten first-course and main-course emergency ideas based on food that I always keep in the house, in hopes the ingredients for one are really on hand: One-Pot Chicken with Carrot and Zucchini Ribbon or Spinach, chicken stock with packaged dumplings or rice and a green vegetable added at the last minute from the freezer, Onion Soup with Thyme Croûtes, an omelette soufflé, quiche, steak, lamb chops, spaghetti, fresh ravioli (from the store, which I keep in the freezer) with broccoli, and so forth. I also have a smaller list of desserts that can be made at the last minute: cobblers, ice cream, brownies, omelette soufflé, and others.

With the help of these lists, I can pull together something even when I am too tired and hungry to think. This does not mean that I don't find pizza, Chinese food, or other carry-out or delivered foods acceptable—I do. Sometimes, however, I really want to offer something home-cooked, or I have to have something to eat sooner than the delivery will arrive, for those emergency times usually come when everyone is already stretched thin and needs sustenance fast.

Some competence with emergency meals is helpful not only for those times when guests are thrust upon you or something explodes in the kitchen, it can also give you the wherewithal to initiate a spur-of-the-moment gathering. Once I had a drink with a blind date who was quite cute. We were with a group of people, and it was time—past time, really—to eat. I decided the only way to move the relationship along a bit was to invite the whole group over for a late supper. What to serve? I had no idea, but I knew I had—always have—a dozen eggs and some cheese on hand. I decided to fix a cheese omelette soufflé, overwhelmingly impressing my date, as well as his friends, because it was so good and unusual and yet easy. (I did enlist help beating the egg whites.) It was by no means my last date with him, and the next time I didn't pay for—or cook!—dinner.

One time Pat Conroy came to Oxford, Mississippi, to talk about his book Beach Music as the keynote speaker at a weekend book conference. He arrived with an entourage—his editor, his publicist, his father, his father's girlfriend, his high school English teacher, and author John Berendt, who was writing a *Vanity Fair* profile of Pat. When I invited Pat for a meal, he pointed out his entourage and said he didn't know how he could, with all those people. But I knew how hard it would be to find a restaurant in Oxford to seat all those people without a reservation.

Sure enough, at 3:00 P.M. Saturday, my husband and I were still sitting at the table after a long lunch with old friends also in town for the conference. I might add that our kitchen was gutted for remodeling. The phone rang. It was Pat. He'd tried to make reservations but to no avail—everything was full. Could we feed him and his friends? I said yes. We cleaned up the dishes, pulled a beef tenderloin out of the freezer, pulled out a bag of charcoal and lit the grill, and were nearly ready when they arrived; the beef, the creamy grits with grated Parmigiano-Reggiano from a hunk I had in the freezer, and the greens cooked in the microwave were read; and the red peppers and other vegetables were on the grill. I made the panna cotta when the lunch guests left. All this was done without a stove using the grill and microwave. Pat and crew were ravenous when they arrived, because no one had fed them all day, and they scarfed up the grits and greens before digging into the beef and vegetables.

The total prep time for the meal was two hours, if that.

Basic Crème Fraîche

MAKES 1½ CUPS

This simple mixture is one of the most useful basic items I know. It adds richness and body to any dish you put it in, be it sweet or savory.

    1 cup heavy cream
    ½ cup sour cream
      Juice of ½ lemon

Mix the heavy cream, sour cream, and lemon juice and allow to stand at room temperature until the mixture has the consistency of lightly whipped cream. Put it into a covered container in the refrigerator. It will keep for up to a month.

Tapenade

MAKES ¾ CUP

This pesto goes well with or on bruschetta crisps or grilled French bread. It can also be used as a dressing for grilled steak, seafood, or vegetables. You could use it in stuffed mushrooms, put it on pasta, or use it on homemade pizza. This is easy to prepare and freezes well. I suggest making extra and freezing it for the unexpected guest.

    3 garlic cloves
    2 anchovy fillets
    1 teaspoon pine nuts
    ⅓ cup pitted black olives
    ⅓ cup pitted black olives, such as Kalamata
      or other brine-cured
    1½ teaspoons extra-virgin olive oil

TIP

Freeze the pesto in an ice-cube tray. When completely frozen, remove the cubes from the tray and store in freezer bags. This way you can defrost what you need and leave the rest frozen.

    1½ teaspoons fresh lemon juice
    ¼ teaspoon freshly ground black pepper

In the bowl of a food processor fitted with the steel blade, put the garlic, anchovies, pine nuts, and olives. Process the ingredients until smooth. Using the pulse button, add the olive oil and lemon juice, a little at a time. Season the pesto with pepper to taste.

Horseradish Sauce

MAKES 2 CUPS

This sauce just couldn't be easier to prepare and is wonderful with any simply cooked beef. It keeps, refrigerated, for up to a week.

    ½ cup prepared horseradish
    ¾ cup mayonnaise
    ¾ cup Basic Crème Fraîche (left)
      Juice of ½ lemon
      Salt
      Freshly ground white pepper
      Hot sauce

Put the horseradish in a very fine sieve and, using the back of a spoon, press out the excess liquid. Whisk together the horseradish, mayonnaise, crème fraîche, and lemon juice. Add salt, pepper, and hot sauce to taste. Refrigerate several hours to develop taste. Taste again after taste develops and correct seasonings if necessary.

VARIATION

Add the grated peel (no white attached) of 1 lime for each 2 cups of sauce and substitute lime juice to taste for the lemon. Or add 2 whole scallions or green onions, thinly sliced, ½ cup chopped cilantro, and 1 small jalapeño pepper, chopped very finely.

Cocktail Sauce

This is an all-purpose sauce for shrimp, crab claws, and oysters. Don't be too serious about the exact amounts of the ingredients. Adjust them so it tastes just the way you want it to.

- 1 **cup (one 8-ounce bottle) chili sauce**
  Juice of 1 lemon
- 2 **tablespoons prepared horseradish**
- ½ **teaspoon Worcestershire sauce**
  Freshly ground black pepper
  Tabasco to taste

Whisk the chili sauce, lemon juice, horseradish, Worcestershire sauce, black pepper, and Tabasco together. Serve at room temperature.

Peggy's Secret Sauce

MAKES 2 TO 3 CUPS

For special occasions, there is no reason not to serve something rich and usually forbidden. After all, it's only one meal—if your guests eat right the rest of the time, you aren't killing them! The sauce is good for a dip or a sandwich spread. It keeps several weeks, refrigerated. Don't leave it out of the refrigerator more than a couple of hours, or you can put it on ice. This recipe can be halved easily.

- ½ **cup yogurt**
- 1 **cup heavy cream**
  Juice of ½ lemon
  Dash of hot sauce
- 1½ **cups of good-quality commercial mayonnaise**
  Salt to taste

Whisk together the yogurt, heavy cream, and lemon juice. Allow this mixture to sit at room temperature until it thickens to the consistency of mayonnaise. This may happen in as little as 1 hour, or it can take up to 6 hours. Refrigerate for several more hours; it will become even thicker. Whisk in the hot sauce and mayonnaise and add salt to taste.

White Sauce

MAKES 5 CUPS

This white sauce, or béchamel sauce, has as its base a milk stock, which adds incredible flavor to the sauce. I keep a "bits and pieces" container in my freezer and add pieces of unused onions, peelings of carrots, parsley stalks, stray herbs, even a tablespoon of leftover vegetables or meat. It all gets strained out, but adds flavor and nutrients.

- 5 **cups whole milk**
- 2 **slices onion**
- 1 **stalk celery**
- 10 **black peppercorns**
  Carrot trimmings
- 1 **teaspoon herbs—thyme, oregano, and/or marjoram**
- 1 **bay leaf**
- 10 **tablespoons butter**
- 10 **tablespoons all-purpose flour**

In a medium, heavy pan, heat the milk with the onion, celery, peppercorns, carrot trimmings, herbs, and bay leaf to a simmer. Remove from the heat, cover, and set aside for at least 20 minutes to infuse the flavors.

Melt the butter in a 3-quart heavy pot. Add the flour and stir until smooth. Strain the hot milk into the butter and flour. Cook, stirring constantly, over medium heat until it comes to the boil. Continue to cook, constantly stirring, for about 3 minutes. Remove from the heat and cover with plastic wrap directly on the surface to prevent a skin from forming if not serving or using right away. Alternatively, keep frozen for up to 3 months and defrost in the microwave.

Garlic-Red Pepper Sauce

MAKES 1½ CUPS

The traditional French sauce is made with egg and is called Rouille. This marvelous sauce can be used for fish, chicken, and potatoes, as well as grilled foods. Traditionally it is added at the end to the bouillabaisse. Jarred red peppers or pimientos can be substituted for the fresh-roasted ones, but fresh are better. As you become familiar with the sauce, you may decide to use fresh hot pepper rather than hot sauce.

- 1 slice French bread, crust removed, torn apart
- ¼ cup strained Mediterranean-Style Fish Broth (page 263)
- ¼ teaspoon saffron threads (several strands)
- ¼ to ½ teaspoon cayenne pepper
- 4 to 6 garlic cloves, crushed to a paste
- 2 medium sweet red bell peppers, roasted, peeled, and seeds removed
  Salt
- ½ cup extra-virgin olive oil
  Freshly ground black pepper
  Hot sauce

Soak the bread in the fish broth with the saffron and half the cayenne until soft. In the food processor fitted with the steel blade or in a mixer, purée the garlic, peppers, and salt. Squeeze the bread to remove excess water and add to the processor. Slowly pour in the olive oil in a thin steady stream until a mayonnaise consistency is reached. Purée. Season well with salt, pepper, the remaining cayenne, and hot sauce.

SHOPPING TIP

Avocado

Don't wait until the last minute to buy your avocados, since they are usually hard as a rock. The best way to speed up the ripening process is to place them in a brown paper bag until soft but still firm, usually 2 to 3 days.

Guacamole

MAKES 1½ TO 2 CUPS

Liz and Joel, my husband Jack's daughter and son-in-law, were in San Diego one night and ordered guacamole. To their surprise, the waiter came to the table and made it right in front of them in two minutes—starting with the whole avocado. When Liz and Joel make their own guacamole, they frequently use lemon juice instead of lime, and sometimes orange juice too. And now they are raising their own cilantro.

- 2 small (6-ounce) ripe avocados
- ¼ cup chopped onion
- ¼ cup finely chopped tomatoes
- 2 garlic cloves, very finely chopped
- 1 teaspoon chopped cilantro leaves
- 2 teaspoons lime or lemon juice
- 1 teaspoon orange juice (optional)
  Salt
  Freshly ground black pepper
- 1 fresh jalapeño pepper, seeded and finely chopped (optional)
  Hot sauce (optional)

Cut the avocados in half, remove the seed, and scoop out the avocado flesh with a spoon. Place the flesh in a medium bowl and coarsely mash with a fork. Add the onion, tomato, garlic, cilantro, lime juice, and orange juice, if using, and mix well. Season to taste with salt and pepper. Add jalapeño and hot sauce if you like. Cover with plastic wrap and store in the refrigerator.

VARIATION

Use ½ cup Pico de Gallo Salsa (page 169) instead of the onion, tomato, garlic, and cilantro.

Cranberry-Orange Relish

MAKES 4 CUPS

This is a recipe from Rich's Cooking School that I have been using for many years. I do not know what the original source was, only that it's so good that Kay, my secretary of twenty-plus years, and I both have used it since she was in my first cooking class.

1 (12-ounce) package fresh cranberries
1¼ cups sugar
¾ teaspoon grated orange peel (no white attached)
1 cup fresh orange juice

In a saucepan, combine the cranberries, sugar, orange peel, and orange juice. Bring to the boil and reduce the heat. Boil gently, uncovered, until cranberry skins pop, 8 to 10 minutes. Stir once or twice. Let cool. The relish will keep for weeks, stored in a covered container in the refrigerator.

Parmesan with Balsamic Vinegar

SERVES 4

The best ingredients make this spectacular. I was served it in Parma, Italy, and will never forget it! I keep Parmegiano-Reggiano tightly wrapped in the freezer, ready to be pulled out at important occasions, when I serve this dish as a "nibble." I once purchased some fifty-year-old balsamic vinegar, and I use that at special times, too. I have also used less expensive varieties with good results, but buy the best you can afford.

8 ounces imported Parmesan cheese, preferably Parmegiano-Reggiano
1 tablespoon balsamic vinegar

Cut the Parmesan into small wedges or chunks. Drizzle with the vinegar. Serve with toothpicks.

Quiche Lorraine

SERVES 8 AS AN APPETIZER,
2 AS A MAIN COURSE

Quiche is an important standby for me. I use it as a starter for breakfast, as a luncheon main course, and for picnics. It can be made one to two days ahead, and the leftovers can be frozen.

1 recipe Basic Pie Pastry (page 279)
3 slices bacon
1 small onion, chopped
1 teaspoon Dijon mustard
1 cup milk
2 large eggs, lightly beaten
½ cup grated Swiss or Gruyère cheese

Preheat the oven to 425°F.

Line a 7- or 8-inch tart pan with removable bottom or a pie pan with the crust and prebake (page 279) until lightly cooked but not brown, using wax paper and rice or beans as weights and removing when done. (You can use the same rice or beans again and again.)

Meanwhile, fry the bacon until crisp, about 3 minutes. Add the onion to the same pan and cook until the onion is soft, about 5 minutes. (Or cook both the bacon and the onion in the microwave). Remove the bacon and crumble it.

In a large bowl or measuring cup with a spout, lightly whisk the mustard, milk, and eggs together. When the crust is done, sprinkle the cheese, bacon, and onion over the bottom. Carefully pour the egg mixture into the crust, taking care to stop before the edge if necessary. Put into the hot oven and reduce the heat to 350°F. Bake until custard is set, a toothpick comes out clean, and mixture is lightly brown, 30 to 45 minutes.

Quiche may be served hot, at room temperature, or cold. If you are not planning to eat the quiche right away, refrigerate or freeze after wrapping carefully in aluminum foil. If frozen, defrost in the refrigerator overnight and bake, uncovered, in a 350°F. oven for 15 minutes.

Steamed Mussels

SERVES 4 AS A MAIN COURSE,
6 TO 8 AS AN APPETIZER

Mussels bring visual excitement to any meal with their shiny black shells. They can make a meal themselves, with just a salad, or be a very dramatic opener when you want leisure, the slow eating of the mussels pacing the meal.

Although not listed in the ingredients, cooked rice or pasta would make a lovely bed for the mussels, particularly for a main course.

3 tablespoons olive oil
1 medium onion, chopped
2 garlic cloves, peeled and chopped
1 to 2 tablespoons Dijon mustard
1½ to 2 cups white wine or nonalcoholic
    wine
4 pounds mussels, cleaned
¼ cup finely chopped fresh mixed herbs
    or fresh parsley
    Crusty bread

Heat the olive oil in a deep pot. Add the onion, and cook until soft, about 5 minutes. Add the garlic and cook another minute. Whisk in the mustard, wine, and bring to the boil over high heat. Add the mussels and herbs, cover, and reduce heat to medium. Cook until the mussels open, about 6 minutes, shaking the pot from time to time. Lift the mussels out with a slotted spoon. Bring the liquid to the boil and reduce a little, about 3 minutes. Tip the pot and ladle out the sauce, leaving any grit from the mussels in the bottom. Discard any mussels that don't open. Serve with crusty bread.

TIP

When adding wine or other alcohol always pour it into a wide-mouthed container such as a measuring cup before adding. Wine fumes can escape from a narrow-necked bottle, causing a flare-up, which can be dangerous as well as ruin your meal.

VARIATION

Leftover mussels can be lovely in a rice and herb salad. Cook the rice with herbs (page 265). Toss with vinaigrette (page 60) and add chilled mussels.

To Clean Mussels

Farm-raised mussels are easier to work with, but they still require some work. To clean, place them in a pan or sink with lukewarm water. Scrub each shell with a stiff brush. If there are barnacles on the shells, scrape them off with a strong knife. Even farm-raised mussels may need debearding. The beard is aptly named. If you don't see anything that looks like a beard, there isn't one! Scoop the cleaned mussels out of the sink, being careful not to tip the mussels out, thereby pouring the gritty water back over them. Do not store mussels in tap water. They will stay alive a week or so if wrapped in wet newspaper and refrigerated, although the longer you keep them the more the flesh will shrink (as they will have nothing to eat).

Yogurt Cheese

Yogurt cheese has become a real staple in my house. It can be used in sweet or in savory dishes and is a good lower-fat substitute for cream cheese in many recipes. You even have control over how much fat will be in the product—use plain, low-fat, or no-fat yogurt, as you see fit. The yield will vary depending on how much liquid the yogurt contains and how long you let it drain.

1 (16-ounce) container yogurt

Empty the yogurt into a cheesecloth-lined strainer and set the strainer in a bowl. Tie the corners of the cloth. Let drain overnight in the refrigerator. Put the drained yogurt in a covered container and refrigerate. It will keep, covered, in the refrigerator until the expiration date on the yogurt.

Soup as a tailgate mainstay is equally memorable. A soup tailgate party can range from a casual affair to a very dressy one. Keep the soup in a good thermos—I have a metal one. Pack everything else well. If using fine china, pack it in china packers for protection. After serving, wipe off with paper towels, then use sheets of paper towels to keep the china packers clean as you repack the china.

Chicken Stock

This full-flavored stock takes a long time on the stove, but it requires very little of your time.

4 pounds chicken bones (necks, backs, and/or wings can be used)
1 medium onion, quartered
1 to 2 carrots, sliced
1 stalk celery, including leaves, sliced
1 bay leaf
4 to 6 sprigs thyme or 1 teaspoon dried thyme
8 parsley stems
2 garlic cloves, unpeeled
12 black peppercorns

Roughly chop or break up the chicken bones and pieces. Place the chicken, onion, carrot, and celery in a tall, nonreactive pot. Add enough cold water to cover.

Bring the mixture to a boil, then reduce the heat and simmer about 45 minutes. Skim off the rising fat and impurities, which come up in a foam. Add water as necessary to keep everything covered.

Add the bay leaf, thyme, parsley stems, garlic, and peppercorns. Continue to simmer for another 3 hours, adding hot water as necessary to keep the bones and vegetables covered. Stir occasionally.

Strain the stock through a fine-mesh strainer or a colander lined with dampened cheesecloth, pressing the solids to release all the juices.

Let the stock cool and then refrigerate overnight. The next day, skim off all the fat that has risen to the surface. The stock will keep refrigerated up to 1 to 2 days, or you can freeze it in 1-cup containers.

BROTH VS. STOCK

For most purposes, broth, bouillon, and stock can be used interchangeably. Broth is simply the liquid left after poaching meat and/or vegetables. Since they don't cook very long, the liquid isn't very flavorful, but it will do as a base for soup or even some sauces. The term bouillon came into use in the mid-eighteenth century and is the same as broth. It came from the French verb bouillir ("to boil") and probably was used to make broth sound more upscale. Stock is made on purpose, not just as a by-product of another process. It is made by simmering meat, vegetables, herbs, and bones a long time. The long simmering extracts all the flavor from the meat and the gelatin from the bones, making a rich liquid.

For a classic brown stock, the meat, bones, and vegetables are all thoroughly browned, usually in the oven, before being put in the stockpot. Since the stock will simmer a long time and will be strained at the end, there is no need to peel the vegetables—especially the onions, since onion skins will add wonderful color to the stock. For a white stock, the ingredients are not browned. In fact, the bones are often simmered for five minutes, drained, and rinsed before being used in the stock to remove any impurities that might color the final product. For this one, onion peels should not be used.

Court Bouillon

MAKES 1 QUART

Court bouillon, which is just flavored water, is usually used for poaching fish. You can use it as a vegetable stock, too.

- 1 small carrot, peeled and sliced
- 1 small onion, sliced
- 6 black peppercorns
- 3 to 4 sprigs thyme
- 6 to 8 parsley stems
- 1 small bay leaf
- ⅓ cup white wine vinegar

Bring 1 quart of water to the boil. Add the carrot, onion, peppercorns, thyme, parsley, bay leaf, and vinegar and simmer about 30 minutes. Use as is or strain. Keeps up to 1 week in the refrigerator, or can be kept frozen for 3 months.

NOTE

If storage space is in short supply, boil the stock down to a cup or so and refrigerate or freeze.

Cold Borscht

SERVES 8 TO 10

When I met my husband, he said he ate everything but beets. "Beets," he said, "are only fit for fodder." Then Tunky Riley made borscht and served it to us for lunch. A well-trained Southern boy, he ate some. Then he lapped it up. And now will eat borscht. The crimson color of this soup makes it particularly appealing, but the beet juice color does stain—hands, clothes, wood—so handle with care.

- 2 to 3 quarts fresh or canned chicken stock or broth
- 6 beets (2 pounds), fresh-cooked (see Note opposite) or canned
- 2 red onions, chopped
- 1 red cabbage, grated or sliced thinly
- ½ cup fresh lemon juice
  Salt
  Freshly ground black pepper
- 1 teaspoon sugar
- ½ cup yogurt or sour cream
- 1½ to 2 pounds (2 medium) cucumbers, peeled and sliced
- 2 scallions, chopped, including green part
- 3 tablespoons finely chopped fresh dill

Bring 2 quarts of the chicken broth to a boil. Add the cooked beets, red onions, and cabbage and cook until soft, about 1 hour. Remove the solids with a slotted spoon, reserving the broth, and purée them in a blender or food processor, adding the beet broth as necessary. Combine the purée, lemon juice, and remaining beet broth. Taste for seasoning and add salt, pepper, sugar, and enough of the remaining chicken broth to have a good consistency and flavor. Chill, covered, if serving cold. The soup may be refrigerated up to 3 days or frozen up to 3 months. Reheat if serving hot. To serve, ladle into individual bowls and add a dollop of yogurt. Slit the cucumber slices, twist them, and set on top of the yogurt. Add a sprinkling of scallions and dill.

NOTE

To cook the beets, preheat the oven to 400°F. Leaving the root and 3 to 4 inches of stem attached, bake the unpeeled beets until tender, 30 to 45 minutes. Alternatively, boil for 25 to 40 minutes, depending on the size. Let cool and peel, wearing rubber gloves, and chop on something that won't stain.

I learned about "refrigerator" soup in Majorca. There was a little restaurant that on Mondays would have a soup that was mostly chicken broth and a little rice. On Tuesdays, green vegetables would show up; on Wednesdays, beans; and so it would go. On Fridays, there was a glorious soup with all the leftovers of the restaurant for the week. My friend Deni Seibert goes so far as to save every liquid she uses to cook vegetables in, adding them to her soup.

Herbed Tomato Soup
MAKES 2 QUARTS

This is the very essence of soup, rich and with the wonderful assertive flavor of tomato and the underlying taste of the herbs. I think the soup is even better the next day. This recipe halves.

2 tablespoons olive oil
2 large onions, chopped
¼ cup flour
½ to ¾ cup chopped fresh basil
½ to ¾ cup chopped fresh parsley
1 (28-ounce) can crushed tomatoes
6 cups chicken stock
Salt
Freshly ground black pepper
1 cup yogurt or heavy cream
Pinch of sugar

Heat the olive oil in a large pot, add the onions, and sauté until they are transparent, about 10 minutes. Add the flour, stir until smooth, and cook a few minutes more. Add ½ cup each of the basil and parsley. Add the tomatoes, stirring briefly, bring to the boil, reduce the heat, and simmer slowly for about 20 minutes, uncovered. Remove from the heat and allow the mixture to cool. Purée the tomato mixture in a food processor or blender and return to the pot. Add the chicken stock and salt and pepper to taste, bring to a boil, reduce to a simmer, and simmer for another 30 minutes. Remove from the heat and add the yogurt or cream. Taste again for seasoning, adding sugar if it seems harsh, as well as salt and pepper and any additional herbs.

This soup can be made ahead and refrigerated for several days, or kept frozen for up to 3 months.

Onion Soup with Thyme Croûtes

SERVES 6 AS A STARTER, 4 AS A MAIN COURSE

This soup, with its rich brown broth, was one of my earliest entertaining efforts. I would call one or two friends and invite them over to our tiny apartment for soup and a green salad. It was easy to prepare, the apartment smelled wonderful, and we had an opportunity to have quiet conversation with our friends. It's particularly nice on Sunday night, when a little bit of socializing is welcome but not so much as to prevent starting off the week rested.

Onions have their own natural sweetness, enabling them to brown and caramelize. Any onion will do, but Texas Sweet, Vidalia, or Walla Walla onions add a particularly lovely caramel flavor and make a very sweet soup. It's better to slice the onions by hand, because using the food processor will make them more watery and it will take longer for them to brown. The temperature of the pan is important—get it hot enough to let them brown, but keep it low enough that the onions do not lose all their water and become hard.

- 2 **tablespoons olive oil**
- 10 **onions, sliced**
- ½ **teaspoon salt**
  Freshly ground black pepper
- 7 **cups canned beef stock or broth (Note: If using condensed stock, dilute to proper strength.)**

Croûtes
- 1 **long loaf French bread**
- 2 **tablespoons grated imported Parmesan cheese**
- 2 **tablespoons butter, at room temperature**
- 1 **tablespoon chopped fresh thyme leaves**

Heat the olive oil in 2 large heavy skillets (not iron) and divide the onions, salt, and pepper between them. Cook the onions over low heat, stirring occasionally, until they caramelize and turn a rich golden brown, about 40 to 45 minutes. Stir 1 cup of stock into each skillet and scrape up all the brown bits in the bottom and on the sides of the pans. Combine the onions and their liquid in a 4-quart pot on medium heat. Add the rest of the stock and water and simmer, partly covered, 45 minutes on low heat. If the soup boils down too quickly and becomes thick or salty, simply add more stock and/or water. Season to taste with salt and pepper. The soup can be made ahead up to this point and refrigerated for up to 3 days, or it can be frozen for up to 3 months.

For the croûtes, preheat the broiler. Slice the French bread into thick slices. In a small bowl, mix together the Parmesan, butter, and thyme. Toast the bread under the broiler until crisp and golden brown, 2 to 4 minutes. Turn, spread the mixture on the other side, and place under the broiler until bubbly and starting to brown, 1 to 2 minutes. Serve the croûtes on top of the soup.

VARIATION
Dilute the beef stock with apple juice, or even white wine, as your taste dictates.

When freezing soups, consider freezing in pint-sized or smaller containers. They can be moved around more easily and tucked away in small spaces. When someone arrives home weary and hungry, there is probably nothing more welcome than a bowl of soup.

Mediterranean-Style Fish Broth

MAKES 2 QUARTS

This broth is what gives Southern Bouillabaisse its full flavor. If you're using whole fish for the bouillabaisse, you can use their bones, heads, and trimmings for the broth. Or you may be able to get some bones and other fish parts from your market. If bones cannot be found, you can substitute fish fillets. Use the cheapest you can find, but stay away from oily fish such as salmon, bluefish, and mackerel. The broth will be flavorful, but it won't have as much body, since the bones provide gelatin.

¾ cup olive oil

2 cups sliced onions

2 carrots, coarsely chopped

1 cup sliced leeks

½ cup finely chopped fresh fennel (optional)
   or ½ teaspoon fennel seeds

3 pounds roma tomatoes or canned Italian
   plum tomatoes, chopped

4 garlic cloves, chopped

3 pounds fish bones, heads, and trimmings,
   well washed

6 sprigs parsley

1 teaspoon fennel seeds

2 bay leaves

1 teaspoon dried thyme

12 black peppercorns
   Peel (no white attached) of 1 small
   orange

½ to 1 teaspoon saffron threads
   Pinch of cayenne

Heat the olive oil in a heavy 12-quart stockpot. Add the onions, carrots, leeks, fennel, tomatoes, garlic, and fish bones and cook over medium heat for 10 minutes. Stir in the parsley, fennel seeds, bay leaves, thyme, peppercorns, orange peel, saffron threads, and cayenne. Add cold water to cover. Bring to the boil, reduce the heat to the simmer, and cook for 30 minutes, uncovered. Let the broth cool enough to handle, then strain it through a large fine sieve or a colander lined with cheesecloth, pressing hard on the solids to extract all the juices. If necessary, bring back to the boil and reduce to 2 quarts. Keep up to 3 days in the refrigerator or freeze up to 3 months.

VARIATION

For a "standard" fish stock, leave out the carrots, fennel, tomatoes, fennel seeds, orange peel, and saffron. Add the juice of 1 lemon and simmer the stock only 20 minutes.

Quick Turkey Stock or Broth

MAKES 4 QUARTS

I use this stock for a soup base as well as for my Thanksgiving gravy. (It's delicious on its own!) Get the butcher to chop the bones, or use a sturdy meat cleaver (not a Chinese-type cleaver) and chop them yourself.

4 to 5 pounds turkey wings, chopped into
   3-inch pieces

2 large yellow onions, unpeeled and
   quartered

1 to 2 large carrots, quartered

1 large bay leaf

3 parsley stems

2 large garlic cloves

Place all the wings and onions, if there is room, in a large baking pan with low sides, without overlapping, and brown under the broiler or in the oven at a high heat (500°F.), whichever is easiest for you, until dark brown but not burned. When brown, remove and set aside. Proceed in batches if necessary. Place the browned wings and onions (with their skins) in a large, heavy pot, turn the heat to low, cover, and cook over low heat until the juices are extruded, about 20 minutes. You should have lovely golden juices. (If they did burn, remove any burned spots.) Add the carrot, bay leaf, parsley, and garlic. Add water to cover.

Bring to the boil, then reduce the heat to a very slow boil. Partly cover and simmer 1 hour, skimming the top occasionally to remove the foam. Avoid boiling the bones, as it makes the stock cloudy.

Remove the wings and set aside. (They are fine to eat.) Strain the stock through a fine-mesh sieve or a colander lined with cheese-cloth. Discard the vegetables. You should have about 2 quarts of stock. Let the stock cool to room temperature. Place in the refrigerator and let cool further until the fat hardens on the surface. Remove the fat. You can keep the stock up to 4 days in the refrigerator, or keep it frozen for up to 6 months.

VARIATIONS

For a "white" stock, do not brown the bones. Cook the bones and onions together until the juice is extruded, 30 minutes, stirring, then proceed as above.

❧

For turkey gravy stock, add only 2 quarts water to the pot.

Grilled Vegetables

SERVES 6

I don't follow this recipe religiously—I add and subtract vegetables according to their size, and usually double this recipe so I have plenty of leftovers for sandwiches or another meal. You could add herbed zucchini, for instance, or sliced eggplant. A quickly grilled tomato is a nice addition, too.

2 red bell peppers
4 onions
**2 (1-pound) bulbs fennel or California anise
   (12 ounces after fronds are removed)**
**10 small new potatoes, washed but not
   peeled**
⅔ cup vegetable oil or olive oil
2 garlic cloves, chopped
6 tablespoons red wine vinegar
**½ to ⅔ cup grated imported Parmesan
   cheese**
Salt
Freshly ground black pepper

Spray the grill or a broiler pan with nonstick spray and preheat.

Place the peppers on the hot grill or on a pan under the broiler and grill or broil, turning occasionally, until blackened all over. Remove and place in a plastic bag to steam off the skin. When cool enough to handle, remove the charred skin and the seeds and ribs. Cut into ¼-inch-wide strips.

Meanwhile, prepare the other vegetables. Quarter the onions, remove the papery outer skin, and brush with a little of the oil. Trim the base of the fennel to remove the discolored portion, but leave the bulb attached at the base. Remove any tough outer layers. Cut off the fronds, chop them finely, and reserve. Cut the fennel into quarters, then each quarter in half, leaving a small section of the base attached to each piece. Brush or spray the fennel and potatoes with oil. Put the onion, fennel, and potatoes on the grill and cook, turning as necessary, about 20 minutes. The inside of the onion and fennel should still be crisp, and the potatoes should be nearly soft.

In a bowl, whisk the garlic and vinegar into the remaining oil. Add the pepper strips, potatoes, onions, fennel, and Parmesan and toss. Season to taste with salt and pepper and the chopped fennel frond. Serve at room temperature or chilled. The vegetables may be prepared 2 days in advance and kept covered and chilled.

Herbed Rice

SERVES 4

This is a real no-brainer. If you have leftover rice, you can put a spiffy starch on the table in about 10 minutes.

- 3 cups cooked rice, hot
- 3 tablespoons finely chopped parsley or other herb
- 4 tablespoons (½ stick) butter, melted
  Salt
  Freshly ground black pepper

Mix the hot rice with the parsley and butter. Season to taste with salt and pepper. Pour into a serving bowl.

> ### TIP
> *To reheat rice, place in a colander over (not in) boiling water for 10 minutes, or reheat in a microwave.*

Spinach and Mushroom Salad with Caper Vinaigrette

SERVES 6

This salad is really green and healthy. Another plus is spinach, which is now available prepackaged without roots (and dirt). It is a nice alternative to regular lettuce and can also be mixed with your favorite lettuce.

- 1 pound spinach, cleaned and stems removed
- 1 pound button mushrooms, sliced

Caper Vinaigrette
- 1 tablespoon capers
- 1 tablespoon chopped fresh parsley
- ¼ cup white wine vinegar
- ¾ cup vegetable oil
  Pinch sugar

Salt
Freshly ground black pepper

Tear the spinach into bite-sized pieces and combine with the mushrooms in a large salad bowl.

In the bowl of the food processor or blender, combine the capers, parsley, and vinegar. In a slow, steady stream, add the vegetable oil to emulsify the mixture. Add the sugar and season to taste with salt and pepper. Toss with the spinach.

Last-Minute Roman-Style Spinach

SERVES 4

Each time I go to Rome, my friend Donna serves me something memorable. This can be made at the last minute or made ahead and reheated.

- ⅓ cup raisins or currants
- 4 to 6 tablespoons butter or olive oil
- 1 garlic clove, chopped
- ¼ cup pine nuts or cashews
- 2 pounds spinach, cleaned, stems removed
  Salt
  Freshly ground black pepper

Plump the raisins in warm water for 15 minutes, then drain. Melt the butter in a large skillet. Add the garlic and pine nuts and cook until the garlic is soft and the nuts are lightly browned. Add the spinach with a little water, cover, and cook over high heat turning once or twice, until the spinach is wilted, 3 to 5 minutes. Set aside to cool. This may be done ahead to this point. When ready to serve, add the drained raisins and heat through. Season to taste with salt and pepper.

Red Bell Peppers with Balsamic Vinegar

SERVES 8

I use these as a side dish, as a garnish surrounding beef or pork roasts, for sandwich enhancers, and as a salad.

10 red bell peppers
2 to 4 tablespoons balsamic vinegar
   Salt
   Freshly ground black pepper

Preheat the grill or broiler. If using the broiler, line a baking sheet with foil.

Place the peppers on the grill or under the broiler. Cook the peppers until they are black all over, turning occasionally. Put the blackened peppers in plastic bags, seal, and let sit until cool enough to handle.

Working over a sieve set over a bowl to catch the juices, remove the skin, seeds, and ribs from the peppers. Tear them into strips and add to the juice in the bowl. Add balsamic vinegar, salt, and pepper to taste.

The peppers may be kept, refrigerated, for 4 days. Serve at room temperature or slightly chilled.

Snow Pea Salad

SERVES 6 TO 8

The crunch of the snow peas and the water chestnuts is a nice foil to the nutty sweetness of the dressing. This dish is great with a broiled salmon fillet or chicken, because it is light enough not to overpower the other dishes.

I have made this without the sugar and it is fine. The sugar adds a smoothness as well as a touch of sweetness. It's very pretty in a glass bowl and will look good on a buffet.

2 tablespoons olive oil
3 tablespoons sesame seeds
3 tablespoons rice wine vinegar or white
   wine vinegar

1 to 2 tablespoons sugar (optional)
3 tablespoons soy sauce
1 teaspoon toasted sesame oil
1 can sliced water chestnuts, drained
1 pound snow peas, tipped and tailed,
   blanched 2 to 3 minutes, drained

Heat the olive oil in a small skillet. Add the sesame seeds and cook 2 to 3 minutes, being careful not to burn them. Add the vinegar, sugar, soy sauce, and sesame oil. Heat until the mixture just barely simmers. Toss together the water chestnuts and the snow peas. When ready to serve, pour the slightly or totally cooled dressing over the vegetables and toss to coat. Spoon into a glass serving bowl. Serve at room temperature.

Oven-Roasted New Potatoes Stuffed with Potato Salad

SERVES 6

The reason for using the little new potatoes is to be able pick them up more easily. Roasting the potatoes really makes a difference in the burst of flavor, and the kosher salt makes them more crunchy on the outside. Adding the potatoes to the dressing when they are still warm lets them absorb the flavors. If you run out of time, you may decide not to stuff the potatoes, but to toss them with all the other ingredients, including the dressing, instead. Or you may find only large potatoes, which will need to be cut into bite-sized pieces, but then you will need forks (see Variation). This recipe multiplies easily and can be a starter or a side dish, with one caveat—what is a manageable task for 6 becomes tiring and time consuming for 10 or 20.

1 to 1¼ pounds medium new potatoes
   about 1½ to 2 inches in diameter (about
   10 potatoes per pound)
7 tablespoons olive oil
   Salt, preferably kosher
   Freshly ground black pepper

1 tablespoon chicken stock or water
1½ tablespoons apple cider vinegar
¼ teaspoon finely chopped garlic
½ teaspoon whole-grain mustard
¼ teaspoon prepared horseradish
2 tablespoons finely chopped scallions, including the green part
1 teaspoon finely chopped fresh parsley
¼ teaspoon chopped fresh thyme leaves

Garnish
  Whole parsley leaves
½ cup finely chopped red or yellow bell peppers
  Small whole leaves of fresh basil
  Chopped chives

Preheat the oven to 400°F. Line a baking sheet with parchment paper or aluminum foil.

Cut the small potatoes in half and toss with 2 tablespoons of the olive oil and kosher salt and pepper to taste. Place the potatoes on the baking sheet cut side down and bake until just fork-tender, about 20 minutes. Remove and let cool.

Meanwhile, in a large bowl, whisk together the chicken stock, 1½ teaspoons of the cider vinegar, and the garlic. Scoop out the inner part of the still warm potatoes, leaving about ⅛ inch of potato inside the skin to make a sturdy shell. Roughly chop the inner potato and toss it with the chicken stock mixture.

Make a horseradish vinaigrette dressing by whisking together the remaining 5 tablespoons olive oil, the remaining 1 tablespoon of cider vinegar, the whole-grain mustard, the horseradish, and ⅛ teaspoon each of salt and pepper.

Discard (or eat) 1 potato shell (to be sure you have enough filling) and gently toss the remainder with the vinaigrette. Add the scallions, parsley, and thyme. Season to taste with salt and freshly ground black pepper. Spoon the potato salad into the remaining potato shells. Garnish with a parsley leaf, red or yellow peppers, basil, or chives, or any combination.

The potatoes may be kept at room temperature for up to 4 hours before serving. Alternatively, they can be covered and refrigerated for several days. Let come to room temperature an hour before serving.

VARIATION

Oven-Roasted New Potatoes in Their Skins

Roast the potatoes and halve if necessary. Mix the stock mixture, vinaigrette, scallions, parsley, and thyme. Toss with the warm potatoes. Serve at room temperature, reheated, or cold.

STEP-UP

Add chopped smoked salmon or chopped grilled shrimp, chopped fresh dill, and a dash of sour cream to the potato mixture. Garnish with a sprig of fresh dill instead of the other garnishes.

TIP

If the potatoes won't sit up straight by themselves, cut a small slice off of the bottoms. Try to purchase potatoes of uniform size.

White Acre Peas with Caramelized Onions and Garlic

SERVES 8

Onions and garlic, sautéed to a light golden brown, give these peas a subtle sweetness. You can substitute any type of bean (lima, butter pea, crowder) for the small white acre pea. If you like, use half the onion-garlic mixture with one meal, and then freeze the rest and add it to cooked peas another night, reheating until the onions thaw and are warmed through.

½ **stick butter or ¼ cup olive oil**
1 **onion, sliced**
12 **garlic cloves**
½ **tablespoon chopped fresh rosemary leaves (optional)**
½ **teaspoon coarsely cracked black pepper**
2 **(10- to 12-ounce) packages frozen white acre peas, defrosted**
3 **cups fresh or canned chicken stock or broth**

In a large skillet, over medium-high heat, melt the butter or heat the olive oil until a drop of water sizzles and pops when added to the pan. Add the onion, whole garlic cloves, rosemary leaves if using, and pepper to the skillet, reduce the heat and cook until the onion and garlic are a nice burnished brown shade, about 20 to 25 minutes. You will need to stir the mixture constantly to keep the garlic from burning.

Meanwhile, in a 3-quart pot, bring the peas and chicken stock to the boil, reduce the heat, and simmer, covered, 18 to 20 minutes. Remove the lid, stir in the onion-garlic mixture and cook 1 to 2 minutes more to heat through. Add water if necessary to keep the peas from getting too dry.

Southern Bouillabaisse

SERVES 6 TO 8

A fine kettle of fish, true bouillabaisse is a marvelously adaptable dish. I've had it in elegant restaurants, as well as in Paris and Marseilles in restaurants where they cut a hole in the table for the debris. One special memory was of an elegant woman who made this soup in a tall copper pot on a hot plate set on her coffee table in front of the fireplace. She didn't have much room but she had a lot of style!

The trick of this dish is a well-flavored broth, made in advance (even frozen). Then the addition of 3 to 4 pounds of seafood at the last minute is all that needs to be done for company. I use Southern fish, but certainly these can be adapted to your favorite fish as long as it's not too oily. Stay away from mackerel, salmon, and bluefish. I've listed some of the options. A true French bouillabaisse has seven kinds of fish.

I usually get my fishmonger to steam the lobsters for me, then I crack the tail and remove the meat. I leave the claws whole, but cracked, and add them to the bouillabaisse at the last minute. The shell goes in the broth. If you are cooking the lobster live, add it 6 to 8 minutes before the rest of the fish.

2 **quarts Mediterranean-Style Fish Broth (page 263)**
½ **pound each of 4 different kinds of seafood or firm, white fish, such as halibut, grouper, rockfish, red snapper, sea bass, haddock, rock cod, monkfish, orange roughy, or scallops, cut into 2-inch pieces, or 4 pounds whole fish, skinned, boned, and cut into 2-inch pieces (skin, bones, and heads reserved for Mediterranean Fish Broth, page 263)**
1 **pound mussels in the shells (optional, see Box page 258)**
1 **to 2 pounds large shrimp (16 to 20 shrimp per pound)**
2 **(1-pound) cooked lobsters, cracked, tail and claws separated (optional)**
Rouille (page 256)
Garlic Croûtes (opposite)

Bring the fish broth to a boil in a large wide-based pan, then add the fish and the mussels. If the shrimp are large, add now. Add smaller shrimp in 1 minute. Reduce the heat to a simmer and simmer for 2 to 5 minutes, until the mussels open and the shrimp are cooked. Discard any mussels that do not open. Do not stir, to avoid breaking up the fish. Add the cooked lobsters and remove from the heat. Taste for seasoning. Ladle the soup into a large tureen.

Thin the rouille with 2 to 3 tablespoons of the soup and pour into a sauceboat. Place a garlic croûte in each soup bowl, add a dollop of rouille, and ladle the soup with much fish over it. Pass more rouille and croûtes separately.

Garlic Croûtes

MAKES 24 PIECES

These homemade toasts, much like thick Melba toasts, are a wonderful snack as well as a good accompaniment to soup. They keep very well in a sealed container for weeks, and they can be frozen.

- **2 or 3 garlic cloves, put through a garlic press**
- **¼ to ½ cup olive oil**
- **24 slices of French bread, each about ½ inch thick**

Preheat the oven to 400°F.

Mix the garlic with the oil and let stand 30 minutes. Lightly brush the slices on both sides with the flavored oil and bake on a cookie sheet for 15 to 20 minutes, turning as necessary until golden brown.

The croûtes can be kept frozen up to a month in an airtight container. Crisp in the oven before serving.

Southern Oyster Casserole

SERVES 10 TO 20 AS A STARTER

This dish is a holiday staple in Southern coastal cities. It can be served with the rest of the meal on the holiday buffet table, but my friend Marion likes to have it ready to go in the oven in case the meal is delayed and tempers get short. It soothes and warms enough to keep the hungry waiting. I'd set out little bread-and-butter plates and forks and put the casserole in the living room.

Not all inland eaters have acquired a taste for oysters; they are especially delicious during winter holidays as either a traditional delicacy or exotic fare.

- **2 quarts oysters**
- **¼ pound (1 stick) butter**
- **3 whole scallions, chopped**
- **1 green or red bell pepper, seeded, deribbed, and chopped**
- **½ pound mushrooms, sliced**
- **¼ cup flour**
- **1 cup heavy cream**
- **¼ cup grated imported Parmesan cheese**
- **Freshly grated nutmeg**
- **½ teaspoon paprika**
- **Salt**
- **Freshly ground black pepper**
- **½ cup bread crumbs**

Preheat the broiler. Grease a 9x13-inch ovenproof serving dish or spray it with nonstick spray.

Drain the oysters and set aside. Melt 2 tablespoons of the butter in a heavy casserole. Add the scallions and pepper and sauté until the onion is soft, about 5 minutes. Add the mushrooms and oysters and sauté for 5 minutes. In a separate pan, melt 2 tablespoons of the remaining butter. Stir in the flour. When smooth, add the cream and stir until boiling and thick. Add the cheese. Stir this cheese sauce into the oyster mixture and season with nutmeg, paprika, salt, and pepper. The casserole may be made ahead to this point and refrigerated overnight. Return it to the simmer on top of the stove before proceeding.

Pour the mixture into the prepared dish and top with the bread crumbs and dot with the remaining butter. Place under the broiler until browned and bubbling—about 10 minutes, depending on the depth of the casserole.

One-Pot Chicken with Carrot and Zucchini Ribbons or Spinach

SERVES 4 TO 6

With sherry and cream added, this is a luscious, beautiful dish for entertaining. It can be made in advance and reheated. For simpler family meals, omit the sherry and cream and everyone will still love it. This elegant dish is practically a meal in one pot.

- 4 tablespoons (½ stick) butter
- 6 chicken breasts, skinned and boned
- 2 carrots, peeled and pared into ribbons
- 5 medium zucchini, pared into ribbons
  Salt
  Freshly ground black pepper
- ¼ cup Madeira or dry sherry (optional)
- 1 cup heavy cream (optional)
- 1 to 2 tablespoons chopped fresh parsley, marjoram, or other mixed herbs

Preheat the oven to 400°F. or cook on the stovetop.

Heat the butter in a heavy flameproof casserole until slightly browned. Add the chicken and brown lightly for 30 seconds on each side. Add the carrot and zucchini ribbons and season to taste with salt and pepper. Cook in the oven

> ### VARIATION
> *Add 2 packages washed and stemmed spinach to the pot with the chicken. Add ¼ cup water or chicken stock, cover, and proceed as above.*

or on the stovetop until chicken is done, 6 to 8 minutes, bouncing back when lightly touched.

Move the chicken and vegetables to a hot platter and keep warm. Serve as is, or add the Madeira and cream to the casserole, bring to the boil, and cook until the cream is reduced and thick. Serve as a sauce.

> *Ribboning of vegetables produces very thin slices that cook quickly, are particularly pretty, and have a fresh-tasting crispness. A good peeler is crucial. Throw away the cheap one and get a good new one—you won't regret it.*
>
> #### HOW TO RIBBON VEGETABLES
> *Place the vegetable on a cutting board and with a sharp vegetable peeler press firmly and peel away from you.*

Roast Chicken with Garlic

SERVES 4

A roast chicken should be part of every entertaining repertoire. It's the kind of thing I do when I don't want to cook ahead but want to have friends in the kitchen talking to me as the aromas fill the kitchen.

Don't worry about the number of garlic cloves. They cook long enough to be tender, loose their pungency, and become almost nutty in flavor. Garlic cloves vary in size. For this dish you want enough to fill the cavity of the bird loosely. Extras don't hurt, however. The peeled garlic cloves for sale in the grocery store are fine to use. Otherwise, place a whole garlic bulb, with the outer skin of the bulb peeled off, in the microwave for 1 to 2 minutes on high until soft, then peel the cloves when cool.

Trussing the chicken adds to the cooking time, because it makes a more compact package, which allegedly cooks more easily and is more presentable. I don't always truss mine, as I usually carve in the kitchen, and I can use the saved time!

I've used the fast roasting method for this chicken, which is the way I cook at home. Many cookbook writers now recommend this method, using 500°F. as the barometer. I find, however, ovens vary so at high heat that 450°F. is a good starting point. Go on to 500°F. if you find that your oven is correctly calibrated, and make sure it is very clean or it may smoke up your whole kitchen!

You will be tempted to bring the whole chicken into the dining room to show off, but it's much kinder to all concerned to do the actual carving in the kitchen.

 2 **tablespoons oil**
 2 **tablespoons unsalted butter**
 25 **to 50 garlic cloves**
 1 **onion, peeled and cut into quarters**
 1 **(2½- to 3-pound) roasting chicken**
 3 **tablespoons finely chopped fresh**
  rosemary, thyme, oregano, or marjoram
 2 **cups chicken broth or stock, preferably**
  homemade
  Salt
  Freshly ground black pepper

Preheat the oven to 450°F.

Heat the oil and butter in a large skillet. Add the garlic cloves and the onions and cook until slightly brown—only a few minutes. Remove the garlic and onions with a slotted spoon, shake off the excess fat, and stuff them inside the chicken cavity with 2 tablespoons of the herbs.

Brush the chicken with any excess oil and butter from the skillet and place it in a metal or ovenproof roasting pan with shallow sides, large enough to accommodate the chicken, onion, and garlic. If desired, tie the legs together or truss. Add enough chicken broth to cover the bottom of the pan and prevent the juices from burning.

Bake 1 hour, adding broth if it boils out. Cook until the chicken registers 170°F. on a meat thermometer in the thick part of the thigh. Remove the chicken from the pan and set aside to rest a few minutes.

Add the remaining broth and the remaining herbs to the pan. Remove the garlic mixture

from the chicken cavity and add to the pan, scraping the sides and bottom to deglaze. Bring to the boil and boil steadily until reduced by half and a thick sauce forms. Skim off the fat. Season with salt and pepper.

Carve the chicken and arrange it on a platter. Spoon a little of the sauce over the meat to moisten and pass the rest of the sauce on the side. The chicken may be refrigerated for up to 2 days and reheated in a 450°F. oven for 15 to 20 minutes or in the microwave, but it's glorious if you time it right and serve it right away.

VARIATIONS

For a simpler roast chicken, put a quartered onion, a garlic clove, and sprig of rosemary in the cavity of the chicken. Brush with oil and proceed to cook as above, adding stock as directed.

ɞ

To add vegetables, use a larger pan to accommodate the vegetables and still brown the chicken. Add peeled carrots, quartered onions, and quartered potatoes to the pan, but don't add the broth. After the vegetables and chicken are cooked, remove them and add the broth to the pan, boiling as above to make a sauce.

The easiest way to practice carving a chicken is to purchase the rotisserie chicken from a grocery store and practice on it. Push the legs out and cut between each leg and the body of the chicken at one joint. Cut the wings off the body of the chicken at the joints where they are attached. Use a kitchen scissors and trim around the breast, severing it from the backbone, and cut in half. There is a tasty piece on either side of the backbone called the oyster. Retrieve it and place under the leg. Arrange attractively, forming back into a chicken shape if you can.

Marinated Boneless Breast of Turkey

SERVES 12 TO 14

A marinated, boneless breast of turkey is a great item to have in your entertaining repertoire. It is easy and inexpensive. It is low in fat, yet tender and moist because of being marinated. It can be broiled or grilled. You can cook the turkey close to serving time if you are offering it as an entrée on a buffet, or you can cook it the day before and refrigerate it if you plan to use it for sandwiches. A cold breast is easy to slice; you can arrange the slices right on the serving platter and bring it out a half hour before serving to take off the chill.

In some supermarkets you may be able to buy a boneless breast half, or you may buy a whole "chest" (both breasts) and have a butcher bone it for you. If these options are not available to you, boning it yourself is a snap, as you'll see. The bonus: throw the skin and bones in a freezer bag. You may keep them in the freezer for at least three months to use for making poultry stock, or the base for your Thanksgiving gravy.

- 1 whole (6-pound) turkey breast, fresh or thawed in the refrigerator
- 1 cup olive oil
- 2 tablespoons fresh lemon juice
- 2 tablespoons coarse-ground prepared mustard
-   Peel of 2 lemons (no white attached) finely chopped
- ¼ teaspoon salt
- ½ teaspoon freshly ground black pepper

Preheat the grill or broiler. (If broiling, cover a baking sheet with sides or shallow roasting pan with aluminum foil, bringing the foil up to cover the sides.)

NOTE

Even though it has been marinated, turkey can dry out if overcooked. After the first 20 minutes, check the temperature. It will continue to rise a little even after you remove the meat from the oven.

Bone the turkey breast (page 112).

Lay each breast half out flat. There should be a thicker part where the meat was the thickest on the breast. Slit this open, laying it out flat but not detaching it from the rest of the meat. This will give you a fairly flat piece of meat that will cook more evenly.

To make the marinade, whisk together the olive oil, lemon juice, mustard, lemon peel, salt, and pepper. Place the boneless breast halves in a plastic bag or nonreactive flat dish. Add the marinade. Turn to coat both sides well. Seal or cover with plastic wrap and refrigerate for 6 hours or overnight, turning occasionally.

Place the meat flat on the baking sheet. Grill or broil for 10 minutes on each side, basting with the marinade when the meat is turned over. Broil for an additional 5 to 10 minutes, or until the temperature reaches 170°F. on an instant-read thermometer inserted in the thickest part of the breast half. Remove the meat from the oven and let it cool for at least 10 minutes before you slice it.

Beef with Celery and Walnuts

SERVES 6 TO 8

I have used this recipe over and over since I learned it at the London Cordon Bleu as a more interesting recipe than beef stew or beef Bourguignon. I make it at least a day ahead so that the flavors will mellow, but I actually keep some on hand in the freezer for cold nights when we want company in front of the fire. The stew is particularly nice served with Herbed Rice (page 265) or Roasted Garlic Mashed Potatoes (page 247).

- 2 pounds braising beef (chuck, stew, round, sirloin tip)
- 2 tablespoons bacon fat or drippings
- 2 onions, sliced
- 1 tablespoon all-purpose flour
- ½ teaspoon dried thyme

1 garlic clove, chopped
2½ to 3 cups canned beef broth or stock
½ cup red wine (optional)
Salt
Freshly ground black pepper
4 to 5 stalks celery
1 tablespoon unsalted butter
⅓ cup walnut halves
Peel (no white attached) of ½ orange, in strips

Cut the beef into 2-inch cubes. Heat the fat in a heavy nonreactive 10- or 12-inch pot. Add enough of the beef to cover the bottom of the pan without the cubes touching and brown well, turning to brown all sides. Repeat with rest of the cubes if necessary. Remove the meat, add the sliced onions, and sauté slowly until they start to brown. Remove from the heat and pour off all but 1 tablespoon of fat. Stir in the flour and cook, stirring, until browned. Add the meat, thyme, and garlic. Add enough stock, wine, if using, and water barely to cover the meat. Season to taste with salt and pepper. Bring slowly to the boil, cover, and simmer gently until tender, 1½ to 2 hours. When tender, remove the meat and boil the sauce until it has reduced enough to have body and a full-flavored taste. Return the beef to the sauce. The beef may be refrigerated at this point up to 3 days or frozen up to 3 months.

Reheat before continuing. Cut the celery in diagonal slices, discarding the leaves and top of stalks. In a skillet, heat the butter until foamy. Add the celery and walnuts, season with a pinch of salt, and cook, tossing occasionally until the celery is lightly cooked but still crisp. While the celery is cooking, cut the orange peel in needlelike strips, blanch in boiling water for 5 minutes, drain, and rinse in cold water. Set aside. Transfer the beef stew to a serving dish or leave in the casserole. Just before serving, scatter the celery mixture and the orange peel over the stew.

POTLUCK SUPPERS

Potluck suppers can be fun. The atmosphere usually is relaxed. And because each guest is contributing, the various dishes often act as conversation ice-breakers.

There are some tips that will help with your potluck supper. The host (the planning person, or "home owner") should be responsible for the main course and should have a backup plan for "undelivered" side dishes to be sure that there will be enough food. The host must either arrange for, or supply, drinks, ice, serving plates and utensils, plates, glassware, flatware.

Getting the right balance of food can be tricky. If the group is large, divide the guest list alphabetically: A to G might be assigned appetizers, H to M, beverages. Or announce that it's BYOB (Bring Your Own Bottle), which allows each guest to bring his or her own beverage.

Potluck suppers work well in "no-host" situations—reunions; neighborhood get-togethers; office, class, or club functions; church socials; or when all the guests are on the same "starting-out" economic level and no one person, or couple, can afford to supply everything. This type of dinner also works for the single host who cooks one dish well and would supply the beverages.

When I take dishes to potluck suppers, I try to use bowls and platters I've purchased at garage sales. I put a tape on the bottom on which I write "Not necessary to return this dish, keep or discard." If I do want a plate or bowl back, I mark the tape on the bottom in waterproof ink with my name and phone number.

Potluck Etiquette:

If there is no organized group, and you just want to have your own potluck, for maximum good manners, invite people to such a gathering by saying, "I'm making my world-famous chili. Please come for potluck." It's best not to say, "What can you bring?"

With that kind of an invitation, your guests will probably ask what they can bring. Since they have offered, you are free to accept. If, however, their response is, "Great! What time?" you should not ask them to bring a salad or dessert. You can say, "I'm not sure what we'll have for dessert," but no further hinting allowed.

Hodding Carter's Roux-less Gumbo

SERVES 8 TO 10

This source recipe was recorded by Marian Burros of the New York Times, *who stood over Hodding Carter III, a Mississippi boy moved north, while he cooked for his annual New Year's Day party. My husband, who is an okra afficionado, adores it. Hodding doubles this recipe, and it makes no pretensions of authenticity or ease of preparation, and I've changed it a bit, of course, according to the way we like it! I've added fresh okra and tomatoes in batches to keep its fresh appeal, and used some of the new California sausages as well as the traditional andouille. Note the range in pepper.*

⅓ cup pork lard, chicken fat, or oil

3 pounds okra, sliced ¼ inch thick (10 to 11 cups), ½ pound slices reserved

2 cups chopped onion

1 cup chopped green bell pepper

2 cups chopped celery

2½ quarts fish stock (page 263)

3 cups canned or fresh chopped tomatoes, 1 cup reserved

1 tablespoon chopped fresh oregano

½ teaspoon to 1 tablespoon freshly ground white pepper

½ teaspoon to 1 tablespoon cayenne pepper

½ to 2 teaspoons freshly ground black pepper

6 to 8 garlic cloves, chopped

1 pound andouille, kielbasa, or other smoked sausage, peeled and cut into ¼-inch slices

2½ to 3½ pounds peeled medium shrimp

1½ quarts shucked oysters

1 cup chopped scallion greens

1 to 2 tablespoons fresh lemon juice
   Additional shrimp and crab meat to refresh (optional)

1 to 2 tablespoons filé powder

18 cups cooked rice, preferably Thai
   Green hot sauce
   Lemon wedges for garnish

Heat the fat or oil in a very large heavy pot until it smokes. Add 6 cups of the okra and cook, stirring often, until the okra is browned, 10 to 15 minutes. Stir in the onions, green pepper, and celery and cook for 5 minutes, stirring to scrape the bottom of the pan. Add 2 cups of the stock and 2 cups of the tomatoes. Cook another 10 minutes, stirring and scraping as needed. Add another 4 cups of stock, the oregano, white pepper, cayenne, black pepper, and garlic. Add the rest of the stock. Bring to the boil, add the sausage, and simmer, covered, about 45 minutes longer, stirring occasionally.

Add 2 more cups of the okra. Cook another 10 minutes. Add the shrimp, oysters, and scallion greens and bring to the boil. Skim any fat from the surface; serve immediately or freeze.

If serving immediately, add the lemon juice, the remaining okra, and remaining tomatoes and heat through. Sprinkle with 1 to 2 tablespoons filé powder, enough to cover about three-quarters of the gumbo's surface with a sprinkling. Do not let reboil.

If frozen, defrost and reheat slowly, proceed as above with the remaining okra and tomatoes, and refresh with crab meat and additional shrimp, if desired. Cook long enough to heat through. Add the filé as above. Serve with rice and green hot sauce. Garnish with lemon wedges.

Osso Buco

SERVES 4

For those of us who love veal marrow, this is a particular treat. Veal shanks are one of the few things I am willing to call ahead to order from the grocery store, and whenever I see them, I buy and freeze some to use at a later time. I have a few marrow bone spoons I use to dig the marrow out to slather it on warm bread, but I find demitasse spoons and some fish implements do quite well.

I enjoy the basil in the gremolata for a change, although parsley is more traditional. Serve in soup bowls with a hearty bread. Risotto is a nice side dish or starter.

It can be kept frozen for up to 3 months.

  5 **pounds veal shank, cross-cut into 6 to 8 pieces, fat removed**
  2 **tablespoons butter**
  2 **tablespoons olive oil**
  ½ **cup all-purpose flour**
 15 **green olives in brine, drained, pitted, and chopped**
  1 **tablespoon fresh rosemary, chopped, or 1 teaspoon dried**
  2 **tablespoons capers, drained and chopped**
  2 **garlic cloves, chopped**
  1 **teaspoon grated lemon peel (no white attached)**
  2 **cups dry white wine (nonalcoholic if desired)**
  3 **cups canned plum (Italian) tomatoes, broken into pieces, juice reserved**
    Salt
    Freshly ground black pepper
    Sugar

Gremolata
  2 **tablespoons grated or chopped lemon peel (no white attached)**
  2 **garlic cloves, chopped**
  2 **tablespoons finely chopped fresh basil or parsley**

In a large nonreactive casserole, heat the butter and oil until bubbling. Meanwhile, place the flour in a small, flat plate and dip the bone ends (tops and bottoms) of the veal pieces to seal the marrow, but not the (meat) edges. Add enough of the shanks to cover the bottom of the pan without touching, and cook until they are brown, about 3 to 5 minutes. Turn with tongs, and brown on the second side, about 3 to 5 minutes. Remove with tongs from the casserole and set aside. Repeat with the remainder of shanks. Spoon off any excess fat, leaving 1 to 2 tablespoons in the pan.

Place the olives, rosemary, capers, garlic, and lemon peel in a bowl and stir in the wine.

Stir the wine mixture into the casserole, scraping the bottom and sides of the pan well to dissolve any browned bits, bring to the boil, and boil until slightly reduced, 3 to 5 minutes. Stir in the tomatoes. Add the veal shanks, cover, bring to the boil, reduce the heat to a slow simmer, and cook slowly for 50 minutes, checking occasionally to make sure the veal doesn't dry out. Add the reserved tomato juice if necessary. Turn the shanks over and cook for an additional 25 minutes. Remove the meat and bones and set aside and bring the sauce to the boil. It should be a moderately thick sauce. Boil down to reduce if necessary. Taste for seasoning, adding salt, pepper, and sugar as necessary.

Make the gremolata: In a small bowl, combine the lemon peel, garlic, and basil.

When ready to serve, place the veal shanks on a platter, pour the sauce over the shanks, and garnish with the gremolata.

VARIATION
Beef or veal stew meat can be used to make a hearty stew—different from osso buco, since there is no marrow, but still very good.

Vegetarian Lasagna

SERVES 6 TO 8

When entertaining today, it's likely that a group of any size will contain a couple of vegetarians. If you are serving your guests a buffet meal, this lasagna can work as a good side dish, or it can stand in as a fine main course.

I am especially fond of this lasagna of Marion Sullivan's, because with low-fat cottage cheese and part skim mozzarella, it is somewhat lighter than the usual. The long simmering further softens the taste of the mild tomato sauce. Using fresh herbs gives the best taste, but dried can be used if fresh are not available. Another choice is in the color of the pasta: you can alternate layers of plain egg and spinach pasta. You can also use tomato/basil or herb-and-cracked-pepper pasta. Experiment.

- 1 **(8-ounce) package lasagna noodles**

Vegetarian Lasagna Sauce

- 6 **tablespoons olive oil**
- 4 **medium yellow onions, chopped (about 4 cups)**
- 7 **garlic cloves, chopped**
- 3 **cups finely chopped carrots**
- 3 **(1-pound 12-ounce) cans diced tomatoes, in their juice**
- 6 **bay leaves**
- 1½ **tablespoons chopped fresh parsley**
- 1 **tablespoon minced fresh rosemary**
- 1½ **tablespoons chopped fresh basil**
- ¼ **cup chopped fresh oregano**
- 1½ **teaspoons dried thyme**

Cheese layer

- 1 **pound low-fat cottage cheese**
- 2 **large eggs, lightly beaten**
- ½ **teaspoon red wine vinegar**
     Freshly ground black pepper to taste
- 1 **pound part-skim mozzarella cheese, grated**
- ½ **cup chopped fresh parsley**

Vegetable layer

- 6 **tablespoons olive oil**
- 3 **medium yellow onions, chopped (about 3 cups)**
- 5 **cloves garlic, chopped**
- 1½ **pounds zucchini, sliced**
- 1½ **pounds mushrooms, sliced**
- ½ **tablespoon chopped fresh oregano**
- 1½ **tablespoons chopped fresh rosemary**
     Salt
     Freshly ground black pepper
- 1 **cup grated imported Parmesan cheese**

Preheat the oven to 325°F. Grease a 12x8x1½-inch baking dish.

Cook the pasta in a large quantity of boiling salted water for 9 to 10 minutes. Drain and set aside.

Heat the 6 tablespoons olive oil in a 5-quart pot or deep skillet. Add the 4 cups onions, the 7 chopped garlic cloves, and the carrots. Cover and cook until just softened, stirring occasionally, about 15 minutes. Add the tomatoes, the bay leaves, the 1½ tablespoons parsley, the 1 tablespoon rosemary, the basil, the ¼ cup oregano, and the thyme and mix well. Bring to the boil, reduce the heat, and simmer over medium heat, stirring frequently, until most of the moisture has evaporated, 1 to 1½ hours. Meanwhile, prepare the rest of the layers. When the sauce is finished, remove the bay leaves and set aside. The sauce may be refrigerated several days, or kept frozen for up to 3 months.

For the cheese layer, mix the cottage cheese and the eggs. Stir in the vinegar, pepper to taste, the mozzarella, and the ½ cup parsley. Set aside.

For the vegetable layer, heat the 6 tablespoons olive oil in a large skillet. Add the 3 cups onions and the 5 garlic cloves, cover, and cook, stirring occasionally, until just tender, about 15 minutes. Add the zucchini and mushrooms, cover, and cook, stirring occasionally, until they soften and wilt, about 10 minutes. Drain off the juices. Stir in the ½ tablespoon oregano and the 1½ tablespoons rosemary, season to taste with salt and pepper and set aside. This may be done several days in advance.

In the prepared dish, layer in this order: a thin layer of the tomato sauce to prevent browning, pasta, sauce, vegetables, and cheese. Repeat, ending with a top layer of sauce. Sprinkle the Parmesan cheese evenly over the top.

Bake until heated through, about 45 minutes. (If made ahead and refrigerated, it will take 15 to 20 minutes longer.) After it has been assembled, the lasagna may be refrigerated for up to 3 days, or kept frozen for up to 3 months.

Ravioli with Broccoli or Spinach

SERVES 4 TO 6

This is my standby emergency meal. I always keep the ravioli in the freezer, and broccoli and spinach are staples in my house.

- 2 (9-ounce) packages fresh cheese ravioli
- 1 head broccoli, florets only
- 2 to 4 tablespoons olive oil or butter
  Salt
  Freshly ground black pepper
- ½ cup grated imported Parmesan cheese

Bring a large skillet of water to a boil. Add the ravioli and cook until tender, about 3 to 5 minutes. Remove with a slotted spoon and keep warm. Add the florets to the boiling water and cook 3 to 5 minutes until done. Drain. Pour out the water and wipe the pan with a paper

---

VARIATION
Substitute spinach for the broccoli. After cooking the pasta, drain off all but ¼ cup of the water. Add 2 (10-ounce) packages prewashed small-leaf spinach, cover, and cook until soft, 3 to 5 minutes. Drain and proceed as above.

---

towel. Heat the oil or butter in the pan. Add the ravioli and broccoli and cook until warmed through. Season to taste with salt and pepper. Toss with half the Parmesan. Pour into a warm serving bowl. Pass the rest of the Parmesan.

Almond Crescents

MAKES ABOUT 60 PIECES

This cookie is perfect as an accompaniment to tea or coffee. It's also a welcome gift. The cookies freeze well, but they may need a little more confectioners' sugar before serving.

- ½ pound (2 sticks) butter, at room temperature
- ¼ cup sugar
- 1¾ teaspoons vanilla extract
- ¼ teaspoon almond extract
  Pinch of salt
- 2 cups all-purpose flour
- 1½ cups finely ground almonds
  Confectioners' sugar, sifted

Preheat the oven to 325°F. Line a baking sheet with parchment paper or foil.

In a mixer bowl, beat the butter, sugar, vanilla, almond extract, and salt until well blended. Beat in the flour and then the almonds, scraping down the sides of the bowl to incorporate everything well. Chill the dough if it is too sticky to handle.

Scoop the dough into balls with the large end of a melon baller and roll them between your palms into crescent shapes.

Place the crescents on the prepared sheet and bake until very lightly browned on the bottom, about 10 to 15 minutes. The tops do not brown.

Let the crescents cool on racks. Gently roll the crescents in the confectioners' sugar.

Store the crescents in an airtight tin between layers of wax paper.

Pecan Crescents

MAKES 60 COOKIES

These crescents are a great company standby because they freeze beautifully and are one of the easiest doughs to make.

They can also be made from almonds, walnuts, or a combination of any of these nuts. When making all-almond crescents, I substitute ¼ teaspoon almond extract for ¼ teaspoon of the vanilla.

It is very important to use a cake flour. Since the cookies are very delicate, let them cool completely on the baking sheets or they will crumble at the touch. Once cooled, they handle fine.

- ½ **pound (2 sticks) unsalted butter, at room temperature**
- ¼ **cup granulated sugar**
- 2 **teaspoons vanilla extract**
  Pinch salt
- 2 **cups all-purpose flour**
- 1½ **cups small pecan pieces, finely ground**
  Confectioners' sugar for rolling

Preheat the oven to 325°F. Line 2 baking sheets with parchment paper or foil.

In a mixer bowl, beat the butter, granulated sugar, vanilla, and salt together until well blended. Beat in the flour and then the nuts, scraping down the sides of the bowl to incorporate. Chill the dough if it is too sticky.

Roll about a teaspoon of dough between floured palms into a 2-inch rope. Place it on the prepared baking sheet and curve to form a crescent. Bake until very lightly browned, 20 to 25 minutes.

Let the crescents cool on the baking sheets. Be sure they are completely cool before you try to pick them up. Sift the confectioners' sugar onto a sheet of wax paper and roll the crescents in it.

Store the crescents in a sturdy airtight container between layers of wax paper. The cookies may be frozen up to 3 months.

VARIATION

Instead of being rolled in confectioners' sugar, the crescents can be dressed up with chocolate. Melt semisweet chocolate chips in a double boiler over water that is no hotter than 120°F. so that the chocolate doesn't get too hot. Remember that chips still hold their shape when they are melted, so stir them up after a couple of minutes to see how much they have really melted. Put the crescents on wax paper. To drizzle, put the melted chocolate in a small, sealable plastic bag and snip off one corner. Drizzle an "M" pattern over the crescents and let dry.

TIP

When you make the cookies ahead and freeze them, let them thaw in the closed tin. Then give them a quick sifting of confectioners' sugar and serve.

Basic Pie Pastry

It takes a bit of practice to make a pie crust, just as it does to hit a tennis ball. Take a cool Saturday morning and make several batches, testing them by cutting off a strip and baking it, until you come up with the one of your dreams. Note on your recipe what you like, then write your own recipe. The size you cut fat into and whether you use shortening or butter can both make a difference. Remember, however, that different flours absorb water differently, and flours absorb water differently according to the weather, so your crust will be different in measure each time—you need to learn the feel.

1¼ cups all-purpose flour or cake flour
½ teaspoon salt
½ cup vegetable shortening, butter, margarine, or a combination
3 to 8 tablespoons ice water

Mix the flour and salt together in a bowl. Cut in the shortening with a pastry blender or two knives until the mixture resembles coarse cornmeal. Divide into three portions. Add some of the ice water to one portion of the mixture, a little at a time, working just until the dough holds together. Set aside. Repeat with each of the remaining two portions. Gather all the dough together into a smooth ball and flatten into a disk. Add more ice water if still dry. Wrap well with plastic wrap and chill for 30 minutes or up to 3 days.

Flour a board, wax paper, or pie cloth and use a floured or stockinged rolling pin to roll out the dough. Place the dough disk in the center of the floured surface. Starting in the center of the dough, roll to, but not over, the top edge of the dough. Go back to the center, and roll down to, but not over, the bottom edge. Pick up the dough and turn it a quarter circle. This will keep it round and keep it from sticking.

Continue rolling, repeating the quarter turns until you have a disk ⅛ inch thick and 1½ inches larger than your pan. Fold in quarters.

Place the pastry in a 9-inch pie pan with the tip of the triangle in the center and unfold. Trim the pastry 1 inch larger than the pie pan and fold the overhanging pastry under itself. To decorate, press the tines or handle end of a fork around the edge. To make a fluted pattern, use both of your thumbs to pinch the dough all around the rim so that the edge of the dough stands up. Place in the freezer or chill in the refrigerator for 30 minutes or up to 3 days, wrapped, before baking.

To prebake, preheat the oven to 425°F. Prick the pastry all over with a fork. Crumple a piece of wax paper, then open it out to the edges of the pan. Weight the paper with raw rice or dried peas. Bake for 20 minutes. Carefully remove the paper and rice or peas and paper. (The rice or peas may be used again the next time you prebake a pie crust.) Now the prebaked shell can be filled with a filling and baked according to the filling directions. If the filling requires no cooking, bake the pie shell 10 minutes more before filling.

> ### TIP
> *If you want a browner crust, use butter or margarine. If you want a less brown crust, use vegetable shortening.*

> ### TWO-CRUST PIE DIRECTIONS
> *If making a two-crust pie, double the ingredients and make the bottom crust larger than the top crust. Dampen the rim of the bottom crust before putting on the top one, then seal the two together. Be very careful not to stretch either dough, so that they stay together when baked.*

Pâte Sucrée
(Sweet Pastry Dough)

MAKES ONE 8-INCH TART
OR 24 TARTLETS

This dough is a sweet short crust dough, which you can treat like a cookie dough. Scraps can be rerolled, and it can be pushed into the tins rather than rolled, if necessary. I find it easier than pie dough to work with, because it doesn't toughen, once I accept the fact that it is the nature of the dough to split, since there is no water. It's easy to patch, and it presses in easily.

This dough is used for many pastries. It is traditionally made by hand, but I use a food processor for this version.

- 1 **cup all-purpose flour**
- 3 **tablespoons sugar**
- ⅛ **teaspoon salt**
- 4 **tablespoons (½ stick) unsalted butter, chilled**
- 1 **large egg, lightly beaten**

Preheat the oven to 350°F.

Combine the flour, sugar, and salt in the bowl of a food processor and pulse several times to mix. Cut the butter into small pieces and add to the dough. Pulse until very finely powdered. Add the egg and continue to pulse until the dough forms a ball that revolves on the blade. Remove the dough, press into a flattened disk, wrap, and chill for 30 minutes or up to 2 days.

Roll out ⅛ inch thick and shape as directed in the tartlet recipe on page 185 or shape by pushing into tins or molds and bake according to the recipe, usually 8 to 10 minutes for prebaking before filling. The dough should never be more than a pale brown, because the sugar will make it bitter if it browns.

Raspberry-Pear Cobbler

SERVES 12

This is a nice change from apple or peach and shows how adaptable cobblers are to other fruits. With the use of frozen raspberries, this can be made year round.

Filling

- 3 **tablespoons all-purpose flour**
- 1 **cup sugar**
- ¼ **teaspoon freshly grated nutmeg**
- ¼ **teaspoon ground cinnamon**
- ¼ **teaspoon ground ginger**
- 4 **pounds Bartlett pears**
- 1 **tablespoon fresh lemon juice**
- 2 **cups frozen raspberries (12-ounce package)**

Dough

- 1½ **cups unsifted all-purpose flour**
- 2 **tablespoons plus 2 teaspoons sugar**
- 1¼ **teaspoons baking powder**
- ½ **teaspoon baking soda**
- ½ **teaspoon salt**
- ¼ **pound (1 stick) unsalted butter, cut into pieces**
- ½ **cup plus 1 tablespoon buttermilk**

Preheat the oven to 375°F.

Make the filling: In a large bowl, mix the flour, sugar, nutmeg, cinnamon, and ginger until well blended. Peel the pears, halve them lengthwise, core them, and cut them crosswise into ¼-

> **TIP**
>
> *If preferred, the dough may also be rolled out between two sheets of floured wax paper into a 12x8-inch rectangle or the shape of the baking dish. Once rolled, gently remove the top sheet of wax paper and invert the dough onto the filling. Brush with 1 tablespoon buttermilk and sprinkle with 2 teaspoons sugar.*

inch-thick slices. Mix the pear slices, lemon juice, and raspberries. Add the fruit to the flour mixture and gently toss until well mixed. Place the filling in a 2½-quart baking dish.

Make the dough: In the bowl of a food processor, combine the flour, 2 tablespoons of the sugar, and the baking powder, baking soda, and salt. Process briefly until well mixed. Add the butter pieces and pulse until the mixture resembles coarse meal. Add ½ cup of the buttermilk and process briefly. The dough will be very sticky. Spread the dough evenly over the fruit and baste with the remaining tablespoon of buttermilk. Sprinkle with remaining sugar.

Bake until the crust is golden and the juice of the fruit starts to bubble, 40 to 45 minutes.

Ray's Sweet Potato Pie

SERVES 8

This is a wonderfully spicy, not-too-sweet dessert to top off a heavy holiday meal—very much like a pumpkin pie. By beating the potato mixture for 3 to 4 minutes and then folding in the whipped egg whites, you achieve a light, melt-in-your-mouth texture. If you do not have any canned sweet potatoes, you can substitute the same amount of solid-pack pumpkin (not pumpkin pie filling). If the edges of the pie begin to brown too quickly, cover the rim of the pie plate with strips of aluminum foil.

- 1 (16-ounce) can sweet potatoes, drained and mashed
- ¾ cup packed brown sugar, light or dark
- ¼ pound (1 stick) butter, at room temperature
- 3 large eggs, separated
- 1 teaspoon ground cinnamon
- ½ teaspoon freshly grated nutmeg
- ½ teaspoon ground cloves
- ½ teaspoon ground ginger
- ½ teaspoon salt
- ½ cup heavy cream
- 1 unbaked 9-inch deep-dish pie crust (page 279)

Topping (optional)
- ½ cup heavy cream
- 1 tablespoon chopped candied ginger

Preheat the oven to 400°F.

In the large bowl of a mixer, combine the sweet potatoes, brown sugar, butter, egg yolks, cinnamon, nutmeg, cloves, ginger, and salt. Beat until light, about 3 to 4 minutes. Add the cream and beat until just combined. In a separate bowl, beat the egg whites until they form soft peaks, about 2 minutes. Stir a large spoonful of egg whites into the potato mixture and then gently pour the potatoes onto the whites. Fold the potato mixture into the egg whites. Pour into the unbaked pie crust. Place the pie on a cookie sheet and bake 10 minutes. Reduce the heat to 350°F. and continue baking until the filling is set, an additional 45 to 50 minutes. Cool on a wire rack. May be made ahead several days or frozen up to 3 months.

If desired, in a small bowl, beat the cream until thick and it holds its shape. Gently fold in the candied ginger. Serve each slice of pie with a dollop of the ginger cream.

Mincemeat Pie

SERVES 8 TO 10

I refuse to be embarrassed about something everybody knows: Jars of mincemeat make an excellent pie, and possibly the easiest pie there is!

- 1 large jar mincemeat, preferably Cross and Blackwell
  Bourbon extract or bourbon to taste
- 1 (8-inch) prebaked pie shell (page 279)

Garnish
  Whipped cream or vanilla ice cream

Preheat the oven to 300°F.

Mix the mincemeat and bourbon extract. Pour into the prebaked pie shell. Heat until warm, 10 to 15 minutes. Serve warm with whipped cream or vanilla ice cream, if desired.

Brownie Truffles

MAKES 120 TRUFFLES

I find these a wonderful house gift or something different for a Christmas gift.

Coating
- 1 cup sugar
- 2 tablespoons instant coffee granules, processed in a food processor
- 2 tablespoons unsweetened cocoa powder

Brownies
- 4 ounces unsweetened chocolate
- ½ pound (2 sticks) unsalted butter
- 4 large eggs
- 2 cups sugar
- 1 cup unbleached all-purpose flour
- ⅛ teaspoon salt
- 2 teaspoons pure vanilla extract

Preheat the oven to 350°F. Butter an 8x16-inch pan.

Make the coating by combining the 1 cup sugar, the powdered coffee, and the cocoa. Set aside.

In a heavy saucepan, or the microwave, melt the chocolate and butter together. Beat the eggs until they are light and then gradually beat in the 2 cups sugar. Stir in the chocolate mixture. Gradually add the flour, salt, and vanilla. This mixture is not meant to be light and fluffy, just fully incorporated. Pour the mixture into the prepared pan and bake 25 minutes. The brownies will be slightly underdone and very moist. Allow to cool in the pan.

When cool enough to handle, cut the brownies into 1x1-inch squares. Roll each square in the palms of your hands into balls about 1 inch in diameter. Roll the balls in the coating mixture. Pack in tins or plastic containers with wax paper between the layers and store in the refrigerator for up to a week. Or place them in a single layer on a cookie sheet in the freezer until frozen, pack in containers, and store in the freezer up to 4 months.

Soufflé Omelette

SERVES 2 AS A LUNCH OR SUPPER
MAIN COURSE, 4 AS AN APPETIZER
OR DESSERT

This recipe is neither a soufflé nor an omelette, but it's light as a soufflé and satisfying as an omelette, and it tastes delicious. It takes just minutes to make and is very easy for something so special! When someone comes unexpectedly and I need to stretch a meal or if a dessert fails, I always have the ingredients. The main recipe is for a savory omelette, but the dessert variation at the end can save you.

- 6 eggs
- 2 to 3 tablespoons finely chopped fresh thyme, marjoram, or basil
- Salt
- Freshly ground black pepper
- 2 tablespoons butter
- ½ cup grated blue or cheddar cheese, at room temperature (optional)

Preheat the oven to 400°F.

Carefully separate the eggs. Beat the yolks until well mixed and pale-yellow. Separately beat the whites until they are in stiff peaks but not rocky. Quickly fold in the yolks, herbs, and salt and pepper to taste.

Heat the butter in an ovenproof 10-inch nonstick skillet or omelette pan until foaming,

---

VARIATION

Dessert Omelette

Substitute 2 tablespoons sugar for the herbs, salt, and pepper. Top one half of the omelette with ½ cup melted raspberry or strawberry jam or ½ cup sliced strawberries or peaches. Slide halfway out of the pan onto the plate, then fold over. Heat 2 or 3 metal skewers on the stove until they are red hot. Sprinkle 2 tablespoons confectioners' sugar over the omelette. Very carefully, mark a lattice pattern on top with the hot skewers.

---

then add the egg mixture. Cook over moderate heat 45 to 60 seconds to brown the bottom. Do not stir. Put the pan in the oven and bake until the top is set, about 5 minutes. Slide the omelette onto a serving platter and sprinkle the cheese on top, if using. Serve at once.

Pumpkin Spice Roulade

SERVES 12 TO 14

This is a special alternative to pumpkin pie at Thanksgiving. It's not too glamorous for an off-season family dinner, either!

- 3 **large eggs, separated**
- ½ **cup packed light brown sugar**
- ⅔ **cup solid-pack pumpkin (not pumpkin pie filling)**
- ½ **teaspoon baking soda**
- ¾ **teaspoon ground cinnamon**
- ½ **teaspoon salt**
- ¾ **cup all-purpose flour**
- ½ **cup granulated sugar**
- ½ **teaspoon almond extract**
  Confectioner's sugar

Filling
- ¾ **cup Cran-Fruit relish (optional)**
- 3 **cups frozen vanilla yogurt, softened**

Garnish
  Confectioners' sugar (optional)
  Grated peel (no white attached) of 1 orange (optional)

Preheat the oven to 375°F. Lightly grease and flour a 15x10x1-inch jelly roll pan. Line it with wax paper and grease and flour the wax paper.

In the large bowl of a mixer, beat the egg yolks until light in color, about 2 to 3 minutes. Add the brown sugar and beat until thick, another 3 to 4 minutes. Add the pumpkin to the mixture and combine well.

Sift together the baking soda, cinnamon, salt, and flour. Gently stir into the pumpkin mixture.

Beat the egg whites until soft peaks begin to form. Add the granulated sugar and almond extract and beat until the peaks are stiff but not rocky. Stir one-third of the egg whites into the pumpkin mixture to lighten it. Gently pour the pumpkin mixture onto the remaining egg whites and fold in until just combined. Pour into the prepared pan.

Bake until the cake springs back when lightly touched, 15 to 18 minutes. Invert onto a tea towel dusted with confectioners' sugar and remove the pan. Tear off the wax paper in strips. When cool, spread the Cran-Fruit relish on the cake. Top this with the softened frozen yogurt. Roll the cake lengthwise using the tea towel as a guide, and chill for at least 2 hours.

When ready to serve, sprinkle the roulade with additional confectioners' sugar and the orange peel, if desired. The roulade keeps well frozen, tightly wrapped in foil, for several months.

Cinnamon Ice Cream

This is a variation of old-time vanilla ice cream—it just has added cinnamon. There are so many ice cream machines on the market now that it is impossible to give directions for them all. The crank kind will need ice and salt, but I use a very easy modern one that requires neither. It has an insert that can be kept in the freezer. Since each machine is different, check to be sure your machine will hold the full quantity of the recipe. You may have to do it in batches. A half recipe works well.

For a quick fix, store-bought ice cream can be used. My friend Anne has been known to add powdered cinnamon to vanilla ice cream and call it her own. And yes, yes, yes, you can add a dash of cinnamon to frozen vanilla yogurt, beat the yogurt briefly in a processor, and use it!

- 2 **cups milk**
- 1 **vanilla bean, halved, or 1 tablespoon vanilla extract**
- 5 **cinnamon sticks, crushed**
- 1 **to 2 teaspoons cinnamon, if needed**
- ½ **cup sugar**
- 2 **large egg yolks**
- 2 **cups heavy cream**
- 8 **to 10 ice cream cones (optional)**

Partly fill a medium bowl with ice and water and set aside for later use. Place the milk, vanilla bean, if using, and cinnamon sticks, if using, in a heavy medium saucepan and bring just to the boil. Remove from the heat. Stir in the vanilla extract, if using. Let sit for 15 minutes or until 180°F. or less. Remove the vanilla bean and large pieces of cinnamon and set aside. Taste the milk to be sure it has a strong cinnamon flavor. Add ground cinnamon if necessary. The flavor will be less in the frozen ice cream.

Meanwhile, using an electric mixer, beat the sugar and egg yolks until pale in color, about 5 minutes. Gradually pour the warm milk into the egg yolk mixture while stirring constantly. Return the mixture to the saucepan. Cook over low heat for 5 minutes, gently stirring constantly to prevent the eggs from cooking, until thickened (approximately 160°F.), and the mixture coats the back of a metal spoon. Do not let the mixture boil. Remove from the heat, strain the mixture into a bowl, and place that bowl in the ice water to stop the cooking process.

Stir in the heavy cream and chill completely. You may choose to scrape in the seeds from the vanilla bean now before rinsing and drying the bean (see box). Freeze in an ice cream machine according to manufacturer's instructions.

Serve in ice cream cones if desired or in small dishes.

TIP

After using vanilla beans, rinse and dry. Once split, you may not have any more of the little seeds, but there's still flavor in the bean. I store them in sugar or in a jar covered with vodka or brandy.

VARIATION

Vanilla ice cream
Omit the cinnamon and proceed as directed.

Ambrosia

SERVES 8

Ambrosia is a fruit dessert that is also a salad. We Southerners always add it to Thanksgiving and Christmas menus to allow us to have the illusion that we're not in too much trouble with our diets, because after all, "We only had ambrosia for dessert!"

The better the oranges in it, the better it is. Splurge and get flavor-filled navel oranges if you can. In any case, seedless oranges are a must. If there are going to be children at the meal, you can add maraschino cherries—sans stems. My mother always did, perhaps because one of my treasured memories from childhood was when my father took me to his men's club and ordered me a Shirley Temple with a maraschino cherry. I ate nearly a whole bottle, thanks to the indulgent waiter.

- 6 navel oranges
- 1 pineapple, peeled, cored, and cut into cubes
- 1 cup coconut, shredded fresh, fresh frozen, or packaged sweetened, according to taste or tradition
- 1 large banana
- 1 small (4½-ounce) bottle maraschino cherries, drained well (optional)

Peel the oranges, taking care to remove all of the white pith. Slice the oranges over a bowl or storage container so that you catch any juice, and add the slices to the bowl. Circular slices look prettiest, hold together best, and are easiest.

Add the pineapple and coconut to the orange slices and gently toss. The ambrosia can be refrigerated up to two days, covered.

When ready to serve, slice the banana and toss it with the other fruits. Add the cherries last.

Serve the ambrosia in your prettiest glass bowl. It will become a tradition.

Fresh Peaches or Pears in Creamy Caramel Sauce

SERVES 4

I used to go to all the trouble of caramelizing sugar with butter and milk to make this caramel sauce. But no more. I just pop open a can of sweetened condensed milk and it's a snap. Obviously, berries would also be wonderful with this.

- 1 (14-ounce) can sweetened condensed milk (regular, low-fat, or no-fat)
- 4 ripe peaches or pears

Pour the condensed milk into a heavy pot and bring to the boil. Reduce heat and boil steadily until a caramel color.

Meanwhile peel, quarter, and stone the peaches or core the pears. Spray a heatproof serving dish with nonstick spray or butter it. Add the fruit and pour the hot sauce over. Cover and chill.

TABLE SETTINGS

The Reality and the Rules

Setting the table simply establishes a place for your guests to eat and provides them with the tools they will need. To set the table "properly" is to do so in a way that is recognizable; ideally, the setting should add to the comfort of your guests. As new generations embrace a more casual lifestyle, the formidable rules of table setting observed by Grandmother and Great-Grandmother are beginning to fade. It may be tempting to say "good riddance," but I'd like to encourage a different attitude. The traditions and customs of table settings serve the function of all traditions and customs: They give us a common set of rules and practices for a particular situation, and they save us from having to reinvent the wheel each time we are faced with that situation. Such customs are also signifiers: A formally set table signals elegance and graciousness to your guests before they've seen the food.

If your style is resolutely casual, remember most etiquette is based on rules that make one's guests comfortable. As long as you keep that in mind, your next steps will be in line.

Equipment

Table Coverings

Tablecloths, place mats, and runners all serve to protect the table, but they also can enhance the mood of the table and of the room.

Traditionally, the only options for a formal table were a crisp, white tablecloth, a colored undercloth with white lace on top, or a white lace cloth alone, but those rules have become more relaxed and now can include solid colors, selected to accent your china, the flowers, or the room's decor.

Fold creases are acceptable, but they should run the length of the table. At formal dinners an eighteen-inch overhang is preferred, since that length allows the cloth to fall gracefully without interfering with the legs of the diners.

A polished, bare table is also appropriate for formal dining. (Consider using trivets or mats under serving dishes.) At England's Trinity College, tables of well-scrubbed oak are set nightly with silver, crystal, white china, and damask napkins.

For a casual table, the rules are looser. The tablecloth can cover the table completely or be draped at an angle. It can reach to the floor (as with buffet cloths) or barely cover the table's edge. A checked, large-patterned, or brightly colored cloth creates a more casual setting. Quilts, bedspreads, or sheets are effective in conveying an even more informal atmosphere. Place mats are used most frequently for luncheons or informal gatherings.

Tents

In the not-so-distant past, if you needed a tent you borrowed it from the local funeral home. Now you can rent a tent for your specific needs. And tents are sold in home catalogues and are quite affordable. There are companies scattered throughout the United States that will tent almost anything, almost anywhere.

A tent can provide insurance against inclement weather—rain, heat, or cold—and can be equipped with cooling and heating systems. It contributes to the presentation, creating a festive or a sophisticated atmosphere. Coming in many styles and with a variety of options, some tops are clear, lovely on a starlit night; others are outfitted with floors, walls, doors, and windows, creating believable rooms that can be rolled up or down if there's a change in the weather.

If atmosphere is your main concern, employ a decorator or event planner. Decorating a tent isn't something you want to take on alone. The designer's knowledge will pay for itself.

If you decide to rent a tent, deal with a professional tenter and only one who will happily supply references. Many tenters will give you the locations of some of their current installations. Check them out. It is important to do your research. Ask if the tent is new. If it's not, ask for a guarantee that it will be clean. Most tenting companies rent lighting, heaters, and fans. Listen to them to be sure they aren't too noisy.

Many larger companies have a cancellation policy, and you will probably be asked for a deposit. If you are renting for rain insurance, the tenter might offer you a window, normally one or two days before the event, to cancel without losing your deposit. Be sure to get a written agreement, covering everything you have discussed, from the tenter and possibly the designer.

Napkins

A napkin is indispensable, but almost anything can be used, from linen tea towels to bandannas.

Cloth dinner napkins, usually range in size from 16 to 20 inches square and are acceptable for most meals, including some formal ones. For very formal occasions, the standard is a 24-inch square of white linen.

Cloth nakins come in all colors, patterns, and easy-care fabrics that need little or no ironing. I love brightly patterned napkins, which do not show stains readily, and I use them daily. Even a peanut butter sandwich can look and taste better when served with a cloth napkin.

One friend, whose Texan mother had instilled in him her own custom following the eighteenth-century French custom, always set a fork, knife, and teaspoon, no matter what was being served. We had many discussions about this practice. Finally, he said to me, "You can't make me do it your way!" And true enough, I couldn't. It is just that at the end of dinner I find it confusing to be left with an unused utensil. Is something else coming? Try to keep your settings uncomplicated.

Flatware

Sterling silver, the standard for formal meals, is appropriate for any meal, though I am certainly not suggesting that you can't serve a formal dinner if you don't own a set of sterling. Through the years I have enjoyed collecting my sterling piece by piece from antiques shops, yard sales, and flea markets. I often use a mixture of patterns when setting the table. Stainless is perfectly acceptable for more casual entertaining.

Glassware

Clear crystal is always acceptable. If you are just starting out, select a pattern that will lend itself to most forms of entertaining. If the cost of crystal is a consideration, there are many less expensive glass patterns available. Whichever you choose, glass or crystal, size is important. Water in a small wineglass is hardly sufficient, and wine in a water glass leads to wasted wine. Unless you are serving more than one kind of wine, an all-purpose wineglass will do nicely for most occasions.

Placement

The way a table is laid varies dramatically from strict to casual, with many gradations between and much overlapping of the two. The degree of formality depends upon the occasion, the appointments, and the service. The twentieth-century American diner probably has no problem envisioning many variations within the term "formal dining." A good etiquette book is a necessity for when it's important to you. It's never good to look ignorant.

Traditional Formal Setting

The cutlery should be as close together as practical and lined up evenly with the edge of the plate, which is placed a half inch to one inch from the table's edge. Generally, English

Covers

A *cover* is an individual place setting at a dining table (hence the cover charge). What was included in the cover was standardized as early as the eighteenth century. A French etiquette manual of 1782 lists the musts: a napkin, a plate, a knife, a spoon, a fork, and a goblet for each guest, and warns "it would be utterly gross-mannered to do without any of these." (I know, I know, but times are changing. I say don't set utensils unless they'll be needed.)

The space required for each cover can vary, depending on the size of the table, but your guests will be more comfortable if they each have twenty-four inches.

"how-tos" specify the plate location as one-half inch from the edge, but I was taught one inch, which I prefer (especially if there is concern that a guest accidently might brush against the table).

☙ Knives, blades inward, are set to the right of the dinner plate and forks to the left, in the order in which they will be used. (First to be used is on the extreme right or left. Last to be used, next to the plate.) The bouillon or soup (the first course) spoon is placed on the extreme right, unless there is a seafood or cocktail fork. If there is, it is placed to the right of the soup spoon.

☙ The dessert spoon and fork can be laid either across the top of the setting (above the plate) with the spoon, handle to the right, above the fork, handle to the left (this arrangement is more often seen in England), or at the sides, closest to the plate, with the spoon on the right and the fork on the left. (The top placement is helpful if the table is crowded.)

☙ Fruit knives and forks also may be laid with the dessert spoon and fork at the top of the setting at the sides, or may be brought with the dessert plate.

☙ The butter knife can be placed either with the knives on the right of the dinner plate or crossed at its top on the bread plate, which is at the upper left of the place setting.

☙ There should be no more than three pieces of flatware on each side of the dinner plate. If necessary, additional flatware can be provided as later courses are served. There should be no unused flatware left on the table at the end of the meal.

There is never an occasion when more than ten implements should be at a place setting. For a meal that elaborate, you would have a serving staff, who would remove the used utensils as they cleared and bring the necessary utensils as they served the final courses.

When I opened my restaurant in Social Circle, Georgia, I was operating on a very tight budget. It was located in an old machine shop warehouse, and the cleaning and other preparation of this space took an enormous amount of personal energy from my husband, brother, and me. We stocked it with antiques, but the bank would only let me spend $1,000 on the kitchen and restaurant part of the conversion. I started with a donated refrigerator from a friend's trailer, a stove from Sears, which I paid for on time, and countertops made by my husband and brother. The napkins came from 25-cents-a-yard remnants. I still have some of them today.

Glasses are arranged in the order of use in a straight line above the right-hand cutlery. The white-wine glass is placed to the far right, with the red-wine glass to the left, with the port or liqueur glass to the left. If you are including a glass for water, it is placed in front of the liqueur glass. The last glass to the left is placed just above the meat knife. After a glass has been used, it should be removed from the table. If you are laying a single wineglass, place it anywhere above the right-hand cutlery.

Napkins can be put in the center of the place setting, on the side plate, or in one of the glasses. Traditionally, the napkins should be folded with the open corner in the lower right corner, allowing the napkin to be picked up and opened with a gentle shake of the left hand and smoothed across the lap with the right.

Informal Setting

Informal here does not mean casual in our contemporary sense but rather a technically informal but still important meal. This placement differs from the formal only in the number of appointments. An informal setting includes a napkin, a plate, and a fork, a knife, or a spoon, as appropriate, for each course placed as they would be for a formal dinner.

The coffee cup and saucer with a teaspoon on one saucer are placed to the right side of the plate for breakfast or lunch. For dinner, however, they usually aren't placed until the dessert course or after the meal.

Serving Utensils and Condiments

Whatever the type of meal, always have the necessary serving utensils on the table. Traditionally, serving spoons and forks are paired, corresponding to the number of dishes.

Salt and pepper, or just a pepper mill, and any other condiments or accompaniments, if using, are positioned centrally. For a large dinner party, it is customary to have more than one set of condiments and two plates of butter, with butter knives placed nearby for passing.

These descriptions are meant to establish the extremes of this vague and flexible subject of table settings, but understand that the majority of entertaining lies somewhere in between.

In America the host or hostess is the first to begin eating, thereby showing the guests the correct implement. In some countries, custom dictates that the most honored guest is the first to start, which can be quite uncomfortable. It's devastating to be staring at unfamiliar food with no idea of how to tackle it.

It's in knowing the basics, the elements, that you and your guests will find comfort. I recall a sit-down dinner in a private home. A foreign guest started eating before the hostess (a custom in his country) and selected the "wrong" fork. The hostess, rather than embarrass him, followed suit, and the other guests took their cues from her—the art of entertaining with grace and style.

INDEX